Cooking Thai
เข้าครัวไทย

Cooking Thai

Heritage and Modern Recipes from My Kitchen Notebooks

Pim Techamuanvivit

with Andrea Nguyen

Photography by Ed Anderson

TEN SPEED PRESS
California | New York

To my grandfather คุณตา for giving me the space to grow into my own self.

For Rayas and Alex, who will always be missed at my table.

Contents

Recipe List

Jatujak Flea market &
Or Tor Kor Food market.

My Cooking Journey

I never met my grandmother. She passed away shortly before I was born. Yet she was the biggest influence in my cooking life. Her name was Somjitr, though everyone, including my grandfather, called her Khun Yai, the formal Thai term for maternal grandmother.

Specters of her were everywhere in our family's home in Bangkok, especially around the kitchen, where her presence was most strongly felt. Her culinary prowess was the stuff of family lore. Everything delicious prepared at our house was said to come from Khun Yai's recipes. "Khun Yai wouldn't have approved" qualified as a grave slight, while "just like Khun Yai's" was the highest compliment. Her most beloved recipe was for namprik pao, an ambrosial blend of fragrant fried shallots and garlic, spicy roasted chili, sour tamarind, salty fish sauce, and sweet palm sugar—the very embodiment of classic Thai flavors.

Khun Yai's namprik pao (page 44) was always present in our family's kitchen, packed in a tall glass jar with a red plastic lid repurposed from an old Nescafé instant-coffee container. The thick, reddish-brown puree could be mistaken for a dark berry jam but for the glistening layer of red chili oil on top.

The chili jam made its way into many dishes in our home. A ladleful to finish a pot of the sour prawn soup called tom yum goong (page 193). Mixed with chopped garlic and bird's eye chili as a base for spicy stir-fries like the clams on page 240. Whisked with lime juice and fish sauce for a basic yum salad dressing, which is good on just about everything (try the seared scallops recipe on page 97). And, my favorite, spread like sweet jam on a slice of toast for a tasty, if a little pungent, breakfast.

After moving to the United States to attend graduate school, first in Washington, DC, then Los Angeles, and eventually ending up at the University of California San Diego, I found myself unmoored in a sea of unfamiliar flavors. My lifeline was always a treasured jar of Khun Yai's chili jam—the comforting taste of home—made for me by her premier disciple, my eldest aunt, Chawiwan Kasemkhun, or Pah Pui, as I called her. The chili jam was always selfishly guarded and carefully rationed to last until the next trip home. Sharing was simply out of the question. I had not, nor have I since, known myself to be so disciplined.

Becoming a Cook

I moved to Silicon Valley to work after graduate school. As I became more settled in California, and the trips back to Bangkok grew less frequent, learning to reproduce the flavors from my childhood became more important, a central project for whenever I did return. Each journey represented an opportunity for kitchen fieldwork: I spent time in the kitchen with Pah Pui and tracked down old relatives and family cooks who apprenticed with my grandmother. I asked them to share her secrets—and perhaps some of their own—with me. I reveled in spending time in the kitchen in Thailand, pounding, chopping, and cooking my way back to my childhood.

The day I mastered Khun Yai's chili jam was a milestone in my cooking life. It was the day I finally considered myself a proper Thai cook. Before that, I'd only been tinkering, making easy stir-fries and curries from store-bought pastes. A few months earlier in Bangkok, I had carefully observed and helped Pah Pui make a batch of chili jam to take home to California. The supply I carried back was depleting at an alarming rate, and the next trip to Bangkok was still far on the horizon. I had to do something about it. I pulled out my little black notebook—oil-stained and a little worse for wear, having spent many a hot and humid day in Bangkok kitchens—and set to work.

Step by step, I cooked through my notes. I began with peeling and slicing a pound each of shallots and garlic. Make sure you use a sharp knife, my note admonished. A dull knife or a food processor would bruise the alliums, turning them bitter. Then I fried the garlic and shallots in a hot wok. I used far more oil than I thought prudent, but that's what my notebook—in lieu of Pah Pui looking over my shoulder—said to do. One ingredient after the next, the gooey mess in the wok began to look and smell more like Khun Yai's chili jam. By the time I was done whirling the final mixture in the blender (the one modern consolation my aunt allowed), it could have been the same chili jam from the red-top jar on the shelf of my childhood.

I made myself a bowl of steaming-hot jasmine rice, stirred in a generous spoonful of the freshly made chili jam, and took the first bite. Leading with a hint of sweetness, followed by the smoky warmth of the chili, a bright acidity from the tamarind, and rounded out with the salty shrimp paste, there it was, my very first batch of chili jam. It wasn't *exactly* like Khun Yai's quite yet, but surely she would have approved.

Becoming a Chef

In the early 2000s, during the initial waves of social media, I launched a food blog—one of the first!—simply named *Chez Pim*. It was highly opinionated (me being me, after all). My day job was at Cisco Systems working on a project that regularly took me to Europe. In Paris and London, I spent my spare time and dollars shopping and cooking from local markets and eating in Michelin-starred restaurants and writing about those experiences. The blog became quite popular, and I was even covered in *The New York Times* and in *The Guardian/Observer* in the United Kingdom.

As a result of the blog's success, I wrote my first book, *The Foodie Handbook* (forgive me the hubris of youth), about those food experiences, mostly with recipes adapted from fancy chefs I'd met.

But all the while, what I actually craved was doing something with my hands. I wanted to *cook*.

Living in California, among some of the most beautiful produce in the world, I decided to learn how to make jam. I read everything by Christine Ferber, my favorite French jam maker, who concocts delicious, surprising jams such as raspberry, rose, and lychee. I tasted every jam that I could get my hands on from June Taylor, my favorite not-French jam maker. Based in Northern California, June makes jams that are clear, pure expressions of the local fruits at their peak ripeness. Then I set out to make my own jams. Aiming for a style that was somewhere in between the two, I wasn't afraid to explore unusual flavor combinations but always preserved the fruit's best savors. The jams were my first foray into cooking outside of the circle of family and friends.

My one-woman jam company took on a life of her own. I was happy with my jams but was surprised by how much people really loved what I made. My Flavor King pluot jam and blueberry and golden raspberry jam won consecutive Good Food Awards in 2011 and 2012. Jeffrey Steingarten raved about my jams in *Vogue* magazine. Nigella, yes, *that* Nigella, tweeted about dreaming of my "peach+saffron" jam. I sold all my jams *en primeur* style, at the beginning of each season to subscribers.

The big success of my little project brought me to a point where I had to decide if crafting jam full-time was the path for me. Things were becoming almost unmanageable. I was still making all the jams on my own, even harvesting some of the fruit that went into them. Did I want to take the success and expand the jam company? Was that really what I wanted to do when I "grew up"?

I knew I made delicious jams. I had access to some of the best fruit available, and I did my best to preserve those fresh flavors. But I didn't really have anything to say. I had nothing groundbreaking to contribute as a jam maker.

Meanwhile, I looked around at the state of Thai food in the United States. When you went to a Thai restaurant, without even glancing at a menu, you likely knew what you could order. That's because the chefs were all cooking the same dishes—crowd-pleasers like pad Thai, tom kha gai, and pad see ew, which they knew would help them cover expenses. You could order curry by the color, then tell the server what protein to add and how spicy you want it. That was the extent of Thai cuisine for many people in the United States.

But that wasn't *my* Thai food, not the flavors I grew up with. Constrained by the economic realities of making ends meet, many Thai restaurants could not afford the care and quality ingredients required to craft the kind of food I had experienced in my family's kitchen.

I wanted to fill that void. I knew I could. I began crafting a plan to open a restaurant. My aim was not to "elevate" Thai food. Thai cuisine didn't need that. Rather, I intended to do it justice. Using the best ingredients, I would show the world the depth and breadth of Thai cuisine beyond the simple dishes people thought they knew. That became my mission.

An opportunity arose when my friend Doug Zeif called about a tiny restaurant space in a downtown San Francisco hotel that the investment company he worked for had just acquired. That space in the Parc 55 hotel in Union Square

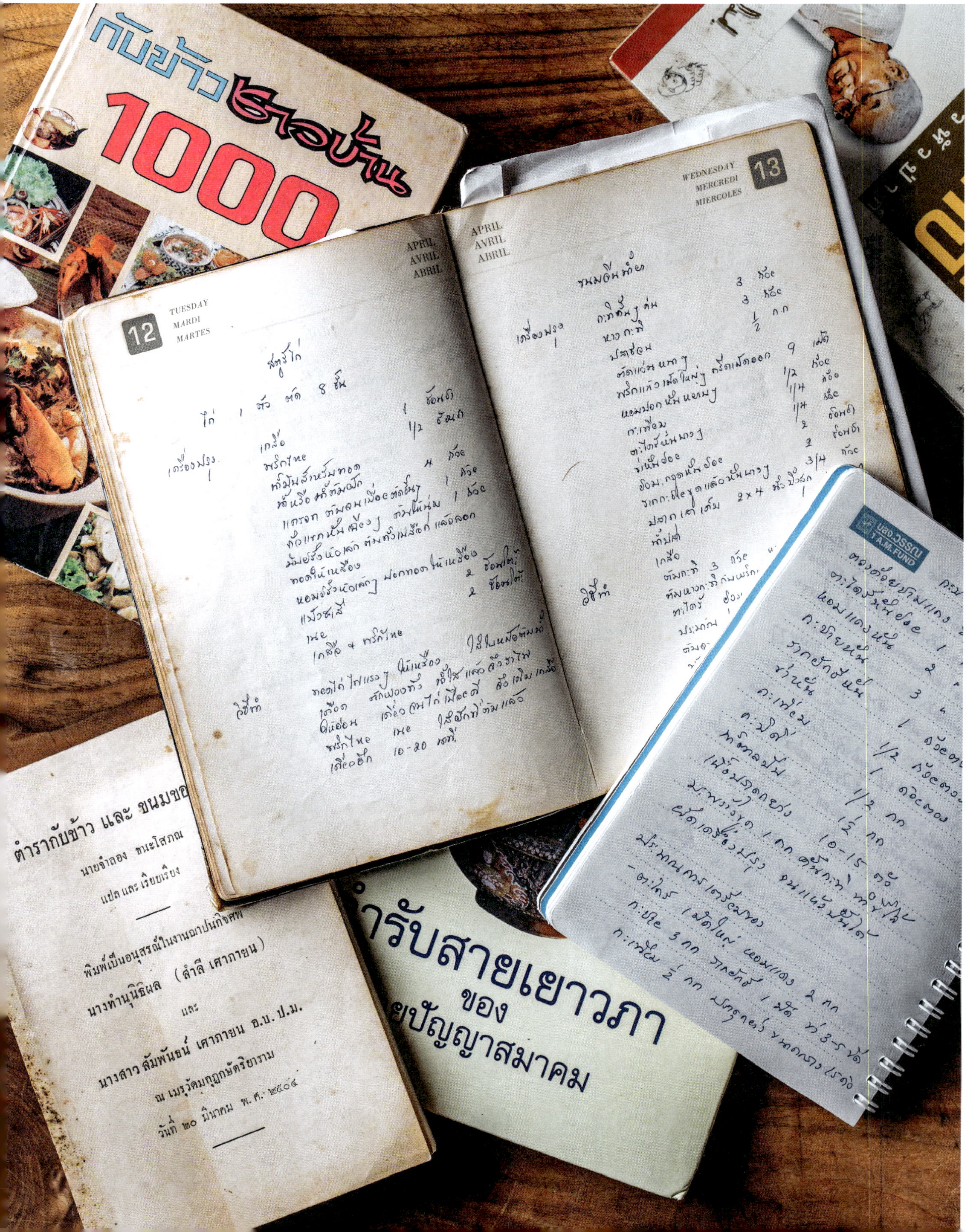
กับข้าวชาวบ้าน
1000
TUESDAY
MARDI
MARTES
12
APRIL
AVRIL
ABRIL
APRIL
AVRIL
ABRIL
WEDNESDAY
MERCREDI
MIERCOLES
13
บลจ.วรรณ
1 A.M. FUND
ตำรากับข้าว และ ขนมขอ
นายจำลอง ธนะโสภณ
แปล และ เรียบเรียง
พิมพ์เป็นอนุสรณ์ในงานฌาปนกิจศพ
นางทำนุนิธิผล (ลำลี เศาภายน)
และ
นางสาว ลัมพันธน์ เศาภายน อ.บ. ป.ม.
ณ เมรุวัดมกุฏกษัตริยาราม
วันที่ ๒๐ มีนาคม พ.ศ. ๒๕๐๔
ำรับสายเยาวภา
ของ
ยปัญญาสมาคม

became my first restaurant. I named the restaurant Kin Khao: *Kin* means "to eat" and *khao* means "rice." For Thai people, to eat is to eat rice. So colloquially when you say "Kin khao," you mean "Let's eat!"

Kin Khao wasn't just my first restaurant. It was my first job in the restaurant business. Looking back, the smartest thing I did when I started planning was acknowledging my naivete. I sat down with a notepad and put together a list of things I didn't know how to do—starting with running a professional kitchen. I had conceived the menu with my recipes, but I didn't have a clue about how to prep and cook for a room full of paying diners.

The Stuff I Don't Know How to Do List became a crucial checklist for building my team. I needed to hire a professional chef to run my kitchen. Check! I knew what wine I wanted to serve with my food, but I needed to hire a proper wine director. Check! I went down the list, finding awesome people to fill the gaps in my experience, and opened Kin Khao in March 2014.

While writing the first Kin Khao menu, I was adamant about not including dishes that American diners would recognize on other Thai menus. Yes, I opened a Thai restaurant without pad Thai! Instead, we had true pad kee mao (page 260) punched up by plenty of locally grown holy basil, the real deal to make that dish properly Thai. We prepared all the curry pastes, base components, and sauces in-house. We used the best-quality seafood and the same locally raised proteins lauded by expensive multiple-Michelin-starred restaurants, like rabbit from Marin County's Devil's Gulch Ranch in our green curry. We collaborated with local farms to grow certain hard-to-find herbs and vegetables for our menu. Basically, I opened the Thai restaurant I wanted to eat in. Of course, my grandmother's chili jam figured into guest favorites, like the chili jam clams on page 240.

Launching Kin Khao was harder than I ever imagined. The first six months flew by in a blur. I was exhausted, but I was also never so energized. I'd finally found my métier. *Bon Appétit* and *GQ* magazine named Kin Khao one of the year's best restaurants. Not long after opening, we had our first rave review in *The New York Times*. Mark Bittman's article led with, "Pim Techamuanvivit is an old-school restaurateur, a person who knows her cuisine inside out."

In September 2015, when Kin Khao was barely eighteen months old, we received our first Michelin star. Despite our success and my energy, it had been a hard year. In addition to opening Kin Khao, I was diagnosed with breast cancer. In fact, I was freshly released from the hospital after my second major surgery just in time to attend the Michelin star award ceremony. My punk Kin Khao team debated carrying me in a palanquin. I conceded to a wheelchair. (In hindsight, I should have gone with the palanquin. Just imagine the entrance!)

Ten years on, I'm still cancer-free. My Kin Khao team and I—including some who've been around since our early days—are still holding on to that Michelin star.

Being a Link in the Chain

In 2018, I added two more restaurant projects to my life. That year, I began building my second restaurant in San Francisco. Named for the Sanskrit-derived Thai word that means "woman," Nari is my love letter to generations of Thai women who are the soul of our cuisine. The restaurant also honors all the women in my family and life who have nourished and taught me and to whom I owe so much of my success.

As I was working on the opening of Nari, another opportunity came knocking. Christina Ong, the owner of the restaurant Nahm in Bangkok, asked me to take the reins of the kitchen when the original chef departed. Returning home to run my own kitchen was a big challenge that meant multiple, lengthy trips to Bangkok to conceptualize the menu and train staff. Whichever continent I was on, I remained in regular contact with my three teams to maintain our quality standards and manage the crises that inevitably happen in restaurant life. I took all of that on believing, like I do with most things in life, that I either succeed or I learn. Nahm received the first Michelin star the year before I took over. I've retained that star every year since.

Nari launched with great fanfare in September 2019, which was unfortunately only six months before the pandemic effectively closed down San Francisco for two years. But she finally got her own Michelin star in 2023. And I still have all of them—the restaurants and the Michelin stars. (And yes, I assign gender and pronouns to the restaurants because, in many ways, I nurture them like my children.)

Having the extensive kitchen at Nari (compared to the tiny one at Kin Khao) plus a kitchen of my own in Bangkok helped me develop as a Thai cook. Being in Thailand gave me access to incredible artisanal ingredients that I didn't have in California, opening my eyes even further to the nuance and delicacy of my cuisine. For instance, I tasted twenty different fish sauces produced by artisans up and down the coast of Thailand just to find the two we would use at Nahm. We did the same with other foundational ingredients too, like palm sugar and gapi (shrimp paste). As a result, I started to import some of those ingredients to use in San Francisco as well.

I returned every few months to Bangkok to work with my restaurant team. I also started building relationships with farmers, purveyors, and craftspeople to source special ingredients and equipment. Of note, I've collaborated with Nguan Lohachalatanakul of Aoon Pottery to design modern pieces inspired by ancient Ban Chiang ceramics for the dining room at Nahm.

It was also then that I began collecting antiquarian cookbooks dating back to the early 1900s; some were original printings and others were reproductions. I was curious about the evolution of Thai cuisine, and those books, mostly written by female home cooks from all walks of Thai society, helped me connect the dots and identify heritage dishes.

Upon learning about my new interest, family members shared their resources with me. My aunt Pah Tas, Tasanee Aryakul, gave me some of her precious notes and old books. She taught me how to make the caramelized pork on page 220 and many other dishes.

My brother-in-law's mother, Dr. Pathum Snitwongse, whom I call aunt Pah Tum, was impressed enough by my culinary interest and diligence that she left me all of her cooking notebooks after she passed away. A nuclear physicist by training, her notebooks were meticulously written, even peppered with subsequent notes from later experiments. Her sensational recipe for kanom jeen nam ya, a luscious fish curry with rice noodles, is on page 265. Chamuang curry (page 176) was also Pah Tum's specialty.

Friends who excelled at Thai home cooking also generously offered knowledge. For instance, Nantana Chitman, Pi Goong (older sister Goong) as I call her, regularly shares her insights and observations about old-fashioned techniques and modern changes in our cuisine. When I asked about the correct way to process rice flour for a recipe, she commissioned a granite rice grinder for me!

These cooking experiences, in home and professional kitchens, shaped me into the cook I am today.

This book, *Cooking Thai*, presents what I've learned about Thai food. Teaming up with my longtime friend and ace cookbook author Andrea Nguyen, I'm documenting recipes, flavors, and techniques that I've practiced in my home kitchen and taught to my teams of professional cooks across the world.

I've had the great fortune to learn so much about Thai cuisine. This is my heritage. I am a link in this chain. This is my chance to write it all down and pass it on. Let me teach you what I've learned so far.

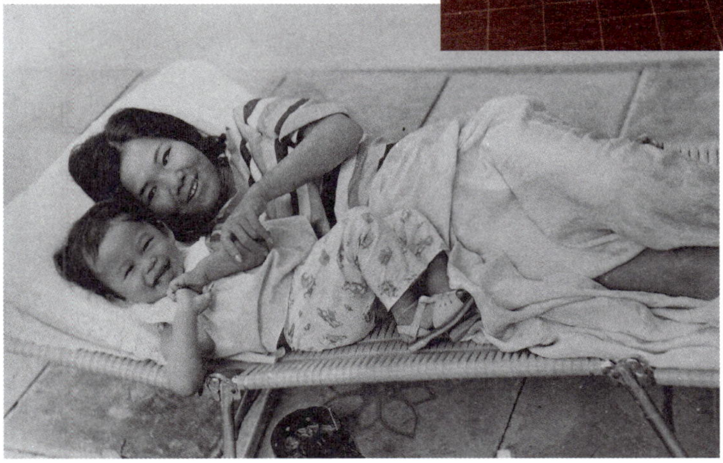

Core Ingredient and Equipment Guide

Even if you are familiar with Asian ingredients, I highly recommend that you read this important section on ingredients and equipment. What's needed for Thai dishes can be different from what is used in other Asian or Southeast Asian cuisines.

With homes and restaurants in three countries, I'm constantly thinking about what it takes to prepare Thai food well wherever I am. Some ingredients are the same as what I use in Thailand, while others need a smart swap. I share my knowledge and preferences in this guide to aid you in understanding and sourcing the necessities. There are also tips scattered throughout to help you be a good Thai cook. Carefully review this section so you can make my recipes work in your kitchen.

Where to shop? The ideal is a Thai market, but there are few of them, even if you live in Los Angeles, the hub of Thai America. That's because the Thai expat population is relatively small. Don't be deterred. Cooking Thai food is partly about sleuthing and community building. For instance, Thai people often congregate at a Buddhist temple (wat), so if there's one nearby, ask visitors there where they shop for food. You can also befriend a favorite Thai restaurant owner, then ask for pointers. One of the recipe testers for this book, a teacher named Hugh, asked a former Thai student about their preferred grocer and found some treasures.

Chances are, they'll direct you to mine Vietnamese, Cambodian, Hmong, and Lao grocers, or Chinese markets that cater to those communities. Those grocery stores should have much of what you need, including hard-to-find items like frozen grachai (fingerroot). Geographically and culturally, we are all neighbors with many culinary overlaps.

What about online vendors? Go for it, but you'll miss out on wandering the aisles of an Asian market and learning. Online vendors such as Weee!, ImportFood.com, TempleofThai.com, and AsianGrocer.co.nz are good sources for specialty ingredients and brands I like.

How about superstores like Ranch 99 and H Mart? They are pan-Asian markets that emphasize Chinese and Korean items, respectively. They will have about 85 percent of the ingredients you need but no frozen grachai and a limited selection of gapi. If you do not need those ingredients, no problem.

Source dried chilies from Mexican or other Latin markets because they have a high turnover of peppers. They may have frozen banana leaves too. Look, too, for independent grocery stores in your area that carry international foods. For example, Buford Highway Farmers Market in Doraville, Georgia, and C Fresh Market in Des Moines, Iowa, are two gems that may surprise you with their eclectic global inventory. In Auckland, I regularly shop at the tiny but well-curated Cambodian-owned produce market called JHC Fruit & Veg on Khyber Pass Road.

Once you have a good understanding of the core ingredients and how to source them, you're ready to make the best Thai food of your life.

Heat Heroes

Many Thai dishes benefit from the fruity heat, vegetal sweetness, and exciting color of chilies. Aside from the common serrano, jalapeño, and mini sweet peppers, you will make good use of the following chilies in fresh and dried forms:

Dried prik chee fa พริกแห้ง, พริกชี้ฟ้าแห้ง and **puya chilies** are medium-hot largish chilies used for curries and more. In Thailand, dried prik chee fa is the default dried chili, which explains why when you see these chilies in the United States, they are simply labeled "dried Thai chili." When unsure, do what I and countless other Thai chefs and home cooks do: Use dried Mexican puya chilies. (If your chili tolerance is low, use milder dried **guajillo, New Mexico,** or very mild **California chilies**.) Good dried whole chilies have even color. Bend the package to ensure you have pliable, relatively fresh ones.

Dried prik jinda พริกจินดาแห้ง and **árbol** are hot chilies that are not often used in large quantities unless you're a thrill seeker. Skinny dried prik jinda are called "small chilies" in Thailand, and just like prik chee fa, they're sometimes ambiguously sold abroad as "Thai chili." To get a chili heat level that works well in my recipes, use dried prik jinda or Mexican árbol chilies.

Fresh Thai chilies พริกสด, basically the typical bird's eye variety sold at supermarkets and Asian markets, are used in this book. They are hot, 2 inches (5cm) long, and available green or red (plus in-between shades like orange and yellow). Buy them fresh or frozen (or grow a bunch and freeze them). Weight is provided in a recipe when it's crucial to have enough heat in a dish. Color is specified when it matters, but otherwise, just use any color of chili.

HOT TIP

Can't find any of the dried chili varieties or need seeded dried chilies fast? In a pinch, some curry pastes can be made with coarse gochugaru (Korean chili powder, see page 137). Go ahead and cheat but don't tell your imaginary Thai auntie.

Chili Pro Tips

It can seem daunting to prep all the chilies required for Thai dishes. But you need to do it because Thai food depends on their vibrancy. Here are some pointers for your journey.

SEED CHILIES STRATEGICALLY

For my recipes, seeding chilies involves removing the inner fleshy membranes (that's the placenta, where most of the capsaicin, or heat source, is produced and stored) plus the seeds attached to them along with any seeds that are just hanging out inside the chili. Some call that "deseeding," but I just use the term *seeding*. By seeding, you're reducing the chili heat.

Save time by seeding a bunch of dried chilies in advance. Start with a 2- to 4-ounce (60 to 120g) bag of large dried chilies (prik chee fa, puya, or a milder variety). Smaller chilies (prik jinda, árbol) are used less often, so unless you're Thai or a heat seeker, just seed 1 to 2 ounces (30 to 60g). Remove the seeds from fresh chilies, such as for making green curry paste (page 162), when needed (you can do it a day ahead but why?). More "seedy" tips are below.

Invest time. Seeding a pile of chilies can take about 45 minutes. Work undisturbed because things will get messy and certainly highly aromatic.

Take precautions. Wear gloves and maybe a mask to protect yourself. Open a window and turn on the range hood exhaust fan for ventilation.

Snip smart. Using kitchen scissors (Joyce Chen is my go-to brand), stem and cut open all the dried chilies lengthwise, dropping them onto a sheet pan to catch any seeds that voluntarily fall out.

Remove seeds well. Open the cut dried chilies and use your gloved fingers to pull away the seeds and fleshy membranes, letting them fall onto the sheet pan. When dealing with fresh chilies, treat them like vanilla beans and cut them open lengthwise with the tip of a knife, then scrape off the seeds. As you seed the chilies, put them into a bowl or on a different sheet pan. More seeds will fall out, so you can discard them too, after you pack up your work.

Store for the future. Transfer the seeded dried chilies to an airtight container or ziplock bag. They will keep at room temperature for months. Fresh chilies are best used as soon as they are processed.

BE FLEXIBLE WITH HEAT

What determines chili heat? It's not just the variety but also the growing conditions, how long the fruit hangs on the plant, and the weather at harvesttime.

Be open to tweaking the heat to your liking. For instance, dial it up with prik pon (page 46) or down with the smaller number of fresh chilies suggested in recipes. Got unusually hot dried puya chilies? Cut their heat with a milder chili like guajillo, New Mexico, or California (make sure the total weight is the same as what the recipe calls for). Chilies make Thai dishes exciting, so don't shy from them. Figure out your tolerance level and be aware of external factors so you can negotiate them.

SAFELY CUT AND GARNISH

Avoid touching chilies with your bare fingers. After slicing or chopping fresh chilies, use one of the trimmed stems to usher the cut pieces onto your knife blade and then push them off to wherever you need them. When garnishing with superthin chili slices, use cooking tweezers for precision and safety. Go ahead and be cheffy!

COLOR-CODE THE HEAT

If you or your guests are chili-heat sensitive, use different-colored chilies so they can be easily identified and picked out of the food. For instance, use fresh red Thai chilies and yellow mini sweet peppers for the basil stir-fries on pages 233 and 260. At the table, you can readily locate the extra heat source and decide to eat it or not.

พริกแห้ง ยอดสน
Dried Chilli - spicy spicy

Savory, Spicy, and Salty

When a recipe ingredient is labeled "Thai," such as Thai thin soy sauce, use a brand from Thailand. It makes a huge difference in how the recipe comes out. Stock your pantry with these condiments to craft great Thai food.

Fish sauce น้ำปลา ❶ is a liquid made from fermented fish and salt and is widely sold. The two brands I use the most are Thai-produced Trachang (scale logo) and Megachef. Two other commonly available Thai brands, Squid and Tiparos, are OK too. Those four Thai brands contain between 1,500 and 1,700 mg of sodium per tablespoon. If your brand differs from mine significantly, adjust as needed.

Golden Mountain Seasoning Sauce ซอสภูเขา ฝาเขียว ❷ has a distinctly savory, slightly sweet flavor that's akin to lighter Maggi Seasoning sauce. It harmonizes well with Thai ingredients, whereas Maggi easily overwhelms. If unavailable, substitute Thai thin soy sauce.

Sea salt เกลือทะเล ❸, particularly fine sea salt that clocks in at about 550 mg per ¼ teaspoon, is what I often use in recipes. Check the nutrition label on your sea salt and adjust the amounts called for in recipes if needed.

Thai black soy sauce ซีอิ๊วดำ ❹ is sweet, salty, and slightly syrupy—like diluted Indonesian kecap manis; this condiment is sometimes labeled sweet black soy sauce. I like the sauces by Megachef and Dragonfly, which is made by the Kwong Hung Seng company in Thailand.

Thai oyster sauce น้ำมันหอย ❺ tastes salty-sweet with a hint of brininess to evoke the piscine origin of the original condiment long ago. I prefer a Thai brand with relatively low sodium. Maekrua brand is mild and fine, but harder-to-find Megachef brand is punchier and better (check online, including Weee!). If you use non-Thai oyster sauce, use about 25 percent less. For **vegan oyster sauce,** we use Lee Kum Kee brand.

Thai sriracha ศรีราชา ❻ is a chili-based hot, slightly garlicky, and mildly sweet condiment that originated in the 1930s in Si Racha, a town on the Gulf of Thailand. Generally available in two heat strengths, medium and strong, Thai-style sriracha works best for my dishes, like the Kin Khao Wings on page 78. I favor Sriraja Panich and Shark brands.

Thai thin soy sauce ซีอิ๊วขาว ❼ is not as dark as Chinese, Japanese, or Korean soy sauce, but it has a strong salinity and deep umami flavor so it pairs well with and can stand in for fish sauce in Thai vegetarian recipes. Healthy Boy thin soy sauce and Megachef gluten-free soy sauce work well.

Umami from Land and Sea

Along with sauces and salt, these umami-laden seasonings help build exciting Thai dishes.

Dried shrimp กุ้งแห้ง ❽ are used whole or chopped to add savory depth. Check the cold case of a Chinese or Southeast Asian market for small or medium ones and keep them frozen to preserve flavor and freshness. When possible, buy dried shrimp without food coloring; those may not be the brightest orange, but they'll be better for you.

Gapi กะปิ ❾ (Thai shrimp paste) is the grounding umami in many Thai dishes. The dark mauve paste is typically sold in plastic jars, shelved in the fermented condiment or Thai section of Southeast Asian and Chinese markets. It is also sold online. Gapi is made from fermented shrimp (krill to be exact) and salt, plus maybe some MSG and sugar. Buy true, pure gapi made from just shrimp and salt, if you can. Brands such as Prateepthong (shrimp logo) and Trachang (scale logo) are good. Store it in the fridge, where it will last forever. Artisanal gapi is hard to find, so use my good gapi hack ❿ (see page 118) to mimic excellent gapi produced in Thailand. Perplexingly, some Thai products labeled "shrimp paste" are not gapi. If the list of product ingredients includes oil and other spices, that's not gapi!

Hatcho miso ⓫ is a dark, thick, strong-flavored paste made from pure soybeans with no other grains (unlike other types of miso), is the best substitute for dried fermented soybeans, or **tua nao ถั่วเน่า**, from Northern Thailand. To make a swap for tua nao, I dehydrate miso and my recipes offer fast- and slow-drying methods. Shop for quality brands of hatcho miso, like Hikari or Marukome, at Japanese markets. When unavailable, use a dark aka (red) miso. If you are lucky enough to find real Thai tua nao, use it.

FAST FAKE FISH SAUCE

In a jar, combine ¼ cup (60ml) Thai thin soy sauce, ¼ cup (60ml) water, and 2 tsp fine sea salt and stir to dissolve the salt. If a recipe in this book calls for fish sauce but is otherwise vegetarian, use this condiment as a substitute for the fish sauce. You're welcome!

Fatty, Sweet, and Sour

What would Thai food be without a complex dance of flavors? These staples are used over and over in my kitchen—and will soon be in yours too.

Coconut milk น้ำกะทิ ❶ defines so many Thai dishes. Use unsweetened full-fat coconut milk, not the stuff for piña coladas. A little emulsifier is OK, but the unshaken box or can of coconut milk should have distinct separation to ensure it will separate well for certain dishes. Thai cooks distinguish gati (coconut milk) by its creamy head, or hua gati **หัวกะทิ**, versus its watery tail, or hang gati **หางกะทิ**. When a recipe needs coconut cream or "thick" coconut milk, you're looking for hua gati. Simply spoon it from the top of an unshaken can of coconut milk (canned coconut cream tastes oddly soapy). What remains is the thinner tail. Most times, you just need gati, so it's fine to use head and tail together. Suggested brands include Aroy-D, Mae Ploy, Chaokoh, PraHom, Whole Foods, and Native Forest.

Lime juice น้ำมะนาว ❷ can help brighten and uplift dishes for a great interplay of flavors. To breeze through prep, juice a bunch of Persian or Key limes, freeze the juice in an ice cube tray, then transfer the frozen juice to an airtight container and store for up to 6 months. See pages 28 and 31 for makrut lime information.

Rice bran oil น้ำมันรำข้าว ❸ is the neutral oil that I use in my home and restaurants. Among its many positives are a clean flavor and a high smoke point of 450°F (230°C). Rice bran has a lighter viscosity than other oils, like corn oil, so rice bran oil does not cling as much to finished fried food, making it less greasy tasting. Because it is naturally rich in antioxidants, it doesn't go rancid as easily as other oils. Rice bran oil is a favorite for tempura frying, so look for it at a Japanese market, or seek it out online.

Rice vinegar น้ำส้มสายชู ❹ is the vinegar I prefer for most dishes. Choose unseasoned rice vinegar. Good distilled white vinegar can be used in a pinch, but use a little less because it's more acidic and stronger tasting.

Tamarind pulp มะขามเปียก ❺ sold as double-wrapped "seedless" slabs is the source of the delicious tamarind liquid (page 52) that's required for some sauces and curries in this book.

Thai palm sugar น้ำตาลมะพร้าว น้ำตาลโตนด ❻ is the unrefined, concentrated sap harvested from cut sugar palms. It is sold as hard, small pucks and large disks or sometimes in a soft, spoonable texture. Some brands include fillers, so always buy brands that contain "pure palm or coconut sugar 100 percent." Suggested brands include Jack Hua and Dragonfly. Note that if your palm sugar comes in a jar with a layer of wax on top, you should scrape off the wax (and a bit of the sugar below too). See opposite page for bonus tips.

Thai sweet chili sauce น้ำจิ้มไก่ ❼ has a garlicky undercurrent that lends good funk to the mildly hot, sweet condiment. Because commercially made sauce tastes cloying right out of the bottle, use the easy recipe on page 54 to doctor it up so it's special. Suggested brands include Aroy-D and Mae Ploy.

PALM SUGAR POINTERS

After opening a new package of palm sugar, briefly microwave the puck(s) to soften, then chop into small chunks. Store the chunks in a tightly capped glass container so they retain moisture, making the sugar easier to measure for recipes. If a recipe has a weight measure for palm sugar, use it for ease; otherwise, do your best to firmly pack the sugar into a measuring spoon or cup. For easier disintegration, you may have to re-chop the sugar before adding it to a dish.

When you need to use palm sugar in a recipe but find that it's rock hard and does not melt easily, try this: Put the palm sugar into a small microwave-safe bowl, add a little water, and then microwave on high power for 15 to 30 seconds, stirring at the midpoint, until the sugar has melted. Just be sure to use it before it rehardens.

To finesse or finish a dish with a pinch of palm sugar, use a vegetable peeler to shave a bit off a hardened chunk.

5
KODA FARMS
A Family Legacy in California Farming Since 1928
Gluten-Free
MOCHIKO
Sweet Rice Flour
BLUE STAR BRAND
6
TAPIOCA STARCH
AMIDON DE TAPIOCA
ERAWAN BRAND
NET WT. 16 OZ. (1 LB.)
POIDS NET. 16 OZ. (1 LB.)
NĂNG. 16 OZ. (1 LB.)
3
RICE FLOUR
2
1

Rices, Flours, and Starches

Learn how to cook jasmine rice on page 256 and sticky rice on page 257, but first, here's what you should shop for.

Rice is the daily go-to grain for many Thai meals and there are many kinds cultivated, as discussed on page 254, but in the main, you'll need two types.

- **Jasmine rice ข้าวหอมมะลิ** ❶ is commonly eaten, and what is cultivated in Thailand not only cooks up fragrant and fluffy but also has unparalleled perfume, texture, and taste. The brands Three Ladies, Golden Phoenix, Golden Star, and Elephant are great. If you want to go for domestic jasmine, try Lundberg from California or Jazzmen from Louisiana.
- **Sticky rice ข้าวเหนียว** ❷ has a good amount of amylopectin (the starch that makes rice grains stick to one another) versus amylose (the starch that makes rice grains firm). That's why the chalky grains cook up very sticky. For certain Isaan dishes, the flavor and texture of the rice counter the heat and soak up sauces. Thai cooking favors long-grain sticky rice (also called glutinous rice and sweet rice). Look for Three Ladies or Golden Phoenix brand.

Rice flour แป้งข้าวเจ้า comes in many forms, but you'll need only the following three kinds of Asian rice flour for recipes in this book. The Thai rice flours we use are water-milled to a very fine, powdery texture; I recommend buying Erawan brand, identifiable by its three-headed elephant logo. Please don't substitute other kinds of rice flour, such as stone-ground flour.

- **Thai (regular) rice flour แป้งข้าวเจ้า** ❸ is made from long-grain jasmine rice. It is sold in plastic bags with **RED** lettering.
- **Thai glutinous rice flour แป้งข้าวเหนียว** ❹ is made from glutinous (sticky) rice and is *not* interchangeable with regular rice flour. Look for bags with **GREEN** lettering.
- **Mochiko** sweet rice flour **แป้งโมจิ** ❺ is ground from dry short-grain glutinous rice so it is slightly coarser than the water-milled Thai flour. I recommend boxed Blue Star brand by Koda Farms.

Starches have multiple purposes in the Thai kitchen. I often use **tapioca starch แป้งมัน** ❻, derived from the cassava plant, to thicken dishes or to combine with regular rice flour to create a crispy coating for deep-fried foods. Choose a Thai brand like Erawan, which is sold in plastic bags with **BLUE** lettering. In a pinch, use a supermarket brand. Any brand of **cornstarch แป้งข้าวโพด** ❼ will do.

Aromatics and Herbs

Whether chopped or pounded, raw or cooked, tropical aromatics and herbs set the tone for Thai food experiences. They inject flavor, color, and perfume.

Basil finishes certain foods and serves as an accompaniment. Anisey and purple-stemmed **Thai basil** ❶ (โหระพา bai horapa) is sold at many Asian markets. If you cannot find Thai basil, use dark **opal basil** ❷, which has similar flavor; you can also combine the two basils, as done for the duck curry on page 147. The softly serrated leaves of rarer **holy basil** ❸ (กะเพรา bai gaprao), whether green or reddish purple, have a distinct aroma and a spicier, more peppery flavor than Thai basil. **Lemon basil** ❹ (ใบแมงลัก bai mang luck), true to its name, has a citrusy scent. Grow these as summer crops or buy them from Southeast Asian farmers or Cambodian or Hmong markets.

Cilantro ❺ (ผักชี pak chee) plays a big role in Thai cooking. The tender leaves and blossoms are used for garnish, and tougher stems and roots are used for curry pastes and seasonings. Cilantro's soapy taste gets neutralized in cooking but if you do not like the herb, omit it for garnishing. **Cilantro root** ❻ (รากผักชี raak pak chee) is widely sold in Thailand but abroad can be hard to source. Trim stubby roots from farmers' market bunches and freeze for future recipes. Cilantro stems are an OK substitute, but the roots are best.

Climbing wattle ❼ (ชะอม cha-om) has a strong, musty aroma that mellows when cooked. Enjoy its vegetal, slightly bitter flavor in the curry and fried omelet on pages 186 and 179. Look for the feathery herb in frozen or fresh form at Southeast Asian markets.

Galangal ❽ (ข่า kha) is related to ginger but it has a sharper, earthier, and more medicinal flavor than ginger. Chinese and Southeast Asian markets sell it fresh and frozen. Spring-harvested galangal has thin skin so buy some to freeze in chunks or thick slices. Ground dried galangal can be used in certain recipes. Please do not substitute ginger.

Grachai ❾ (กระชาย fingerroot, Chinese keys) lends an earthy, pungent pepperiness and menthol-like medicinal note to certain curries. Buy the fingerlike rhizome fresh or frozen at Thai and Vietnamese markets (it is imported from Vietnam as ngải bún). I never use jarred pickled grachai.

Lemongrass ❿ (ตะไคร้ takrai) costars in many dishes in this book, so find a source for fresh stalks or purchase frozen stalks (resist prechopped frozen lemongrass) from an Asian market. Thinly slice fresh stalks for raw uses. See page 30 for prep tips.

Makrut lime leaves and fruits ⓫ (ใบมะกรูด bai makrut, ลูกมะกรูด luk makrut) are both used in Thai dishes, but the leaves are called for more often. You'll crumple or sliver the leaves for recipes (see page 31). Need makrut rind? Use a paring knife to cut the skin and a bit of pith (ditto if swapping in regular lime rind). Makrut lime leaves and fruits freeze beautifully.

Mint (สะระแหน่ saranae) leaves, whether spearmint or peppermint (see page 122, in the center), impart refreshing zip to Thai dishes. Grow it for the best flavor and perkiest texture.

Pandan leaves ⓬ (ใบเตย bai toey) offer jade color and grassy, vanilla-ish notes to sweets and savories. Frozen pandan is great because fresh is rare. Partially thaw the package of leaves (which resemble giant blades of grass) at room temperature for 15 to 20 minutes, then peel off what you want and refreeze the package in a ziplock bag. Pandan is sold as lá dứa at Vietnamese markets.

Sawtooth herb ⓭ (ผักชีฝรั่ง pakchee farang) is a spiny-leaf herb with an earthy cilantro flavor. The skinny, long leaves, usually folded over in their packaging, are sold at many Chinese, Southeast Asian, and some Latin grocers. At Vietnamese markets, look for packages labeled "ngò gai."

Shiso ⓮ (ใบชิโสะ bai shiso), whether the Japanese or Viet variety (called tía tô), is great with laab and other dishes. The matte, broad leaves may be ruffly or serrated, green, red, or purple and green. Shiso's unique flavor blends elements of basil and mint.

Wild betel leaves ⓯ (ใบชะพลู bai chaplu) have an inviting peppery, nearly incense-like flavor. The glossy, heart-shaped green leaves of *Piper sarmentosum* and *P. lolot* are mostly sold at Viet markets as lá lốt and are in season from late spring into fall. Do not mistakenly buy thicker, matte betel leaves (*P. betle*), which are meant to be chewed as a mild stimulant. Fresh is best for raw eating. Sold at Viet grocers, frozen lá lốt (sometimes labeled "piper la lot") will work fine for cooked dishes.

Vietnamese coriander (ผักไผ่ pak pai) is available at Vietnamese and some Chinese markets. With cilantro-ish heat, the miniature bamboo-like leaves (in the lower right of the photo on page 122) are a worthy swap for sawtooth herb. Use 50 percent less because pak pai is strong! In Vietnamese markets, this herb is labeled "rau răm."

2
12
9
7
5
15
1
10
4
8
11
6
13
14

Tips for Aromatics and Herbs

Beyond knowing what to buy, these tips offer basic insights for making the most of the aromatics and herbs that you'll soon be using for cooking Thai food.

PREP LEMONGRASS WISELY

Lemongrass looks like an inedible baton, but you can eat it if you prep it right. To trim a stalk, chop off the tough bottom base with its hard V-shaped core and the green, woody tops. Remove any loose or dry outer layers to reveal a smooth, tight stalk.

To slice, firmly hold the trimmed stalk with your nondominant hand and cut crosswise into thin (⅛-inch | 3mm) rings. If the lemongrass is to be eaten raw, slice it super thin (1⁄16 inch | 1.5mm) or thinner so it can be easily chewed. (Or cut the stalk into roughly 3-inch | 7.5cm lengths, then split in half lengthwise before cutting crosswise into half circles. It's steadier on the cutting board but less handsome in the dish.)

To chop or mince lemongrass, go at the thin circles or half circles with a sharp knife. For ¼ cup (25g) or more, chop the sections into ¼-inch (6mm) pieces, then blitz in a food chopper. A food processor can handle 1 cup (100g) or more.

When you spy gorgeous fresh lemongrass, buy five or six stalks, trim off the base and the woody tops, and remove the loose, dry outer layers. Freeze the trimmed sections in a ziplock bag for up to 3 months. Frozen lemongrass is easier to chop, but the slices aren't as fresh tasting for raw garnishes.

If your lemongrass is weak on flavor, use more. You can never have enough, it seems.

KEEP BASIL FRESH FOR DAYS

Avoid refrigerating basil, as the moisture of a refrigerator will darken and spoil the leaves. Trim the ends of the stems at an angle, then stand the sprigs like flowers in a water vase. Cover loosely with a large plastic produce bag (poke four or five holes on each side of the bag for ventilation) and keep at room temperature, changing the water every few days. The basil should last for a good week or more, depending on the type and its freshness.

CUT LIME LEAF SLIVERS LIKE A PRO

The delicate slivers of makrut lime leaf in Thai dishes are not there for show. They inject aroma and flavor. For chewability, a makrut leaf needs to be rendered into delicate threadlike slivers.

Separate each figure eight–shaped leaf into a big and small leaf. With the big-leaf spine running vertically, roll the leaf up into a cylinder as wide as a thick pencil.

Press two fingertips on the center spine to hold the leaf in place as you slowly and methodically cut the leaf (rushing yields uneven cuts). Wield a sharp, thin knife, such as a santoku, nakiri, or vegetable cleaver. Alternatively, snip with kitchen scissors, like a pair by Joyce Chen. When using a knife, curl your knuckles to avoid mishap.

Whatever your tool, make superfine cuts to yield threadlike pieces. When you come uncomfortably close to the spine, rotate the leaf 180 degrees and cut the other side. When done, discard the leftover inedible spine. If the smaller leaf is big enough, cut it too (or save it to add whole to dishes). Slivers sometimes break into short lengths, so don't fret. Transfer to an airtight container with a damp paper towel touching the slivers and refrigerate for up to 3 days.

Weigh or measure the slivers as loosely packed quantities, but be generous because a little more makrut leaf won't hurt a dish.

Alliums

Thai food involves lots of alliums. Luckily, you likely already keep these on hand.

Garlic กระเทียม appears often and in large amounts. Purchasing already-peeled garlic is fine as long as it is fresh. For the pickled garlic recipe on page 55, make sure the cloves are very fresh (peel them yourself).

Green onions ต้นหอม (scallions) add verdant pungency to laab salads and other dishes. Unless specified otherwise, use a medium green onion, which is about ½ inch (1.25cm) wide where the green melts into the white part. Slender ones are as thin as pencils. In the main, Thai food's bold flavors can handle the entire green onion (all the green and white parts). Trim off the root end, then prep what remains for my recipes, unless otherwise specified.

Onions หอมใหญ่ vary in size, so here are rough benchmarks: small (5 oz | 150g, tangerine size), medium (8 oz | 225g, orange size), and large or jumbo (11 oz | 330g, grapefruit size).

Fried shallots หอมเจียว lend sweet, nutty richness to Thai dishes. We fry them at my restaurants, but for home cooking, my advice channels Ina Garten: "Store-bought is fine!" Look for brands from Thailand, which may be labeled as "fried shallots," "fried onions," or "fried red onions" (usually a red-skinned shallot on the label verifies what is inside). Once the jar or package is opened, refrigerate to keep the shallots good for months.

Shallots หอมแดง add delicate, sweet pungency to curry pastes, laab salads, and many other Thai dishes. Because shallots vary in size, use the weight measurement as a guide.

Spices

Whole spices offer the most perfume and flavor, so my recipes call for them. In a few cases, such as fresh turmeric and mace blades, you may see an equivalent in ground form.

Certain spices, like **sand ginger** เร่วผง, **dried galangal** ข่าผง, and **black cardamom** ชะโก, are best sourced from Chinese and Southeast Asian markets. Otherwise, purchase from a spice shop or online importer, such as Diaspora Co. or Burlap & Barrel.

Core Equipment Needs

Aside from the basic tools and equipment, such as a digital scale, food processor, blender, spice grinder, and good knives, you need just a few other affordable items to cook recipes from this book.

I use the following tools and pans quite often.

Thai cooks make frequent use of a granite **krok** (ครก) to pound, crush, and bruise ingredients efficiently. To be precise, the mortar is the krok and the pestle is the sak, but in Thai we often use the shorthand "krok" for both because you can't use one without the other, and the krok is the main tool. The pestle is great for smacking lemongrass, making pesto, and much more. See page 37 for krok tips.

A large **wok** (กระทะ grata) is perfect not just for stir-fries but also for toasting rice for laab salads and charring chilies for curry pastes. Mine is a lightweight, inexpensive carbon-steel wok. For induction burners, a wok with an extra-wide flat bottom will distribute heat well. Don't have a wok yet? Use a similarly shaped pan or a skillet made of carbon steel or cast iron.

When charring aromatics and vegetables, employ **a perforated skillet** or **vegetable grill pan.** Recipes in this book were developed using a Közmatik pan from Turkey plus the OXO perforated carbon-steel pan. In the absence of those, you can char your aromatics and vegetables by grilling over an open flame, broiling very close to the heat source, or trying a ripping-hot cast-iron or carbon-steel skillet.

A **microwave vented splatter cover** allows you to heat food in the microwave without having to cover the container with parchment. It also enables the microwave to function like a steamer. It is great for small tasks like cooking sticky rice in 30 minutes (page 257) and steaming potatoes for curry puffs (page 81).

Bonus! Although not requisite, I do love these items for cooking Thai food and more.

- **The Chef's Press** by Bruce Hill keeps wobbly ingredients (like chilies) in place for charring and searing.
- Washable natural fabric **spice bags** hold aromatics for apothecary soup (page 202) and duck noodle soup (page 273). If unavailable, use a large piece of unbleached muslin. Cheesecloth is pricey and cannot be reused as much.
- A **fine-mesh Asian skimmer** efficiently removes impurities, like pesky scum and errant bits, from broth and oil.
- The OXO Good Grips **collapsible steamer** stands taller than others to facilitate decent steaming sessions in tallish pots for the curries on pages 225 and 227 and the custard on page 286.
- A basic **Thai fruit carving knife** with a long bird's beak-like blade makes digging cucumber tunnels a cinch for the soup on page 201. It's fab for cutting arty pieces of other produce too.
- **Nitrile medical gloves** make such messy tasks as seeding chilies and chopping fresh turmeric easier. Choose biodegradable ones for sustainability.
- **Quarter and eighth sheet pans** are a godsend for organizing food prep and mise en place.

THAI TABLE SETTINGS 101

Keep it simple. Spoon and fork plus a dinner plate comprise the everyday table setting for Thai meals. Your dominant hand holds the spoon while the nondominant hand wields the fork. Use both utensils to combine foods on your plate, then usher a morsel onto the spoon to eat. For wraps, sticky rice, and other finger foods, dive in with your hands to eat.

When there's a soup on the menu, add a small bowl for each person. Knives are not traditionally used at Thai tables, but you can use them if you like. In Thailand, chopsticks are used only for noodles, never for rice.

POT AND PAN SIZES

Using too small or too large a pan impacts how a dish cooks, potentially changing the timing or how quickly moisture evaporates, for example. You don't have to match exactly what we use, but if you choose equipment wisely, you will cook through recipes more easily. Here are two tables to guide you.

SAUCEPANS, POTS, DUTCH OVENS, AND BRAISERS	U.S. VOLUME	METRIC VOLUME
Very small	1 quart	1L
Small	1½ to 2 quarts	1.4 to 1.9L
Medium	2½ to 3 quarts	2.3 to 2.8L
Medium-large	3½ to 4 quarts	3.3 to 3.8L
Large	5 to 6 quarts	4.7 to 5.7L

SKILLETS AND WOKS	U.S. WIDTH	METRIC WIDTH
Small skillet	8 inches	20cm
Medium skillet	10 inches	25cm
Large skillet	12 inches	30cm
Medium wok	10 to 12 inches	25 to 30cm
Large wok	14 to 16 inches	35 to 40cm

Thai Mortar and Pestle Pointers

Now and then, it's a good idea to slow down to pound ingredients rather than chop them in a processor. You'll release their essence and witness their transformation much better. Also, some ingredient quantities are so small that a krok (shorthand for Thai mortar and pestle) does the job more efficiently than a machine—and with less cleanup involved. Pound with confidence.

Shop wisely. A granite krok, about 7 inches (18cm) wide from outer edge to outer edge, is big enough for most tasks. It will be heavy but manageable for washing without first having to train for the Olympics. The pestle needs to be hefty to effectively crush ingredients, but it should also be comfy for you to hold and use. Shop for a Thai-made granite mortar and pestle set at Thai, Cambodian, and Lao markets. Asian kitchen supply and houseware shops are good sources, as is online. No, you do not need a separate earthenware mortar and wooden pestle for the green papaya salad on page 92.

Absorb shock. Set the mortar atop a folded thick dish towel or, better yet, a layer of cork 1 inch (2.5cm) thick (if needed, stack two high-density round cork trivets). The towel or cork will protect your work surface while you use the krok.

Pound strategically. Depending on the ingredients and your stage in the process, wield the pestle accordingly so you'll use less effort to get more done. Here are my favorite pestle moves:

- *Aim for the center* to bruise, crush, or flatten small amounts of spices, chilies, or garlic cloves.
- *Aim for the side* to smash bulky ingredients (lemongrass, galangal, shallot, peanuts) against the wall of the mortar. Then let gravity naturally pull the pestle downward, allowing its residual force to keep crushing the ingredient as it drags the ingredient toward the mortar's center. You can often achieve more by striking the side of the mortar than the center. The side strike yields the ubiquitous "pok, pok" sound of Thai kitchens.
- *Make a well in the center* of already pounded ingredients to add new ingredients, like peppercorns, that you'll then pound only to crack before working them in. The well allows you to layer and build flavors efficiently.
- *Gently twirl* the pestle to remove ingredients sticking to it. Believe me, it works.

Scrape as needed. When pounding a lot of ingredients and they're mostly climbing up the wall of the mortar, pause to use a metal spoon (or silicone spatula) to scrape, flip, and push the ingredients to the center, then continue pounding. It's like scraping the wall of a blender jar or processor bowl.

Shield yourself. If you're concerned about bursting chilies flying into your face, partially cover the mortar with a piece of paper towel as you pound. When pounding more congenial but bulky ingredients that can fly out, like peanuts or curry paste, use your hand to cover partially.

Anatomy of a Recipe

THE **YIELD** PREVIEWS HOW MUCH YOU'LL MAKE OR HOW MANY PEOPLE YOU'LL SERVE.

This book is organized to help you craft the flavors and dishes that I cherish. Each chapter leads with an essay to illuminate what is to come. To explain how recipes are structured, this page is designed like a recipe. What you're reading now is the recipe headnote, a brief introduction on why and how the dish is made. Sometimes the headnote offers extra pointers, like time required or menu planning, so never skip the intro!

Ingredient listings are easy to interpret if you keep certain standards in mind and look for signposts built into them. Below are samples to guide you.

One 400ml | 13.5 oz can coconut milk Measurements often include both metric and an equivalent in U.S. standard units or a count. Ingredients lines generally begin with metric followed by U.S. standard units, as we prefer metric's precision for key measures; there are a couple of places where we flip the order as it's crucial for measurement.

2 Tbsp fish sauce When the measure is 3 tablespoons or less, only the volume is offered in U.S. standard units; we break that rule for tricky ingredients like spices in curry pastes.

10g | 3 slices peeled galangal, smashed Prep techniques are stated in order of operation. Here, the ingredient line means that you should weigh a 10-gram piece of peeled galangal, cut it into 3 slices, and then smash the slices.

30g | 1 oz seeded dried prik chee fa or puya chilies Interpret this to mean that the seeds were removed from the chilies before they were measured. You'll find seeding tips on page 20.

5 green Thai chilies Fresh chili peppers come in many colors. Unless noted, fresh chilies are used unseeded. If the recipe does not call for a specific color, use any color.

40g | ¼ cup garlic cloves Unless otherwise stated, peel shallots, garlic, and onions and then measure.

25g | ¼ cup chopped green onions Employ whole green onions, both green and white parts, unless otherwise specified.

40g | 2 Tbsp Thai palm sugar Weighing the sugar is easiest, but when using volume measurements, be sure to chop and soften the sugar before firmly packing it into a measuring spoon or cup.

6 makrut leaves Each double-lobed makrut leaf counts as one leaf. Employ them both when whole leaves are needed.

2 Tbsp chopped sawtooth herb (optional) If you can find the ingredient, use it. However, it is not required for your success.

1½ Tbsp fish sauce, plus more to taste Understand that you may need to add more than the baseline amount stated to tweak flavors and garnish, as you like.

5 to 8 Thai chilies, to taste Use as much as you like per your taste. The range is simply a guide.

Skim the instructions first: Before getting to work, know how things will flow and the equipment and time needed. Instruction subheads provide an overview of the process and serve as handy placeholders (if you pause mid-recipe). When measures are provided in instructions, they are in U.S. standard units, and on occasion, followed by metric.

Organize for efficiency: Recipe ingredients are presented in order of use, not in their prep order. Identify advance prep and other tasks you can do while something else is cooking. Put ingredients that go into the pan together in one bowl. Prep vegetables before proteins to minimize cutting-board washing.

Know your stove: All of the recipes were developed in my home kitchens in San Francisco and Auckland, tested by Andrea, and cross-tested by volunteer home cooks with gas, electric, or induction ranges. Stoves vary in power, and our average gas burner was between 9,000 and 12,000 BTUs. "Wok burners" were up to 21,000 BTUs. You may need to adjust cooking time or heat level. Employ the recipe's visual, tactile, and flavor cues as your guide.

Use sugar judiciously: Some dishes, like na tung (page 71) and caramelized pork belly (page 220), are sweet and savory, but most savory Thai dishes are not sugary sweet. You can coax complex, natural sweetness from coconut milk, shallots, and other ingredients by proper cooking and patience. When in doubt, rest and cure flavors for 10 to 15 minutes. Let them meld and fully develop, then retaste and adjust as needed.

NOTES

Look for bonus tips: Recipe endnotes contain ingredient swaps, advance prep, and sourcing pointers.

Variations let you play: They have all been tested.

Follow the recipe the first time: We all need standards and parameters when making new dishes. After tweaking things to your liking, write down your changes for next time.

RECIPE BUILDING BLOCKS

I sometimes divide recipes into discrete building blocks to help you better understand recipe components or accomplish long projects. Building blocks are used by many chefs and recipe developers to organize their professional kitchen. They are handy tools for advance prep too.

For example, in the pork belly hunglay curry on page 181, there are three recipe building blocks: the masala, curry paste, and curry. Each block contains a grouping of ingredients followed by corresponding methods. Think of each one as a mini recipe or project to tackle before combining them to assemble the finished dish. That means you can make the masala and paste weeks ahead and cook up the curry when you want.

WEIGH WHEN POSSIBLE

When both a weight measurement and volume measurement are provided, choose the weight measurement and use a digital scale (it rarely lies). That way, you'll closely match my flavors and have good benchmarks to craft your own. If you don't have a scale yet, use the volume measurement. If there is only a count, like "3 lemongrass stalks," aim for medium ones or use big ones if you like the aromatic. You won't ruin the recipe.

THE ORDER OF THINGS

There's something quite uncommon in the way old-school Thai cooks talk about the correct composition or balance of flavors in a dish. For instance, a dish is not just spicy, salty, and sour. Its identity depends on a very specific order in which you taste each distinct flavor. I've never heard cooks or chefs from other cultures describe flavors that way.

As I cook these heritage recipes, I often hear my aunties' voices. For instance, there's Pah Pui telling me that her gaeng som (page 179) must lead with acidity, followed by salinity, then spicy chili heat, and finally just a slight roundness of sugar. "**แกงส้มต้องหวานปะแล่มๆ อย่าหวานนำเด็ดขาด** [It must never lead with sweetness]," she admonished. On the other hand, for gaeng moo chamuang (page 176), Khun Pah Tum (who taught me how to make it) would say you *must* taste the balance of sugar and acid, followed by salt and heat.

I find this Thai way of describing flavor sequence quite helpful as I am finishing a dish, dialing up or down certain elements to achieve the correct order of things. Look for similar cues in the recipes as you finesse dishes. The world is messy enough. We should be grateful to my aunties for sorting us out!

1 เครื่องปรุง ของแห้ง

Larder

800
750
900
950
700
650
480
620
700
680

It's Worth It

My life these days is split among three countries: the United States, where my husband, Mark, and I have our home base and my two restaurants in San Francisco; New Zealand, where we now keep two homes, a city apartment in Auckland near Mark's family and our vineyard farmhouse in Martinborough; and Thailand, at my family home in the Sukhumvit neighborhood of Bangkok, although while in the city, I mainly cook at my restaurant, Nahm.

But no matter where I am, cooking in my own home kitchens is how I stay grounded. That entails keeping a pantry of store-bought ingredients I like and growing a garden of herbs and other hard-to-find produce that I need for Thai cooking. What is most important is creating a larder of super-useful base ingredients for crafting my flavors, my food.

At my restaurants, making everything we serve in-house has been our ethos from the start. Offering our own unique flavors and style is how we have established and distinguished ourselves from other restaurants. Barring things that are not logistically possible for us to do, like making fish sauce or operating our own coconut plantation, we do the rest ourselves.

But at home, without an army of prep cooks and dishwashers to help, I approach cooking-from-scratch Thai food a bit differently.

"Is it worth it?"

That's the question I always ask myself. Indeed, fried shallots (which are called for in quite a few recipes in this book) are best when freshly fried, but are they worth using up a quart of oil that spatters everywhere? Not really, given that store-bought fried shallots are pretty good. I'm not going to fry my own at home.

On the other hand, toasting and grinding dried chilies for prik pon (page 46) gives me the ability to dial up or down the smokiness and heat of the chili blend to meet my personal taste. Excellent bespoke prik pon is among the levers I pull to calibrate flavors in many dishes, including curries, laab salads, and jaew sauce. I'll do that myself.

Isaan-style khao kua (rice powder) is sold commonly enough, but that stuff from the bag tastes like sawdust. Making your own khao kua (page 47) yields an ambrosial powder that is so far superior that it hails from an entirely different universe. Absolutely worth it.

And, of course, my home is never without my grandmother's namprik pao (page 44). You *could* buy commercial chili jam, and many people do, but taste my homemade magic once and you will never go back.

Ranging from hot and heady seasonings to fluid accents and pungent notes, the recipes in this chapter are ones I find worthy of spending a bit (and, OK, sometimes a *little* more than a bit) of time and energy to make for my larder. But with these homemade ingredients on hand, I feel like I have my secret culinary superpowers. They'll soon be yours too—for your flavors, for your Thai food.

Trust me.

น้ำพริกเผาคุณยาย | Namprik Pao

Grandmother's Chili Jam

MAKES ABOUT 2 CUPS (570G)

Excellent chili jam is not just a workhorse in the Thai kitchen. It is the soul of my kitchen. The recipe by my khun yai (grandmother) seeded my Thai cooking journey, many favorite dishes at my restaurants, and this cookbook. Richly balanced with beguiling tart-sweet-salty flavors and not too fiery (the way it should be!), this namprik pao comes together with basic Thai staples and supermarket ingredients. Mexican dried puya chili closely mimics the bright, smoky, citrusy notes of prik chee fa, the big, medium-hot pepper typically used in Thailand for this condiment.

A batch of namprik pao has many uses. Plop some into tom yum soup (page 193), stir-fry it with clams (page 240), use it to define a coconutty sauce for seared scallops (page 97), or simply spoon it on top of rice or noodles. You can even spread it on toast! See Notes for more tips, including one on how to lower the jam's chili heat.

50g | 1.8 oz seeded dried prik chee fa or puya chilies

240ml | 1 cup neutral oil, such as rice bran

100g | ⅔ cup garlic cloves, sliced lengthwise about ⅛ inch (3mm) thick

150g | 5 medium shallots, sliced crosswise about ⅛ inch (3mm) thick

40g | 2 Tbsp packed gapi (Thai shrimp paste), either Gapi Dee (Good Gapi, page 118) or store-bought

80ml | ⅓ cup Nam Makam (Tamarind Liquid, page 52), plus more to taste

100g | 5 Tbsp firmly packed Thai palm sugar, plus more to taste

60 ml | ¼ cup water

2 Tbsp fish sauce, plus more to taste

Prik Pon (Toasted Chili Flakes, page 46; optional)

Toast the chilies: To mitigate the indoor aromas, turn on the range hood exhaust fan and open a window. Set a large wok over medium heat. When the pan is hot (to test, flick in a couple of drops of water; they should sizzle and evaporate within seconds), add the chilies. Use a spatula to stir vigorously and constantly until they begin to smoke and darken in a few places, 1 to 2 minutes. Pour into a medium bowl. Wipe the wok clean.

Fry the alliums and process: Add the oil and garlic to the wok and set over medium heat. As the oil heats up, stir with the spatula to fry the garlic evenly until lightly golden, 4 to 5 minutes. (Don't go over to a solid gold color now, as the garlic will be recooked later.) Remove the pan from the heat to slow the cooking efficiently, then use a fine-mesh skimmer to transfer the garlic to a small bowl, leaving the oil in the wok.

With the wok set over medium heat, add the shallots and fry, stirring often with the spatula to prevent hot spots, until at least half of the pieces are golden brown, 4 to 10 minutes. Remove the pan from the heat and use the fine-mesh skimmer to scoop the shallots into the bowl of garlic, leaving the oil in the pan.

Transfer the toasted chilies to a food processor, add the fried garlic and shallots, and process, pausing to scrape down the bowl sides as needed, until a very fine, crumbly, moist mixture forms. Transfer to a small bowl.

Cook and tweak the jam: For faster and more even cooking, form the shrimp paste into a ball, then use the back of a spoon to flatten it into a disk ½ inch (1.25cm) thick. Set the wok with the remaining oil over medium-high heat. When the oil is hot (a small pinch of shrimp paste should gently sizzle), add the shrimp paste and fry, turning often, until fragrant, about 1 minute. The shrimp paste will naturally fall apart, and that's OK.

Lower the heat to medium and stir in the processed chili mixture. Add the tamarind, sugar, water, and fish sauce and stir well with the spatula to blend and dissolve the sugar. To check your seasoning, move the wok off the heat, let cool briefly, and taste. You should taste a good balance of sour, sweet, and salty flavor notes followed by a lingering smoky, slightly spicy finish. The mixture should not be too spicy at this point. To tweak the flavor balance, add tamarind liquid by the 1½ tsp to boost fruity tang and tame spiciness, palm sugar by the 1 tsp to amplify sweetness and cut spicy heat, prik pon (if using) by the 1 tsp to boost heat, or fish sauce by the 1 tsp to increase savory notes.

When satisfied with the flavor notes, continue cooking over medium heat, scraping the sides and bottom of the wok to avoid burnt spots, until slightly thickened and the texture of loose jam, 3 to 5 minutes.

Remove from the heat and let cool completely in the pan. Transfer to a jar, cap tightly, and refrigerate for nearly forever. Always use a clean metal spoon to scoop up jam from the jar.

NOTES

Hand slice the raw garlic and shallots so they don't clump up during frying. Resist prepping them with the food processor. But do use the food processor to grind the chilies and fried aromatics.

For milder heat, make a fifty-fifty blend of puya and guajillo (or New Mexico) chilies. For even gentler heat, make the chili jam with only guajillo, New Mexico, or California chilies. Regardless of what chilies you use, snip them into 2-inch (5cm) pieces to ensure even toasting.

The wok is the most efficient vessel for making chili jam. If unavailable, toast the chilies in a large skillet but fry the aromatics and cook the jam in a medium saucepan.

Without a fine-mesh skimmer, pour the garlic and oil through a fine-mesh strainer set over a heatproof bowl, then return the oil to the wok. Repeat with the fried shallots.

พริกป่น | Prik Pon

Toasted Chili Flakes

MAKES ABOUT ⅔ CUP (160ML)

Certain Thai dishes need lots of dried chili for heat, aroma, and color, or they look and taste anemic. But be not afraid! Using lots of chilies in dishes doesn't necessarily lead to screaming-hot flavors. One Thai tool for balancing flavors and calibrating heat is prik pon (photographed on page 48 on the left). My recipes liberally use it, but it is always tempered by salt, acid, and some fat. Restaurants offer it in condiment caddies, but you can easily make your own with a bespoke selection of chilies and a spice grinder.

Use your prik pon to define Thai icons like laab salads (pages 106 and 107) and nam jim jaew (page 209) or to fine-tune curries and chili jam (page 44). If you don't want to commit to a super-spicy curry paste, make it milder by tweaking the chili blend and then season with prik pon during cooking. Add spices to prik pon to yield prik laab (page 49), a spice blend required for certain northern Thai dishes.

You can make and keep prik pon at different heat levels, as different dishes have different chili needs. From the options at right, pick two to match your spice tolerance. Make a batch of each (halve them, if you like) and use them for recipes in this book. Create your own blends. Before you begin, see page 20 for pointers on seeding chilies to protect yourself. It can be challenging to seed a large quantity.

SPICY

60g | 2 oz seeded dried prik jinda or árbol chilies (aim for uniform size)

MEDIUM SPICY

30g | 1 oz seeded dried prik jinda or árbol chilies (aim for uniform size)

30g | 1 oz seeded dried prik chee fa, puya, or guajillo chilies, cut into 1-inch (2.5cm) pieces

MILDLY SPICY

60g | 2 oz seeded dried prik chee fa, puya, guajillo, or New Mexico chilies, cut into 1-inch (2.5cm) pieces

Toast the chilies: Because the chilies are of different sizes, toast each type separately in a large wok or skillet. To mitigate the indoor aromas, turn on the range hood exhaust fan and open a window. Put the chilies into a cold pan and set over medium heat. Stir rhythmically and constantly with a spatula until they begin to darken. Lower the heat to medium-low and keep stirring until the chilies have darkened and dulled a bit, smell aromatic, and feel crisp under the weight of your stirring. Total toasting time is 4 to 6 minutes, depending on the chili size and type. Remove from the heat, dump the chilies into a bowl, and leave to cool to room temperature. Let the pan cool completely before beginning to toast a different chili.

Grind, tweak, and store: Using a clean spice grinder or coffee grinder, pulse each variety of toasted chili into small flakes, stopping before the chilies turn powdery. Combine your chilies in a bowl, taste, and then wait a minute for the flavor to bloom on your tongue. Does it taste spicy, medium spicy, or mildly spicy? If needed, toast and grind more chilies to add to the mix. For instance, if your prik pon is too hot, add some ground toasted guajillo, New Mexico, or California chili to shift down the heat.

Store the prik pon in a tightly capped glass jar in a cool, dark cupboard for up to 1 year. Use a dry metal spoon to measure it to avoid introducing moisture.

ข้าวคั่ว | Khao Kua

Isaan Fragrant Rice Powder

MAKES ABOUT 1½ CUPS (360ML)

Toasted rice powder adds nubby texture and nutty flavor and slightly thickens innumerable Isaan (Northeastern Thai) dishes, such as laab (pages 106 and 107), nam tok salad (page 112), and jaew sauces (pages 209 and 224). It's so simple to make, costs little, keeps for months, and yields results far superior than what you can buy. Preparing it typically involves only toasting rice in a skillet, but if you add aromatics (they're all in the photo on page 48), as is done here, the khao kua acquires a citrusy heat that will make your dishes superspecial. To honor Isaan culinary tradition, use white sticky rice (see page 27). When it is unavailable, use jasmine rice. Instead of arduously hand pounding the toasted ingredients, use an electric spice grinder, coffee grinder, or blender (see Notes).

35g | scant ⅓ cup chopped, peeled galangal (see Notes)

35g | generous ⅓ cup thinly sliced lemongrass rounds

250g | 1¼ cups raw sticky rice or jasmine rice

5g | 5 makrut lime leaves, torn

Dry-fry the aromatics: Set a dry large wok over low heat, add the galangal, and stir around until slightly dried and darkened a tad, 2 to 4 minutes. Add the lemongrass and continue stirring until most of the rounds are dry and some have browned edges, 3 to 5 minutes.

Toast and perfume the rice: Dump the rice and lime leaves into the pan, increase the heat to medium-high, and continue stirring until the rice is well toasted and a rich blond, 6 to 15 minutes, depending on the stove and the pan. If smoke rises from the pan, lower the heat slightly. As they dry, the galangal and lemongrass will shrivel and the lime leaves will curl and crisp. Transfer to a heatproof bowl (or spread on a sheet pan if you're in a hurry) and let cool completely, about 15 minutes.

Grind the rice: Using a clean spice grinder or coffee grinder, and working in batches, pulse the rice mixture to a medium-fine texture. It should be the consistency of cornmeal or coarse sand. It's OK to leave some pieces of the rice a bit chunkier and the rest powdery, as that will add a nice textural crunch to your khao kua. If hard, unchewable galangal pieces linger, sift the khao kua through a medium-mesh strainer and buzz the stubborn bits in the grinder before letting them join the rest.

Transfer the powder to an airtight container and refrigerate or store away from any light or moisture. Your khao kua will keep for up to 3 months. Always use a clean, dry spoon to scoop out what you need.

NOTES

For even cooking and efficient grinding, cut the galangal no bigger than ¼ inch (6mm).

To grind the toasted rice in a blender, work in two batches. After grinding each batch, sift the batches through a medium-mesh strainer, then pound any hard bits in a mortar.

พริกลาบ | Prik Laab

Northern Thai Chili-Spice Blend

MAKES ½ CUP (120ML)

Use this unique blend of toasted chili flakes and spices to create stunningly delicious dishes like the artichoke laab on page 110 and the cookies on page 293. Chili and long pepper lead the flavor of prik laab, while the other spices collectively contribute citrusy, floral, sweet, and pungent notes. Southeast Asian makwaen is more citrusy and slightly less tingly than its better-known relative, Sichuan peppercorns. When cooking in the States, I favor Burlap & Barrel's, which sources it from Vietnam, where it is called mắc khén. Check the spice section of a Chinese or Southeast Asian market for galangal, ground sand ginger, and long pepper (see Notes for details on the latter two).

The heady perfume and unusual flavor of prik laab reflect the rich traditions of places like Chiang Mai and the surrounding region's ancient Lanna culture. You won't regret spending time to gather and weigh all of the spices.

- 2g | 1½ tsp Sichuan peppercorns, or 2 tsp makwaen
- 2g | 2 big long peppers, each snapped into 2 or 3 pieces
- 1g | 1-inch-piece cinnamon stick, snapped into 3 or 4 pieces
- 1g | 5 green cardamom pods
- 1g | 5 robust star anise petal-like segments
- 1g | ¾ tsp coriander seeds
- 1g | ¼ tsp plus ⅛ tsp dill seeds
- 1g | ¼ tsp plus ⅛ tsp fennel seeds
- 1 pinch of ground nutmeg
- 1 pinch of ground mace (see Notes)
- 1g | ½ tsp ground sand ginger or galangal
- 30g | brimming ⅓ cup Prik Pon (Toasted Chili Flakes, page 46)

In a small saucepan, combine the whole spices: Sichuan peppercorns, long peppers, cinnamon, cardamom, star anise, and coriander, dill, and fennel seeds. Set over medium-low heat and toast, shaking the pan frequently, until heady, about 2 minutes. Remove the pan from the heat, immediately add the ground nutmeg, mace, and sand ginger, and stir to activate their perfume.

Let the spices cool completely, then transfer them to a clean spice grinder or coffee grinder and whirl to a powder. Add the prik pon and pulse to mix well. Transfer to a glass jar, cap tightly, and store in a cool, dark cupboard for up to 1 year.

NOTES

You can use a slender mace blade in place of the ground mace and toast it with the whole spices. Dill seeds here stand in for the traditional malaeb seeds (*Peucedanum dhana* A. Ham), which are all but impossible to find, even in Thailand.

Sand ginger (*Kaempferia galanga*) is related to ginger and galangal (see page 28), but with a spicier, more camphorous aroma. Check the spice section of a Chinese market for 沙姜 (shā jiāng) because sometimes the package of cream-colored spice is mislabeled as "dried ginger powder." Sand ginger is also used for the Hunglay pork belly curry on page 181 and duck noodle soup on page 273.

Long pepper (*Piper longum*) contains wonderful notes of warm spices. They are reminiscent of miniature elongated pine cones. A big long pepper can be up to 1½ inches (3.75cm) long. Like sand ginger, long pepper is also used for Hunglay curry.

ข้าวตังแห้ง | Khao Tung

Crispy Rice Crackers

SERVES 8

Thai cooks don't waste rice. Long ago, when rice was made in large woks, the crusty layer at the bottom was removed, sun-dried, and then deep-fried into khao tung. The crispy shards were perfect for scooping up dishes like beef tartare laab (page 68) and hor mok steamed curries (pages 225 and 227). At Nari, I serve some incredible fried black rice crackers. We use leftover rice and a dehydrator for big batches. Andrea developed this recipe so that you can consistently make the rice crackers in small batches at home. Jasmine rice and a low oven yield thicker but equally ethereal crackers full of toasty rice flavor. These are a great snack on their own too.

240g | 1¼ cups raw jasmine rice

400g | 1⅔ cups water

¼ tsp plus ⅛ tsp fine sea salt

Neutral oil, such as rice bran, for deep-frying

Cook the rice: For minimal cleanup and efficient cooking, measure the rice and water directly into the pan. Stir in the salt, then bring the pan to a boil over high heat, stirring often with a silicone spatula, until the grains expand and swim about in the starchy, thickish liquid and a few craters form on the surface, 1 to 2 minutes. Turn the heat to low, cover, and cook for 10 minutes. Turn off the heat and let sit for 15 minutes to finish cooking.

Press and dry: While the rice finishes cooking, position a rack in the middle of the oven and preheat the oven to 200°F (95°C). If available, use the convection mode for good air circulation. Place a large wire cooling rack on a sheet pan. For the "mold," line the bottom and sides of a 9 by 13-inch (23 by 33cm) cake pan or sheet pan with parchment paper, extending the parchment above the rim on all sides to provide handles. Perfect corners are not crucial! Have ready a large cutting board.

Use the silicone spatula to transfer the hot rice to the parchment-lined pan. Dip the spatula in cold water to prevent sticking, then spread the rice to cover the bottom. Dipping the spatula in water as needed, firmly press the rice into an even layer ¼ to ⅓ inch (6 to 8mm) thick. Lift the longer sides of the parchment to transfer the sheet of rice, still on the parchment, from the pan to the cutting board.

Lightly wet the bottom of the mold pan, set it on top of the rice sheet, and press down to compress further and flatten to an even thickness of ¼ inch (6mm); the rice will spread a bit. Dip a bench scraper in cold water, cut the entire sheet in quarters, then cut each quarter into credit-card-size pieces.

Use the cutting board to help you slide the parchment paper with the cut rice sheet onto the cooling rack on the sheet pan. Bake the rice pieces until they are mostly dry but still slightly damp (expect fissures to appear), usually 1½ to 2 hours. The time involved depends on how moist the rice is to start and the height of the rack.

Remove from the oven and let cool for 5 minutes. Slide a flexible spatula under the rice pieces to detach them from the parchment and ease them directly onto the wire rack; discard the parchment. Gently turn over each rice piece, then return the pan to the oven. Bake until the pieces are fully dry, 1 to 1½ hours. (If the rice pieces won't release from the parchment after the first baking, slide the parchment with the rice pieces off the cooling rack, invert the rack over the rice, and flip the rack and parchment so the parchment faces up. Return the rack to the pan and bake as directed. When done, the parchment will have released; gently snap the rice pieces off the precut lines.) Let the rice pieces cool completely, then store in an airtight container in the cupboard for up to 3 months.

Fry into puffy crisps: Line a sheet pan with a cooling rack and paper towels. Pour oil to a depth of 1½ inches (3.75cm) into a large wok and heat over medium heat to 350° to 375°F (175° to 190°C). Working in batches of one or two pieces, deep-fry until puffy, crispy, and golden, 45 to 60 seconds (it's fast frying). Using a spatula or a spider, turn or gently press for even frying. If the crackers break into shards, they'll be extra arty. Transfer to the towel-lined sheet pan to drain. Let cool, then eat right away or store in an airtight container at room temperature for up to 2 weeks.

NOTE

No time for whipping up a batch of khao tung? Purchase dried square-shape rice pieces sold in packages at Chinese markets; deep-fry them like you would in this recipe.

น้ำมะขามเปียก | Nam Makam

Tamarind Liquid

MAKES 3½ TO 4 CUPS (840ML TO 1L)

Tangy tamarind plays a key role in balancing flavors in many Thai foods. The pulp of the podlike fruit is easily transformed into a liquid for adding to condiments, salads, curries, and more. Asian markets sell premade tamarind liquid concentrate, but I find it to be inferior—texturally thin, too tart, and lacking in tamarind's fruity charm. Annoyingly, most brands even need to be strained to remove lingering seed bits before using! Your time and money are better spent on creating the thick liquid from a slab of seedless tamarind pulp. At an Asian market, press on the packages to make sure the tamarind is somewhat soft and fresh.

One 400 to 450g | 14- to 16-oz package seedless tamarind pulp

About 1L | 4 cups lukewarm water

1 Tbsp citric acid dissolved in 2 Tbsp warm water (optional)

Hydrate the tamarind: Unwrap the tamarind and use your hands to pull it apart into small pieces, dropping them into a medium bowl. Add 3 cups (720ml) of the water and then massage the tamarind. After a few minutes, the solids will loosen up and dissolve to turn the liquid sepia brown. The mixture will eventually thicken to the texture of chocolate cake batter. Once you feel mostly solid bits in the liquid, pause.

Strain twice: Set a coarse-mesh strainer over a large measuring cup (or a medium bowl), then strain the tamarind liquid, stirring and firmly pressing against the solids with a silicone spatula to expel as much liquid as possible. Return the solids to the first bowl and mix in ½ to 1 cup (120 to 240ml) of the water, using the larger amount if you began with the bigger tamarind package. Stir with the spatula (or your fingers) to release more flavor, then strain again to yield more liquid. It's normal to see a few shiny bald seeds in the strainer at the end. If you prefer a sharper flavor, pour the diluted citric acid into the liquid.

Stir to combine well before using or storing. Keep in an airtight container in the refrigerator for up to 1 week or in the freezer for up to 6 months.

NOTES

Citric acid powder, sometimes labeled "sour salt," is sold online and in the canning section of some supermarkets.

Freeze tamarind liquid in 2- to 4-Tbsp portions in an ice cube tray. Or pour the liquid into a large ziplock bag, secure closed, lay the bag on a quarter sheet pan or other flat pan, and freeze, then store the bag in the freezer. To use, gently tap the bag against a sink divider or similar edge to break off a chunk, thaw the chunk, and measure for recipes.

ขี้โล้ | Kee Lo

Cracked Coconut Milk

MAKES 1 TO 1⅓ CUPS (240 TO 320ML), DEPENDING ON INITIAL QUANTITY

When you patiently crack coconut milk, cooking it down until the oil separates from the milk solids, the overall mixture concentrates and slightly caramelizes into kee lo. It tastes elegantly rich and is as alluring and useful as French brown butter. Add kee lo to certain curry pastes to help build svelte texture and preserve their fresh flavor. Instead of frying curry paste in creamy, thick coconut milk, use kee lo. It can also be used in place of oil in stir-fries and magically elevates the grilled golae dipping sauces on pages 214 to 218.

The only trick to making kee lo is using coconut milk that has minimal (or no) emulsifiers, thickeners, and preservatives. My go-tos are Aroy-D and PraoHom brands in 1-liter UHT boxes. Devoid of emulsifiers, Native Forest coconut milk works well too. Creamy, silky coconut milk containing too much of the thickener guar gum tends not to crack easily. Whatever you use, carefully read the label to ensure success.

Two 400ml | 13.5-oz cans, or one 1L | 33.8-oz box coconut milk

Simmer the coconut milk: Pour and scrape the coconut milk into a pristine large wok or medium saucepan. Set over medium heat and bring to a boil, stirring with a wooden or silicone spatula. Lower the heat slightly to a gentle simmer (on my stove, that's almost medium-low but not quite). To prevent the coconut milk from boiling over and to minimize sputtering, leave the spatula resting in the pan. It works!

Let cook, stirring occasionally, until reduced by a good two-thirds, 40 to 50 minutes. Near the end of cooking, as the bubbly sounds of liquid simmering start to change to what sounds like raindrops pelting a window, the coconut oil will separate from the remaining milky solids, which may look like small curds. Regardless, coconut oil will eventually float to the top to signal doneness. You are essentially concentrating the coconut milk into a fragrant, rich, slightly sweet liquid.

Cool and store: Remove from the heat and let cool completely uncovered. Measure your yield. If you used two cans, you should have 1 cup (240ml). If you used a big box, you should have 1⅓ cups (320ml). If you have a lot more than that, return the coconut milk to the stovetop and cook briefly to reduce further.

Transfer the cooled coconut milk to a jar and refrigerate for up to 1 month. To freeze the coconut milk, stir to mix together the oil and milky solids, then fill large ice cube trays and slip into the freezer. Once the cubes are frozen, transfer them to an airtight container and freeze for up to 6 months. In recipes, always use both the oil and the milky solids (warm the jar in hot water or the microwave, if needed).

NOTE

About 15 to 20 minutes into cooking, if the coconut oil doesn't start breaking from the milk, you may add a spoon of virgin coconut oil to help nudge it along.

น้ำจิ้มไก่ | Nam Jim Gai

Sweet Chili "Chicken" Sauce

MAKES 1½ CUPS (360ML)

There are times when making things from scratch is worthwhile, and there are times when it's fine to use a purchased product. The latter applies to Thai sweet chili sauce, which is cloyingly sweet right out of the bottle. However, if you simply add two ingredients to the sauce, you'll have a not-too-sweet, pleasantly spicy sauce to enjoy with Thai grilled chicken (page 208), fish cakes (page 72), and pork meatballs (page 235). My cheat is lightning fast and marvelous.

When shopping for Asian brands of Thai sweet chili sauce, you'll likely see grilled chicken on the label. That's because what's labeled "sweet chili sauce" for English speakers is known as chicken sauce—nam jim gai—by Thai speakers. And Thai people love it with grilled chicken, which is why it's included in the photo on pages 210 and 211! Language aside, whenever a dish needs a sunny, tangy, spicy lift, grab your jar of semi-bespoke sweet chili "chicken" sauce. If you have chili garlic vinegar handy (it's the next recipe!), use it instead of store-bought chili garlic sauce.

240ml | 1 cup Thai sweet chili sauce

60ml | ¼ cup unseasoned rice vinegar

2 to 4 Tbsp chili garlic sauce

In a measuring cup, stir together the sweet chili sauce and rice vinegar. Amp up the heat by stirring in 2 Tbsp of the chili garlic sauce, then gradually add more until you have a not-too-sweet, slightly hot flavor. Use immediately, or transfer to a tightly capped glass jar and refrigerate for up to 6 months.

น้ำส้มพริกตำ | Nam Som Prik Tum

Chili Garlic Vinegar

MAKES ¾ CUP (180ML)

Sprinkle this orangish table condiment into a bowl of rich noodle soup, like the spiced duck noodles on page 273, to add bright, spicy, pungent notes. Earthy, bitter greens like broccoli rabe or collard greens get a nice lift from it too. So does a plate of fried rice. Nam som prik tum (photographed opposite at the lower right) is easy to make and keeps for months in the fridge. Using red chilies ensures the signature cheery color of this condiment. It is easy to make with a mortar and pestle, which yields a hand-crafted texture and look, but you can also just blitz all of the ingredients in a blender or food processor.

20g | 6 garlic cloves

10g | 1½ Tbsp coarsely chopped, seeded fresh red Fresno, serrano, or jalapeño chili

10g | 1½ Tbsp coarsely chopped fresh red Thai chilies (about 8)

¼ tsp granulated sugar

1 big pinch of fine sea salt

10g | 1 Tbsp Gratiem Dong (Pickled Garlic, page 55), coarsely chopped

1 Tbsp brine from pickled garlic

120ml | ½ cup unseasoned rice vinegar

Pound and mix: Using a mortar and pestle, pound together the fresh garlic, all of the chilies, the sugar, and salt to a fine paste. Add the pickled garlic and pound to incorporate. Scrape into a jar, then stir in the brine and vinegar.

Finesse the sauce: Taste and if the result is not sour, hot, and garlicky, adjust with extra vinegar, chili, or fresh garlic. Cap and store in the refrigerator for up to 3 months. Stir well before using.

กระเทียมดอง | Gratiem Dong

Pickled Garlic

MAKES 1½ CUPS (360ML)

An everyday pickle, gratiem dong is sold in jars at Southeast Asian and Chinese markets. It is made from tiny, tender unpeeled garlic cloves. Purchased gratiem dong is OK in a pinch, but if you make it yourself, yours will taste brighter and fresher. Every March, I hunt down heads of springtime garlic, which have mild-tasting cloves that are perfect for putting up a batch of this Thai staple. (But don't worry if you don't have spring garlic. This recipe will work with all kinds of fresh garlic.) Pickled garlic is used in such recipes as chili garlic vinegar (page 54) and hunglay curry (page 181). It's also a side nibble with items like crisp curry fish cereal (page 239) and fried rice seasoned with namprik kai kem (page 258). Feel free to double the recipe because, kept in the fridge in a vinegar bath, it never dies.

240g | 1½ cups garlic cloves

240ml | 1 cup distilled white vinegar

1 Tbsp granulated sugar

½ tsp fine sea salt

Assemble the pickle: Put the garlic in a 2-cup (480ml) jar. In a small bowl, stir together the vinegar, sugar, and salt until the sugar and salt dissolve, and then pour into the jar, submerging the garlic. Cover tightly and refrigerate for 3 months before using. The garlic will have a strong taste at the 3-month mark, but it is ready to deploy in recipes in which it will be tamed by other ingredients.

Enjoy over time: Expect the garlic to keep mellowing and develop more flavor as it sits in the brine. This pickled garlic will keep practically forever in your fridge.

กระเทียมกรอบ | Gratiem Grob

Fried Garlic Chips

MAKES ¼ CUP (60ML)

Thai salads, noodle soups, and many other dishes often need a little pungent flavor pop at the end. That's when these garlic chips (photographed on page 55, on the right) come into play. They're sold at Asian markets, but when you need just a small amount for dishes like artichoke laab (page 110) and burnt eggplant salad (page 99), fry them yourself. And after frying the garlic, while the tasty oil remains hot, you can fry any extra components for your recipe, such as the dried chili garnish for the laab and the dried shrimp for the eggplant. Leftover garlic-frying oil is fab for stir-frying too.

40g | 12 medium garlic cloves

120ml | ½ cup neutral oil, such as rice bran

Prep the garlic: Very thinly and uniformly slice the garlic cloves lengthwise. Pat with a paper towel to remove excess moisture.

Fry and cool: Transfer the garlic to a very small saucepan, add the oil, and set over medium-low heat. Bring to a gentle bubble and fry, frequently swirling the pan, until the garlic chips are crispy and very pale blond, 7 to 10 minutes.

Remove the pan from the heat, swirling it to slow the cooking quickly and avoid burning. When the chips are near golden, use a slotted spoon to transfer them to a bowl to finish crisping and darken further, about 5 minutes. (If a few slices still aren't crisp, very briefly refry them and let cool.) Use immediately or store in an airtight container at room temperature for a couple of days. Strain the leftover oil through a fine-mesh strainer so it's extra clean and ready for frying another batch or for making another dish.

NOTE

For even frying, do your best to select garlic cloves of the same size. When doubling the recipe, use a bigger saucepan so the garlic moves freely and expect to fry the slices a little longer.

TOASTED COCONUT FLAKES HOW-TO

Occasionally, as with the classic miang recipe on page 63, it's easy to work toasting coconut flakes into recipe prep. Other times, you just want to grab pre-toasted coconut from a container. I prefer toasting coconut on the stovetop for better control of the process (coconut burns easily!). Lowish heat and slow toasting coax the coconuttiest outcome. You'll want to eat the flakes out of the pan.

To toast 1 cup (240ml) unsweetened dried coconut flakes: Add the coconut to a heavy medium skillet and set over medium-low heat. Toast the flakes, initially stirring now and again and then more actively after the flakes are fragrant, start turning blond, and eventually become golden brown in many places, about 10 minutes total. Pour onto a sheet pan and let cool completely before using or transferring to an airtight container for storage. The toasted coconut will keep at room temperature for up to 2 months. Use a bigger skillet for a bigger quantity.

สามเกลอ | Saam Kleur

Three Buddies Paste

MAKES SCANT ½ CUP (120ML)

Yes, plenty of Thai flavor is crafted without chilies. One of the classic seasonings is saam kleur (three buddies), a punchy trinity of pounded garlic, cilantro root, and peppercorns. Included on the left in the photo on page 55, the paste adds remarkable pungency (garlic), spiciness (pepper), and aroma (cilantro) to meats, marinades, soups, and stir-fries.

White peppercorns are traditionally used for this paste, but because the quality of white pepper varies so much, I blend white and black peppercorns in my paste. Make a batch of saam kleur and keep it frozen or refrigerated like many Thai cooks do. You'll speed through preparing dishes like coconutty pork and peanut dip (page 71), stuffed cucumber soup (page 201), fried meatballs (page 235), and garlicky spareribs (page 244). Those recipes include small-batch instructions, in case you need to make the buddies on the spot.

80g | ½ cup garlic cloves

40g | ⅓ cup finely chopped cilantro root, or 20g | 2½ Tbsp finely chopped cilantro stems

5g | 1 tsp coarse sea salt

6g | 2 tsp white peppercorns, plus more to taste

6g | 2 tsp black peppercorns

Using a mortar and pestle, aggressively pound together the garlic, cilantro, and salt to a coarse, moist paste. Make a well in the center of the paste, then, working in three or four batches, add the white and black peppercorns to the well and pound to smithereens, gradually working the pounded garlic and cilantro into the pepper and continuing to pound until you have a finely textured mixture. Do your best to chase down and pound any hairy cilantro root. Smell the paste, and if you want more pepperiness (some peppercorns are wimpy), pound in an additional ¼ to ½ tsp of white peppercorns.

Alternatively, process the garlic and cilantro in a small food chopper. Because the machine doesn't pound peppercorns well, pound them in a mortar before whirling all of the ingredients together in the chopper. You'll have more dishwashing and won't get to practice old-school Thai cooking.

Use the paste immediately, or transfer to a tightly capped glass jar and refrigerate for up to 1 week. To freeze the paste, spread it in a thin layer in a small ziplock bag, seal, lay the bag on an eighth sheet pan or other flat small pan, and freeze, then store the bag in the freezer for up to 3 months. To use, break off pieces as needed for recipes.

12 13
19 20

2 กินเล่น

Snacks

ภูแล

Play Eating All Day Long

Thai cuisine turns snacking, or what we call kin len (**กินเล่น**, literally "play eating"), into an art form. Walking around Bangkok, at any time of day, you'll see food-stall vendors hawking not-quite-a-meal foods of various kinds.

Not just candies and cookies, these foods are often substantial enough to tide you over the many torturous hours between lunch and dinner, between elevenses and lunch, and between dinner and midnight dinner. (Yes, Thai people are hobbits when it comes to food. I am always hungry.)

My favorite childhood food of this genre is khao tung na tung (page 71), a coconutty shrimp and pork dip served with crispy rice crackers. At once sweet and savory, quite rich in protein, and hefty enough, it filled me up after a long day at school and helped power me through tennis practice before dinnertime. I never tire of it and make it at home as well as for guests at Kin Khao. Ditto for the more grown-up beef tartare with rice crackers on page 68, which we serve at Nari.

For a restaurant chef like me, many of these not-quite-part-of-a-meal dishes provide an interesting avenue to present Thai food. I serve several of them in bite-size portions to whet the appetite as a prelude to a meal. One mouthful of something tantalizing like a miang, a punchy interplay of textures and salty-sweet-spicy-fatty flavors wrapped in herbaceous chaplu (wild betel) leaf, never fails to capture a diner's attention and provides a perfect launching point to a deliciously complex Thai meal.

Most cooks stick with traditional miang, the choose-your-own-adventure one-bite leaf wrap that's presented with an assortment of toppings, including dried shrimp, shallot, and lime rind. But there's so much you can do with this beloved Thai snack once you understand how it comes together. This chapter not only teaches you the basics of miang but also gives you many ways to enjoy it—from the classic version to ceviche, mushroom, and seasonal fruit iterations (pages 64 to 67).

When a more substantial snack is in order, who can resist the deep-fried curried fish cakes on page 72? So easy to prepare, their flavor and aroma transport me to Thailand. The crispy fish cereal and grilled seafood (page 76) and curry puffs (page 81) are more labor-intensive but can be made in stages with advance prep.

Even though the recipes in this chapter are meant to be eaten as snacks, there's nothing stopping you from serving them as a part of a meal. In fact, the tod mun fish cakes would be great with rice and a salad.

By the same token, certain dishes in other parts of this book—like the hor mok steamed curries on pages 225 and 227 will satisfy four people as part of a multi-dish meal or titillate eight to ten snacky folks when served with crispy rice crackers! Eat the grilled squid on page 219 as a main course or present it with fancy bamboo toothpicks and let guests stab away at them while sipping drinks. The golae lamb, chicken, and tofu (pages 213 to 218) are all snackable too.

This chapter's recipe collection aims to inspire your Thai "play eating."

น้ำเมี่ยง | Nam Miang

Miang Sauce

MAKES ¾ CUP (180ML)

If you want to kick off a fun, impressive Thai meal, make the one-bite leaf-wrap snacks called miang. Just focus on preparing the signature ingredient of miang: an enchantingly salty-sweet palm sugar sauce accented by galangal and lemongrass (photographed on page 65). With miang sauce in the fridge (or freezer), the rest is a matter of gathering or chopping a handful of ingredients and setting them out for folks to assemble their own thrilling snacks (or do it for them like we do at my restaurants). Miang iterations are endless, and the recipes on pages 63 to 67 will get you going. But first and foremost, make this sauce to glue everything together.

12g | 1½ Tbsp finely chopped, peeled galangal (from 3 slices)

9g | 1½ Tbsp super-thinly sliced or 1 Tbsp finely chopped lemongrass

180g | ½ cup plus 1 Tbsp firmly packed Thai palm sugar

2 Tbsp water

3 Tbsp fish sauce (see Variation for vegan substitute)

1 Tbsp lime juice

Pound aromatics: Using a mortar and pestle, pound together the galangal and lemongrass to a fine, crumbly mixture. (This tiny amount isn't great in a small food chopper.)

Cook the sauce: In a very small saucepan, combine the palm sugar and water and set over medium heat. Warm the mixture, stirring continuously with a silicone spatula, until the sugar is completely melted. Lower the heat slightly, stir in the pounded aromatics, bring to a boil, and boil until caramelized to a rich orange brown, 2 to 3 minutes.

Lower the heat to medium-low, stir in the fish sauce, and let the mixture cook and bubble until it subtly darkens a shade to a rich amber, about 2 minutes.

Turn off the heat and continue stirring to avoid scorching. Within 1 minute or so, slowly lift the spatula. The sauce will have thickened enough to coat the spatula and then slide off, leaving a drip clinging to it. (If that's not the case, cook the mixture over medium heat for a bit longer and test again.) Let the sauce cool for a few minutes, then taste for a pleasant salty sweetness followed by a galangal nip.

Stir in the lime juice. Scrape into a small heatproof bowl, cover partially, and let cool completely, then stir down the sugar film that inevitably forms. The cooled sauce should be spoonable and somewhat gooey, like a very soft caramel. If you ended up with a firm, set caramel, stir in a bit of just-boiled water to loosen, then reheat the sauce on the stovetop or in the microwave to incorporate fully.

Use the sauce at room temperature. Refrigerate in an airtight container for up to 1 week or in ¼-cup (60ml) portions in the freezer for up to 6 months. Thin slightly with water and microwave to warm if needed. A little goes a long way.

NOTE

For a fermented, briny edge, replace the 3 Tbsp fish sauce with 1½ Tbsp fish sauce, 1 Tbsp water, and 1 Tbsp gapi (Thai shrimp paste), preferably Gapi Dee (Good Gapi, page 118).

VARIATION

น้ำเมี่ยงเจ | Nam Niang Jae

Vegan Miang Sauce

Replace the fish sauce with 1½ Tbsp Thai thin soy sauce, 1½ Tbsp water, and 1 tsp fine sea salt.

เมี่ยงคำ | Miang Kam

Classic One-Bite Miang

SERVES 4

Begin a special meal with an appetizer of raw ginger, shallot, lime, and chili along with fried dried shrimp, toasted coconut, and peanuts? Yes, and do it Thai style: Put a bit of each plus some miang sauce atop a palm-size leaf and pop it into your mouth as a one-bite nosh. The word *kam* (คำ) literally means "a mouthful," and miang kam is all about building your personal mouthful of deliciousness. Included in the photo on page 65 at the top right, this classic version is the ultimate flavor bomb. Make it to understand how miang works, then try out the shrimp, mushroom, and fruit renditions that follow. Learn more about wild betel leaf (bai chaplu) on page 28. Don't hesitate to eat raw lime rind (peel plus pith). It's super Thai or, as we say, Thai-Thai ไท้ย-ไทย.

- 60ml | ¼ cup Nam Miang (Miang Sauce, page 62)
- 120ml | ½ cup unsweetened dried coconut flakes
- 120ml | ½ cup small or medium dried shrimp (omit for vegan version)
- 1 to 2 tsp neutral oil, such as rice bran
- 120ml | ½ cup roasted peanuts, coarsely chopped if large
- 60ml | ¼ cup small diced, peeled ginger
- 60ml | ¼ cup thinly sliced or finely diced shallots
- 1 lime, sliced into wheels, then each wheel cut into 6 to 8 triangles
- 2 fresh Thai chilies, very thinly sliced
- 12 to 16 wild betel, radicchio, or Little Gem lettuce leaves

Prep the sauce and cooked toppings: Make or thaw the miang sauce and keep in a small bowl at room temperature.

Add the coconut flakes to a heavy medium skillet and set over medium-low heat. Toast the flakes, initially stirring now and again and then more actively after the flakes are fragrant and beginning to color. Continue toasting, stirring almost continuously, until golden brown, 3 to 5 minutes. Transfer to a small bowl or arrange them in a pile on a serving platter.

If the shrimp are hard to chew, soak them in hot water to cover until beginning to soften, 1 to 2 minutes, then drain well. Return the medium skillet to medium-low heat and warm 1 tsp of the oil. Add the shrimp and fry gently, stirring occasionally and adding more oil if needed to prevent sticking, until bright orange and fragrant, about 2 minutes. Slide them into a small bowl or arrange them in a pile on the platter. If your shrimp are chewable, skip the soaking and frying!

Assemble and serve: Arrange the peanuts, ginger, shallots, lime, and chilies in individual small bowls or make discrete piles of them on the platter. If the wild betel leaves are bigger than 5 inches (12.5cm), trim them down, matching each leaf's contour. If using radicchio or Little Gem leaves, trim off the thickish bottom of each leaf so it is pliable for wrapping. Stack the leaves on the platter or present them on the side with the sauce.

Invite diners to build their own miang kam. Use a small spoon to smear about ¾ tsp of the sauce on a leaf, then top with a three-finger pinch of each mild topping: coconut, dried shrimp, and peanuts. Finish with several pieces of each assertive topping: ginger, shallots, lime, and chili. Gather up the leaf and eat. Repeat to build each bespoke one-biter until all is gone.

NOTES

For juiciness, select a lime with very smooth, thin skin.

Cook ahead! With the exception of the lime and chilies, the toppings can be prepped up to 3 days in advance.

เมี่ยงกุ้งสะเออะ | Miang Goong Sa-uh

Shrimp Ceviche Miang

SERVES 6 TO 8

Sa-uh สะเออะ is an antiquated Thai culinary term similar to ceviche, that's to say, "cooking" seafood proteins with citrus juice. I found this recipe in a very old cookbook and adapted it for serving as miang, on a wild betel leaf, as included in the photo here at the bottom left. The bright, gingery morsels of citrus-cured shrimp make for a perfect counterpoint to nutty, caramelized miang sauce. Double the recipe for a party because your friends will want more. If you must avoid raw seafood, see the Note for an easy workaround.

- 225g | 8 oz peeled, deveined shrimp (from 300g | 10 oz shell-on)
- 75ml | ¼ cup plus 1 Tbsp lime juice, divided
- 120g | 1 small, slightly unripe nectarine, tart apple, or other crunchy, tangy fruit
- 60ml | 4 Tbsp Nam Miang (Miang Sauce, page 62), divided
- 10g | 1½ Tbsp super-thinly sliced shallots
- 7g | 1 Tbsp super-thinly sliced lemongrass (see page 30)
- 7g | 1 Tbsp slivered, peeled ginger
- 1½ Tbsp finely slivered makrut lime leaves (2 to 3 leaves; see page 31), divided
- 15 g | ¼ cup fried shallots
- 10g | 1 Tbsp coarsely chopped roasted peanuts
- 5g | 1 Tbsp toasted unsweetened dried coconut flakes (see page 56)
- 16 to 20 wild betel, radicchio, or Little Gem lettuce leaves
- 2 fresh Thai chilies, thinly sliced

Prep the shrimp and fruit: Cut the shrimp into chunks no larger than ¾ inch (2cm). Transfer to a small bowl, add ¼ cup (60ml) of the lime juice, and mix to coat well. Press down gently on the shrimp to ensure they are submerged in the lime juice, then cover and chill until pinkish and fairly firm, about 30 minutes.

Meanwhile, halve and pit or core the fruit, then cut the halves lengthwise into wedges ¾ inch (2cm) thick. Slice each wedge crosswise into triangles no more than ¼ inch (6mm) thick. Aim for about ⅓ cup (50g) and snack on the leftovers.

Mix the shrimp: Drain the shrimp in a fine-mesh strainer, pressing gently to remove excess lime juice. In a medium bowl, stir together 1 Tbsp of the miang sauce with the remaining 1 Tbsp lime juice. Stir in the sliced shallots, lemongrass, ginger, and a rounded 1 Tbsp of the lime leaves and then fold in the shrimp and fruit. Put the remaining 3 Tbsp (45ml) miang sauce and the remaining lime leaves in separate small bowls and set aside for serving.

Prep the toppings and leaves: In a small bowl, mix the crunchy bits: Combine the fried shallots and peanuts, smooshing them to crush the shallots slightly; add the coconut flakes, crumbling them if big. If the wild betel leaves are larger than 5 inches (12.5cm), trim them down, matching each leaf's contour. If using radicchio or Little Gem leaves, trim off the thickish bottom of each leaf so it is pliable for wrapping.

Assemble and serve: Put the chilies into a small bowl and set out with the wild betel leaves, miang sauce, shrimp mixture, crunchy bits, and makrut slivers for guests to build their own miang, or do it for them and present the bites on a platter. For each one-biter, use a small spoon to smear ½ to ¾ tsp of the miang sauce on a leaf, then top with 1½ to 2 Tbsp of the shrimp mixture, a three-finger pinch of the crunchy bits, 1 or 2 chili slices, and a few makrut slivers. Gather up the leaf and eat the whole thing as a single mouthful.

NOTE

Instead of curing raw shrimp, poach them first: Bring a small pot of water to a boil, add the whole shrimp, and turn off the heat. When the shrimp start to curl, after 20 to 30 seconds, drain them and let cool to room temperature before cutting and curing in lime juice.

เมี่ยงเห็ด | Miang Hed

Mushroom Miang

SERVES 6 TO 8

Make miang magic with mushrooms! Use one kind or combine a few different types (even button mushrooms will do) for this wondrous one-bite snack photographed on page 65, in the center. Sometimes I grill the mushrooms in a banana leaf for extra depth, but it's just fine to sear them in a ripping-hot pan to create a caramelized, savory base for all of the citrusy, pungent, salty, sweet, rich miang components.

300g | 10 oz fresh mushrooms (any kind or a combo)

Fine sea salt

1 Tbsp neutral oil, such as rice bran

1½ Tbsp lime juice

60ml | 4 Tbsp Nam Miang (Miang Sauce, page 62), divided

10g | 1½ Tbsp super-thinly sliced shallots

7g | 1 Tbsp super-thinly sliced lemongrass

7g | 1 Tbsp slivered, peeled ginger

1½ Tbsp finely slivered makrut lime leaves (2 to 3 leaves; see page 31), divided

15g | ¼ cup fried shallots

10g | 1 Tbsp coarsely chopped roasted peanuts

5g | 1 Tbsp toasted unsweetened dried coconut flakes (page 56)

16 to 20 wild betel, radicchio, or Little Gem lettuce leaves

2 fresh Thai chilies, thinly sliced

Caramelize the mushrooms: Cut the mushrooms into irregular ¾-inch (2cm) pieces. Season lightly with salt. Set a heavy large skillet over high heat. When the pan is hot, add the oil and swirl the pan to coat the bottom. When the oil is nearly smoking, add the mushrooms and sear and sauté to caramelize lightly, remove some moisture, and concentrate flavor, 4 to 5 minutes. Set aside to cool to room temperature.

Mix the mushrooms: In a medium bowl, stir together the lime juice and 1 Tbsp of the miang sauce. Stir in the sliced shallots, lemongrass, ginger, and a rounded 1 Tbsp of the lime leaves and then fold in the mushrooms. Put the remaining 3 Tbsp (45ml) miang sauce and the remaining lime leaves in separate small bowls and set aside for serving.

Prep the toppings and leaves: In a small bowl, mix the crunchy bits: Combine the fried shallots and peanuts, smooshing them to crush the shallots slightly; add the coconut flakes, crumbling them if big. If the wild betel leaves are larger than 5 inches (12.5cm), trim them down, matching each leaf's contour. If using radicchio or Little Gem leaves, trim off the thickish bottom of each leaf so it is pliable for wrapping.

Assemble and serve: Put the chilies into a small bowl and set out with the wild betel leaves, miang sauce, mushroom mixture, crunchy bits, and makrut slivers for guests to build their own miang, or do it for them and present the bites on a platter. For each one-biter, use a small spoon to smear ½ to ¾ tsp of the miang sauce on a leaf, then top with 1½ to 2 Tbsp of the mushroom mixture, a three-finger pinch of the crunchy bits, 1 or 2 chili slices, and a few makrut slivers. Gather up the leaf and enjoy the whole thing as single mouthful.

เมี่ยงผลไม้ | Miang Polamai

Seasonal Fruit Miang

SERVES 6 TO 8

If you haven't caught on, Thai cooks use fresh fruit for sweets and savories. For this delicious snack (photographed on page 65, in the lower right), choose fruit with tang, or combine a sweet-tasting fruit with one that's tart. You can't go wrong as long as you have the miang blueprint in place—the sauce, aromatics, and leaves. Beyond the basic framework, play around with flavors, colors, and textures. Here are some fruity ideas to consider:

- crisp pluots + nectarines
- crunchy, tart green plums
- unripe (green) mango
- pineapple + jicama
- Fuyu persimmon + Asian pear
- Granny Smith + Fuji apple
- blood orange + pomelo
- lychee or rambutan + star fruit

300g | 10 oz tangy seasonal fruit (from above)

1 Tbsp lime juice, plus more to taste

60ml | 4 Tbsp Nam Miang (Miang Sauce, page 62), divided

10g | 1½ Tbsp super-thinly sliced shallots

7g | 1 Tbsp super-thinly sliced lemongrass

7g | 1 Tbsp slivered, peeled ginger

1½ Tbsp finely slivered makrut lime leaves (2 to 3 leaves; see page 31), divided

15g | ¼ cup fried shallots

10g | 1 Tbsp coarsely chopped roasted peanuts

5g | 1 Tbsp toasted unsweetened dried coconut flakes (see page 56)

16 to 20 wild betel, radicchio, or Little Gem lettuce leaves

2 fresh Thai chilies, thinly sliced

Chop and season the fruit: As needed, peel, core, or pit the fruit before cutting it into irregular pieces. Slice and chop to produce an artful mélange of fragments no bigger than ½ inch (1.25cm). Cut wedges and uneven chunks; if using citrus, cut supremes (pith and membrane-free sections) and then drain off the juice. Some fruit can be hand torn. Create small pieces that fit on the leaf and avoid dainty, characterless perfection. Aim for 1½ cups (200g) total.

In a medium bowl, combine the lime juice and 1 Tbsp of the miang sauce. Stir in the sliced shallots, lemongrass, ginger, and a rounded 1 Tbsp of the lime leaves and then fold in the fruit. Taste and if it's too sweet, add more lime juice by the ½ tsp until the flavor suits you. Put the remaining 3 Tbsp (45ml) miang sauce and the remaining lime leaves in separate small bowls and set aside for serving.

Prep the toppings and leaves: In a small bowl, mix the crunchy bits: Combine the fried shallots and peanuts, smooshing them to crush the shallots slightly; add the coconut flakes, crumbling them if big. If the wild betel leaves are larger than 5 inches (12.5cm), trim them down, matching each leaf's contour. If using radicchio or Little Gem leaves, trim off the thickish bottom of each leaf so it is pliable for wrapping.

Assemble and serve: Put the chilies into a small bowl and set out with the wild betel leaves, miang sauce, fruit mixture, crunchy bits, and makrut slivers for guests to build their own miang, or do it for them and present the bites on a platter. For each one-biter, use a small spoon to smear ½ to ¾ tsp of the miang sauce on a leaf, then top with 1½ to 2 Tbsp of the fruit mixture, a three-finger pinch of crunchy bits, 1 or 2 chili slices, and a few makrut slivers. Gather up the leaf and eat the whole thing as a single mouthful.

ลาบจิ้น | Laab Jin

Beef Tartare Laab

SERVES 4

Not your average French-style tartare de boeuf, laab jin is a fireworks display of vibrant flavor, textures, and color. The alluring flavor comes from prik laab, a traditional Northern Thai blend of chilies and other warming spices. Serve this tartare with vegetables and sticky rice (the traditional way) or gild the lily (like we do at Nari) by pairing it with puffy fried rice crackers. My dear friend Madeleine Fitzpatrick, who regularly drives an hour from Tomales Bay down to Nari in San Francisco just for this laab, threatened to stop talking to me if I ever took it off my menu. Laab jin can kick off a special meal or be a sumptuous one-dish lunch for two. Choose a favorite steak cut that's free of gristle to ensure a beautiful dice. Have your accompaniments ready before mixing the tartare so you can enjoy it as soon as it's done.

225g | 8 oz beef steak (such as tenderloin, New York strip, or top sirloin), very well chilled

2 Tbsp fish sauce

2 Tbsp neutral oil, such as rice bran

40g | about ⅓ cup thinly sliced shallots

10g | 2 Tbsp super-thinly sliced lemongrass

1½ Tbsp Prik Laab (Northern Thai Chili-Spice Blend, page 49), plus more to taste

80ml | ⅓ cup chopped mixed fresh herbs (such as cilantro, mint, sawtooth herb, or green onion)

3 makrut lime leaves, finely slivered (see page 31)

2 to 2½ Tbsp fried garlic chips, homemade (page 56) or purchased

60ml | ¼ cup fried shallots

2 dried puya chilies, fried (optional)

Cut and season the beef: Trim the steak into a small brick, then cut the brick into cubes no bigger than ¼ inch (6mm). My technique for cutting the cubes is to cut the steak across the grain into slices ¼ inch (6mm) thick, then cut the slices into sticks ¼ inch (6mm) thick, and, finally, cut the sticks crosswise into cubes. Transfer to a medium bowl, sprinkle with the fish sauce, and toss to coat evenly.

Bloom the aromatics and assemble: In a very small saucepan, combine the oil, sliced shallots, lemongrass, and prik laab. Set over medium-low heat and heat, stirring and sweating the ingredients, until the shallots just soften, 1 to 2 minutes. Remove from the heat, scrape into the bowl holding the beef, and stir and fold gently to mix.

Add the chopped herbs and most of the lime leaf to the beef, saving a little for garnish. Add the garlic chips, crumbling and breaking them up as you drop them into the bowl. Add most of the fried shallots, saving a little for garnish. Stir and fold gently to mix well, then mound the mixture on a plate. Garnish with the reserved makrut slivers and fried shallots, then crown with the fried chilies, if using.

ACCOMPANIMENTS

½ batch Khao Tung (Crispy Rice Crackers, page 50), or 1 batch Khao Niew Neung (Microwave Sticky Rice, page 257)

Vegetables, such as lettuce leaves, radicchio leaves, fresh herbs (such as cilantro, mint, and/or sawtooth herb), thickly sliced cucumbers, thinly sliced radishes, and green or long beans (see page 104 for tips)

Ready the accompaniments and serve: Prepare the accompaniments of your choice and set them at the table, along with the tartare. When serving with fried rice crackers, invite diners to spoon some of the tartare onto the rice crackers for a scintillating mouthful. Or they can pair each mouthful of the tartare with sticky rice. Either way, they should chase the tartare with raw vegetables and herbs to cool the palate.

ข้าวตังหน้าตั้ง | Khao Tung Na Tung

Coconutty Shrimp, Pork, and Peanut Dip with Fried Rice Crackers

SERVES 4

Crunchy, salty, mildly spicy, candy-like na tung was my favorite after-school snack growing up. Kid- and adult-friendly, it features creamy coconut, sweet palm sugar, savory pork and shrimp, and nutty peanuts. You spoon the concoction onto a crispy rice cracker and shove the whole thing into your mouth. I adore na tung so much that it's on our restaurant menus and in rotation at home. If you have saam kleur in your larder, use it to save time.

SAAM KLEUR (THREE BUDDIES PASTE) OR 1 TBSP PREMADE FROM LARDER (PAGE 57)

- 10g | 3 garlic cloves
- 5g | 2 tsp finely chopped cilantro root, or 1 tsp finely chopped cilantro stems
- 0.7g | 15 white peppercorns
- 0.7g | 12 black peppercorns

Prep the saam kleur: If using the 1 Tbsp premade saam kleur, put it into a small bowl and skip to the next step. To make the paste from scratch, use a mortar and pestle to aggressively pound the garlic and cilantro into a coarse paste. Make a well in the center of the paste, add the white and black peppercorns to the well, and pound the peppercorns to smithereens, gradually working the pounded aromatics into the pepper until you have a finely textured mixture, then scrape the paste into a small bowl.

- 150g | 5 oz peeled, deveined large shrimp (from 200g | 7 oz shell-on)
- 1½ tsp neutral oil, such as rice bran
- 150g | 5 oz ground pork
- 1½ Tbsp fish sauce, plus more to taste
- 100g | about 1 cup thinly sliced shallots
- 160ml | ⅔ cup thick coconut milk (see Notes)
- 70g | 3½ Tbsp firmly packed Thai palm sugar
- 40g | mounded ¼ cup roasted peanuts, chopped
- 1 Tbsp oil from Namprik Pao (Grandmother's Chili Jam, page 44; optional)
- Cilantro, for garnish (optional)
- 1 batch Khao Tung (Crispy Rice Crackers, page 50)

Chop the shrimp: Cut the shrimp into uneven ½-inch (1.25cm) chunks. In the finished dish, you want identifiable shrimp pieces that are also scoopable onto the rice cracker. Don't make them too big or too small.

Cook the dip and serve: Set a medium saucepan over medium heat. When the pan is hot, add the oil and swirl the pan to coat the bottom. Add the saam kleur and stir until aromatic, about 30 seconds. Add the pork, poking and mashing it into small pieces to coat it with the seasonings. After about 1 minute, when the pork is half cooked, season it with the fish sauce and continue cooking, stirring occasionally, until the pork is fully cooked, about 45 seconds more.

Add the shallots and cook, stirring, just until softened, about 1 minute, then stir in the coconut milk and sugar. Continue cooking, stirring, for 1 minute to meld the flavors. Stir in the shrimp and peanuts and, when the shrimp is just cooked through, about 1 minute, remove from the heat. Taste, and if more saltiness is needed, stir in fish sauce by the ½ tsp until the taste suits you. This dish should be a little bit sweeter than it is salty. If using, stir in the namprik pao oil for color and aroma.

Transfer the warm dip to a serving bowl, garnish with cilantro (if using), and enjoy with the rice crackers.

NOTES

Peanuts are the go-to for na tung, but if you're allergic to them, use cashews.

For the thick coconut milk, collect it from the top of an unshaken can or box of coconut milk.

ทอดมันปลา | Tod Mun Pla

Curried Fish Cakes

MAKES 16 CAKES; SERVES 4 TO 6

In Bangkok markets, these favorite fish cakes sell so quickly that vendors often impale several on a skewer for easy counting. Vibrant orange from red curry paste, crenulated tod mun are easy to make. They are chewy—with a slightly bouncy bite—so don't expect tender, genteel French quenelles. In Thailand, these cakes are made from the collagen-rich flesh of specific fish species that fish-paste vendors scrape from bones. In the United States, I've found that you can use a fresh fish fillet and a food processor for equally good results. I do practice the traditional splat method of throwing the paste against the wall of a bowl to increase its bouncy texture (it's a fun stress reliever). A good stir with a silicone spatula will do, if you're not in a throwing mood. Form tod mun like good Thai cooks do: Using one hand, squish and press the paste hard enough to leave finger imprints, and then release it into the oil to fry. (The imprints add crispness.) This dynamite snack is great with rice too.

SAUCE

225g | 8 oz Persian or English cucumbers, halved lengthwise, seeded, and thinly sliced crosswise

2 mini sweet peppers, quartered, seeded, and cut on the diagonal

60 to 80ml | ¼ to ⅓ cup thinly sliced shallots

60 to 80ml | ¼ to ⅓ cup Nam Jim Gai (Sweet Chili "Chicken" Sauce, page 54)

Mix the sauce: In a medium bowl, combine the cucumber and peppers with as much shallot and nam jim gai as you like. Let sit while you prepare the fish cakes.

FISH CAKES

500g | generous 1 lb skinless mild white fish fillet, such as rockfish, halibut, or sole

1 to 2 Tbsp Prik Gaeng Ped (Red Curry Paste, page 144)

1 Tbsp fish sauce

½ tsp fine sea salt

1 Tbsp tapioca starch

60g | ½ cup thinly sliced green or long beans

4 or 5 makrut lime leaves, finely slivered (see page 31; optional)

Neutral oil, such as rice bran, for deep-frying

Season the fish: Cut the fish into 1-inch (2.5cm) cubes. In an extra-large bowl, combine 1 Tbsp of the curry paste, the fish sauce, salt, and tapioca starch and mix well. Add the fish and stir to coat evenly.

Make the paste: Transfer the fish to a food processor and process until it forms a paste. Check the flavor by microwaving a small amount and then tasting. If you don't taste elements of the curry paste, pulse in up to an additional 1 Tbsp curry paste. Don't add more than that, however. Tod mun pla is purposefully not spicy.

Using a silicone spatula, scrape the paste back into the bowl. Use one hand to gather the paste into a ball and throw it against the wall of the bowl to make a "splat" sound. Do this eight to ten times. (Use the spatula to gather the paste as needed.) Use your hand to massage in the green beans and lime leaves (if using) to distribute them evenly.

Fry and serve: Pour oil to a generous 1-inch (2.5cm) depth into a large wok and heat over medium heat to about 350°F (175°C). Place a wire cooling rack on a sheet pan and set it plus a small bowl filled with water near the stovetop. Divide the fish paste into 16 equal portions, arranging them on a sheet pan or large plate, and set it near the stovetop as well.

When the oil is ready, dip one hand into the water and then pick up a portion of the fish paste and position it at the base of your four fingers. Fold your four fingers over to lightly press the ball into a flattish cake about 2¼ inches (5.5cm) in diameter. Aim for your fingers to leave their imprints in the cake so the edges fry up nice and crisp. Gently release it into the hot oil. (If the paste falls apart as you're working with it, knead it back into a ball and re-squish.) Fry in batches of 4 or 5 cakes, turning the cakes occasionally, until slightly puffed, 2 to 3 minutes. Using a spider, transfer them to the cooling rack to drain (they will deflate and darken slightly). Return the oil to temperature before re-dipping your hand into the water to shape and fry the next batch.

Serve warm or at room temperature with the sauce.

ปลาดุกฟู | Pla Duk Foo

Fish Cereal

SERVES 4

Whoever first thought of cooking a small amount of mild-tasting fish, then flaking and drying it before frying it into crispy clouds was a genius. Moreover, the resulting fish cereal can be kept for a couple of weeks and refreshed for dishes like the simple green mango salad on page 100 or the sumptuous seafood saeng wah on page 76. The fish cereal can also be refried with a coating of curry paste for the rice topping on page 239. Double the recipe to practice and have plenty on hand. Catfish is traditionally charcoal grilled, but briefly baking the fish works just fine. I often use sole or other mild white fish fillet when catfish is unavailable.

300g | 10 oz skinless sole, catfish, cod, or rockfish fillet

Neutral oil, such as rice bran, for deep-frying

Bake the fish: Position a rack in the middle of the oven and preheat the oven to 375°F (190°C). Line a sheet pan with parchment paper and lay the fish on the parchment. Bake the fish until fully cooked, about 10 minutes for sole and longer for catfish or other firmer fish. To check for doneness, poke the fish with a fork or finger. It should flake easily.

Pour off the accumulated liquid from the sheet pan, then let the fish cool completely on the pan, 15 to 20 minutes. If you like, carefully slide the parchment off the pan, leaving the fish on the pan so you can segue into flaking it.

Use your fingers to break the fish up into pieces no bigger than ½ inch (1.25cm), spreading them out in a single layer on the pan. Blot off excess moisture with paper towels and then let the fish air-dry for about 30 minutes to make it easier to flake.

Make fluffy fish flakes: Using two forks with the curved back of the tines facing down, press and drag the forks crosswise on the fish to break it up (see photos). Occasionally turn the forks on their side to fluff the fish. Your goal is to mush, separate, and then fluff! Aim for tiny pieces like finely grated fresh coconut. Discard any errant big bones that appear (tiny ones will fry fine).

Spread the flaked fish out in a thin layer and leave, uncovered, to dry further. It is ready when it has shrunken slightly yet still feels damp, about 2 hours. Midway through this drying time, re-flake the fish with a fork or rub it between your fingertips to fluff further. (To expedite this step, you can set the pan on the stovetop and turn on the exhaust fan for extra ventilation.) Or instead of leaving it to dry at room temperature, you can refrigerate it uncovered overnight or up to 12 hours. Regardless of which method you use, you'll have about 1½ cups (360ml) flaked fish when it has dried sufficiently.

Fry fish clouds: Pour oil to a generous 1-inch (2.5cm) depth into a large wok and heat over medium-high heat until nearly smoking, about 375°F (190°C). Set a fine-mesh strainer over a medium bowl and place the bowl near the stovetop. Line a sheet pan with a cooling rack and paper towels and set it near the stovetop as well.

Lower the heat to medium, then grab a handful (⅓ to ½ cup | 80 to 120ml) of the fish flakes and scatter them onto the surface of the hot oil. Gently shake the wok a bit to distribute the fish flakes so they fry evenly. Let fry for 5 to 10 seconds before nudging the fish bits toward the center so they stick to one another and form a light and airy cloud-like piece (see photo). Fold one side over the other so your cloud is roughly rectangular, then fry, flipping the cloud a few times, until crispy and browned. All of this will take about 2 minutes. Use a fine-mesh skimmer to transfer the finished fish cloud to the strainer, then scoop up any bits lingering in the oil (as long as they're not burnt, they're good, so don't waste them). Repeat to make another cloud. As one fish cloud finishes frying, carefully transfer the draining fish cloud from the strainer to the towel-lined sheet pan to absorb excess oil. Repeat until all the fish flakes are fried; as you're working, return any oil that drains into the bowl back to the wok.

When all the fish clouds are fried, assess them. If they browned before they fully crisped (it easily happens), position a rack in the middle of the oven and preheat the oven to 300°F (150°C). Arrange the fish clouds on a sheet pan and bake until crisp, about 10 minutes.

Use right away, or refrigerate in an airtight container for up to 2 weeks. To refresh before serving, bake in a preheated 300°F (150°C) oven, until warm and re-crisped, 5 to 10 minutes.

แสร้งว่า | Saeng Wah

Fish Cereal and Grilled Prawns with "Pretend" Sauce

SERVES 6

This is a splurge dish, luxurious in composition with both fried crispy fish and grilled fresh seafood. In Central Thai, the word *saeng wah* means "pretend." King Rama II, who ruled from 1809 to 1824 and was a talented poet and artist, described the court dish in his epic poem *Kap He Chom Khrueang Khao Wan* (กาพย์เห่ชมเครื่องคาวหวาน). The original version featured fermented fish guts in the sauce, but squeamish palace cooks replaced the guts with a trompe l'oeil tamarind dressing. Their dish looked the same but was palatable to elegant society. In Thailand, I use somsa (a type of Thai citron) for the tart, salty, spicy sauce, but in America, lime or calamansi juice works just fine. Use all the toppings for vibrant flavors.

---

1 batch Pla Duk Foo (Fish Cereal, page 75)

½ tsp firmly packed Thai palm sugar

60ml | ¼ cup lime or calamansi juice (see Notes)

1 Tbsp plus 1 tsp fish sauce

120ml | ½ cup Nam Makam (Tamarind Liquid, page 52)

60g | 2-inch section ginger, peeled and cut into fine matchsticks

60g | 2 mini sweet peppers, seeded and cut into fine matchsticks

2 Tbsp super-thinly sliced lemongrass (1 stalk), loosely separated into rings

3 Tbsp finely slivered makrut lime leaves (5 to 7 leaves; see page 31)

2 or 3 fresh Thai chilies, thinly sliced

500g | 6 shell-on, head-on langoustines, or 12 large shell-on, head-on shrimp

Cilantro, for garnish (optional)

Ready the fish cereal: Make the fish cereal, or if already on hand, re-crisp as directed in the recipe, then let cool.

Prep the sauce and gather the toppings: Use the back of a spoon to smash the sugar against the side of a small bowl, then gradually stir in the lime juice until the sugar dissolves. Stir in the fish sauce and tamarind and let the sauce sit until serving. Have the ginger, sweet peppers, lemongrass, lime leaves, and chilies ready for assembly, keeping them separate.

Grill the seafood: Prepare a charcoal or gas grill for direct-heat cooking over a medium-hot fire. Or heat a cast-iron grill pan over medium-high heat on the stovetop closer to cooking time.

If using langoustines, soak six bamboo skewers, each about 8 inches (20cm) long, in hot water for at least 20 minutes. One at a time, lay a langoustine on its back. To remove the soft shell along the belly, use kitchen scissors to cut along the two sides of the tail section, from the base of the legs to the tail. Snip at the base of the head and the top of the tail to detach and remove the shell section. Remove the legs but leave the big front claws for good looks. Snip through the middle of the head to make it easier for diners to suck out all the goodness. Stick a skewer up the tail to keep the langoustine straight during grilling. Grill the langoustines, uncut-side down, until tender firm and just barely cooked through, 2 to 3 minutes (no need to turn them); if you prefer well-done seafood, cook longer. Hold on a plate until assembly time.

If using shrimp, keep the shrimp whole with the shell intact for grilling (no skewering needed). Grill until tender firm and just cooked through, 2 to 3 minutes, turning once; cook longer if you prefer well-done shrimp. Let cool until handleable, then peel and devein the shrimp, keeping the head intact for eating.

Assemble and serve: On a large platter, make a bed of the fried crispy fish, breaking it apart to distribute evenly. Arrange the grilled seafood on top; if using langoustines, remove the skewers and place them belly-side up. Drizzle about one-third of the sauce over the top of the seafood (aim mostly for the exposed flesh), then add the ginger, sweet peppers, lemongrass, lime leaves, and chilies; garnish with cilantro (if using). Set the remaining sauce in a bowl alongside the platter.

To eat, take a little bit of everything, extracting the seafood from its shell as needed, and mix together with extra sauce if you like.

NOTES

Popular in many parts of Southeast Asia, calamansi is the small, tart citrus hybrid of kumquat and mandarin orange. If you want to use calamansi juice but cannot find fruits, you can mimic its flavor by combining the juice of 2 limes and ½ mandarin orange.

Grill the seafood up to 1 hour in advance of serving, cover, and leave at room temperature. If you can't find langoustines or head-on shrimp, grill shell-on, headless shrimp for about the same amount of time.

ปีกไก่กินข้าว | Peek Gai Tod

Kin Khao Wings

SERVES 4

When I opened Kin Khao, I wanted a fun, standout Thai take on buffalo wings. I fried up crispy chicken wings seasoned with saam kleur, a garlic-cilantro-pepper paste that's part of every decent Thai kitchen. The wings were glazed with a glossy concoction of tamarind, palm sugar, and the original Thai-style sriracha made by Sriraja Panich (you can swap in Shark brand, but Huy Fong's aggressive Rooster sauce won't work here). The tasty wings looked rather sexy, so I named them Pretty Hot Wings, though most people know them as Kin Khao Wings. They've never gone off our menu. You'll know why once you make a batch. If you prefer to bake the wings, see the Note.

SAAM KLEUR (THREE BUDDIES PASTE) OR 1 TBSP PREMADE FROM LARDER (PAGE 57)

10g | 3 garlic cloves

5g | 2 tsp finely chopped cilantro root, or 1 tsp finely chopped cilantro stems

0.7g | 15 white peppercorns

0.7g | 12 black peppercorns

Prep the saam kleur: If using the 1 Tbsp premade saam kleur, put it into a large bowl and skip to the next step. To make the paste from scratch, use a mortar and pestle to aggressively pound the garlic and cilantro into a coarse paste. Make a well in the center of the paste, add the white and black peppercorns to the well, and pound the peppercorns to smithereens, gradually working the pounded aromatics into the pepper until you have a finely textured mixture, then scrape the paste into a large bowl.

---

1 Tbsp plus 2 tsp fish sauce, divided

900g | 2 lb whole chicken wings or drumettes and flats

40g | ⅓ cup Thai rice flour

40g | ⅓ cup tapioca starch

25g | 4 tsp firmly packed Thai palm sugar

2 tsp water

120ml | ½ cup Nam Makam (Tamarind Liquid, page 52)

120ml | ½ cup Sriraja Panich or Shark sriracha sauce

Neutral oil, such as rice bran, for deep-frying

2 fresh Thai chilies, thinly sliced (optional)

1 small lime

Marinate the wings: Add 1 Tbsp of the fish sauce to the saam kleur and mix well. Then add the wings to the bowl and rub and massage them all over with the seasoning. Cover and refrigerate for at least 6 hours or up to 3 days.

Prep the wings and glaze: About 1 hour before frying, in a large bowl, stir together the rice flour and tapioca starch. Add the wings and toss to coat each wing evenly, then transfer the wings in a single layer to a large sheet pan. Let sit, uncovered, to remove most of the chill and develop a coating that will later cook up extra crispy. (If opting to bake, see the Note.)

Meanwhile, to make the glaze, in a small saucepan, combine the sugar and water and heat over medium heat, whisking to melt the sugar. Whisk in the remaining 2 tsp fish sauce, the tamarind, and sriracha. Let come to a vigorous bubbly simmer to develop flavor, 1 to 2 minutes. Remove from the heat, let cool briefly, then scrape the glaze into a medium bowl.

Fry the wings: Pour oil to a depth of 1½ to 2 inches (3.75 to 5cm) into a large wok or medium-large pot, using the deeper oil if frying whole wings. Heat over medium-high heat to between 350° and 375°F (175° to 190°C). Set a large wire cooling rack on a sheet pan and place the pan near the stovetop.

When the oil is ready, fry the wings in three batches, lightly shaking the wings to release excess coating before dropping them into the hot oil. Cook, using a slotted spoon to stir and turn often, until golden brown and crisp, 8 to 12 minutes (whole wings take longest). Use the spoon to transfer the wings to the wire rack to drain. After each batch is cooked, use a fine-mesh skimmer to remove and discard any bits in the oil and return the oil to temperature before adding the next batch.

Glaze and serve: Have ready a serving platter. Working in batches, add the wings to the glaze, turning them in the glaze and spooning the glaze over them as needed to coat evenly, then transfer to the platter. Top the wings with the chilies, then finish by grating the zest from the lime over the glorious pile. Enjoy your Pretty Hot Wings with lots of napkins.

NOTE

To prep the marinated wings for baking, rub them with 3 Tbsp neutral oil, such as rice bran, then coat in the rice-and-tapioca mixture. Let sit uncovered for 1 hour. Preheat the oven to 450°F (230°C) with a rack in the middle spot. Line a sheet pan with parchment and lightly oil the paper. Tap excess coating from the wings, then put them on the pan, equally spaced apart. Bake until pale gold, about 20 minutes. Pull from the oven, briefly cool to coax easier release, and then flip each wing. Continue baking, turning once or twice, until golden brown and crisp, 10 to 15 minutes longer. Glaze and serve as usual.

กะหรี่ปั๊บอบ | Karee Puff Op

Baked Chicken Curry Puff

MAKES 12 PUFFS

In Thailand, there are Buddhist temples galore, but in the Bay Area, we're lucky to have a handful. I usually accompany my aunt Wandee to Wat Buddhapradeep of San Francisco. While she prays, I peruse the temple's food concessions. Deep-fried chicken curry puffs crafted from spiral-cut rounds of Chinese puff pastry always catch my eye. At Nari, we serve deep-fried curry puffs prepared with duck confit, but at home I prefer a simpler route: I bake the puffs with a foolproof flaky pastry and stuff them with a sweet-salty chicken-and-potato curry. The pastry and baking make the puffs easier to achieve, and my decadent, tender dough rivals the Chinese puff pastry. To counter their richness, pair the puffs with ajaad, the quick pickle on page 113.

These are a project. To avoid feeling rushed, make the pastry and filling on day one, then assemble and bake the puffs on day two or three. Review the entire recipe to gather all ingredients. Your time investment will be worth it. Unbaked puffs freeze like a dream. See page 84 for a vegetarian filling.

DOUGH

250g | 1¾ cups bread flour, preferably King Arthur (12.7 percent protein)

113g | ½ cup chilled salted butter (dairy or plant based)

113g | ½ cup chilled leaf lard or vegetable shortening

3 to 4 Tbsp water (room temperature is fine)

Make the dough: Put the flour onto the center of a large cutting board and spread it into an 8-inch (20cm) round. Using a bench scraper, cut the butter and lard into pats or chunks ¼ inch (6mm) thick. Put them on top of the flour and then, using the bench scraper, turn them to coat well.

Now, apply the French fraisage technique for building flaky dough. Using the heel of one hand, methodically press to flatten and smear the fat pieces into thin, long streaks coated by flour. Work all over the flour pile, using the bench scraper to fold and shovel the mixture toward the center. The fat pieces will become superthin and then break into pieces resembling a messy pile of giant mashed potato flakes.

When powdery flour is no longer visible and the pile begins coalescing into a very rough dough mass, gather it into a volcano shape and make a hole in the center. Pour 2 Tbsp of the water into the hole. Use the bench scraper to scoop and fold the dry ingredients into the liquid middle. Sprinkle 1 Tbsp of the water on top of the pile, then, working around the perimeter, keep gathering and folding the mixture toward the center. If the dough isn't moist enough to press together into a block, work in the remaining 1 Tbsp water.

Scrape and shape the mixture into a 5-inch (12.5cm) square block. Press firmly to compact, adding a bit more flour if it's overly sticky. Neaten the block so it is straight and flat. If it's tacky, sprinkle on a little flour. Wrap the block in plastic wrap and chill for 1 to 2 hours to firm and hydrate.

FOR FILLING AND FINISHING

180g | 6 oz boneless, skinless chicken thigh or breast

180g | 1 medium-large Yukon Gold potato, unpeeled and quartered

1 Tbsp neutral oil, such as rice bran

20g | 2 Tbsp chopped shallots

1 garlic clove, finely chopped

2 tsp Madras curry powder

1 Tbsp Thai oyster sauce

1½ Tbsp fish sauce

40g | 2 Tbsp firmly packed Thai palm sugar

1 large egg, lightly beaten (for egg wash)

Cook the filling: While the pastry chills, freeze the chicken until semihard, about 1 hour, then cut into pea-size pieces. Put the potato into a microwave-safe bowl, add water to a depth of ¼ inch (6mm), cover with a vented microwave splatter guard, and then microwave on high power until tender firm, 3 to 4 minutes. (Or steam the potato over boiling water on the stovetop until tender firm, 15 to 20 minutes.) Let cool, remove and discard the peel, and cut the potato flesh into pieces about the same size as the chicken.

CONTINUED

Set a wok or medium skillet over medium heat. When the pan is hot, add the oil and swirl the pan to coat with the oil. Add the shallots, garlic, and curry powder and cook, stirring, until fragrant, about 15 seconds. Add the chicken and stir constantly until it no longer looks raw, about 30 seconds, then add the potato and the oyster and fish sauces. Add the sugar, smooshing it on the side of the pan to help it melt and caramelize. Keep cooking, stirring gently and constantly, until the liquid is no longer visible and the mixture smells heady, 1 to 2 minutes. Transfer the roughly 1⅓ cups (320ml) filling to a bowl or plate, press to compact (it's OK to mash the potato), and then divide into 12 equal portions. Partially cover and let cool completely before using. Or let cool, transfer to an airtight container, and refrigerate for up to 2 days.

Roll out and trifold the dough six times: Heavily dust the work surface. Unwrap the dough, set it on the floured surface, and top the dough with a dusting of flour. Use a rolling pin to firmly press and roll the dough into a rectangle 6 inches (15cm) wide, 10 inches (25cm) long, and ½ inch (1.25cm) thick. Employ the bench scraper (or a ruler) to gauge the size and neaten the edges. Press any lingering bits of the dough into the rectangle, then brush off the excess flour before you trifold the dough: With a longer side of the rectangle closest to you, fold the left third inward and then fold the right third inward so the two folds overlap completely (see the photo). (If the narrower side of the rectangle is closest to you, fold the top third down and then fold the bottom third up to overlap completely.) Rotate the dough 90 degrees, lightly dust it with flour, and then repeat to roll out the dough and fold it five more times. Between each repetition, remember to rotate the dough 90 degrees and dust with flour; before each trifold, be sure to brush off excess flour. As the dough becomes sturdier, you will need to dust with less flour.

When the dough slightly resists your rolling, you are at dough perfection. (If in doubt, roll the dough out and trifold again; you won't ruin this dough!) After your last fold, wrap the roughly 3½ by 6-inch (8.75 by 15cm) dough rectangle in plastic wrap and chill for about 30 minutes to firm up and rest.

Make a spiraled dough cylinder: Lightly dust the work surface. Unwrap the dough and set it on the floured surface with one of the narrower (3½ inch | 8.75cm) edges closest to you. Then roll the dough into a rectangle measuring 6 inches (15cm) wide and a scant ¼ inch (6mm) thick. It will be 18 to 20 inches (45 to 50cm) long. Pause occasionally to lightly flour the underside of the dough to prevent sticking.

Lightly brush the top of the rectangle with water, then working from a narrow side, tightly roll up the dough jelly roll style into a spiraled cylinder (avoid air in the spiral!). Wrap the dough cylinder in plastic wrap and chill until hard, at least 3 hours or up to 2 days.

Fill and shape the puffs: Unwrap the dough cylinder and set on the work surface. Mark and then slice 12 equal rounds, each about ½ inch (1.25cm) thick, along its length. (It's OK to shave some dough off biggish rounds to press onto skimpy ones.) Let the rounds sit, without overlapping, until malleable, 15 to 30 minutes. Line two sheet pans with parchment paper.

To make a puff, first use the heel of your hand to press a dough round to half its original thickness, then use a skinny dumpling rolling pin (or smooth bottle or drinking glass) to roll the round into a round wrapper 4¼ inches (10.5cm) wide, rotating the dough 90 degrees with every roll to prevent sticking. Aim to preserve a poochy belly in the center by rolling from the center and exerting more pressure on the edge. Ideally the finished wrapper is thicker in the middle and the spirals are somewhat preserved.

Place a portion of filling (about 1½ Tbsp) above the midline, moisten the dough edge with water, fold up to close into a half-moon, then press to seal well. Crimp the edge as you like (it's fine to press with fork tines). Place on a prepared sheet pan. Repeat with the remaining dough rounds and filling, placing the puffs about 2 inches (5cm) apart and dividing them evenly between the prepared pans. Chill, uncovered, for 15 to 30 minutes.

Bake and eat: Position a rack in the middle of the oven and preheat the oven to 400°F (200°C). Bake the sheet pans one at a time. Lightly brush the puffs with egg wash and bake until golden brown and puffed, 22 to 25 minutes. Let cool on the pan on a wire cooling rack for at least 10 minutes. Repeat with the second sheet pan of puffs. Enjoy the puffs warm or at room temperature.

NOTES

Freeze unbaked puffs on a sheet pan until hard, then transfer to an airtight container and return to the freezer for up to 3 months. Thaw in the refrigerator and then bake as directed.

For a different chicken filling, swap out the curry powder and oyster sauce for 3 Tbsp of Prik Gaeng Golae (Golae Curry Marinade, page 212). Keep all the other ingredients and cooking techniques the same.

กะหรี่ปั๊ปเห็ด | Karee Puff Hed

Mushroom Curry Puff Filling

MAKES 1⅓ CUPS (320ML), ENOUGH FOR 12 PUFFS

To make a vegetarian version of the curry puffs on page 81, make the dough with vegetable shortening rather than lard, and swap out the chicken-and-potato filling for this mushroomy one.

180g | 6 oz fresh mushrooms (any kind)

180g | 1 medium-large Yukon Gold potato, unpeeled and quartered

1½ Tbsp neutral oil, such as rice bran, divided

Fine sea salt

20g | 2 Tbsp chopped shallots

1 garlic clove, finely chopped

2 tsp Madras curry powder

1 Tbsp vegetarian oyster sauce

1 Tbsp Thai thin soy sauce

20g | 1 Tbsp firmly packed Thai palm sugar

Prep the mushrooms and potato: Chop the mushroom caps and stems into large pea-size pieces. Put the potato into a microwave-safe bowl, add water to a depth of ¼ inch (6mm), cover with a vented microwave splatter guard, and then microwave on high power until tender firm, 3 to 4 minutes. (Or steam the potato over boiling water on the stovetop until tender firm, 15 to 20 minutes.) Let cool, remove and discard the peel, and cut the potato flesh into pieces a little smaller than the mushroom.

Assemble the filling: Set a wok or medium skillet over medium heat. When the pan is hot, add 1½ tsp of the oil and swirl the pan to coat with the oil. Add the mushrooms, season with 2 big pinches of salt, and cook, stirring occasionally, until the mushrooms have shrunken to about half of their original volume, about 2 minutes. Stir in the remaining 1 Tbsp oil.

Add the shallots, garlic, and curry powder and cook, stirring, until fragrant, about 15 seconds. Add the potato and oyster and soy sauces and stir gently to combine. Add the sugar, smooshing it on the side of the pan to help it melt and caramelize. Keep cooking, stirring gently and constantly, until only a little liquid remains and the mixture smells delicious, 1 to 2 minutes. Transfer to a bowl or plate, press to compact (it's OK to mash the potato), and then divide into 12 equal portions. Partially cover and let cool completely before using. Or let cool, transfer to an airtight container, and refrigerate for up to 2 days.

3

ยำ ตำ ดอง

Salads and Pickle

มะม่วง
เขียวเสวย
กกละ 130.-

An Interplay of Flavors and Textures

The concept of "salad" doesn't exist in Thai cuisine. By that I mean we don't eat a big bowl of leaves tossed with some kind of dressing. The closest approximation to salad is a category we call yum. The word *yum* (ยำ) means "tossed together" or "mixed together," often by hand. (It also means beating someone senseless, but that's not about food, so let's skip it.)

A wealth of Thai dishes fit into this category of mixing or tossing together. And Thai yum salads incorporate not just greens or leaves but also meats, seafood, and even fruits. In fact, Thai people are quite fond of using sweet seasonal fruits in savory salads.

Yum som-o (page 90), or pomelo salad, is a great example of fruit-filled Thai-style salads. In Thailand, pomelos are peeled, broken into big chunks, and tossed with a spicy, tangy dressing that sometimes incorporates minced pork or even shrimp. In this book, I adapt the classic into a vegan version and swap out the pomelos (because they're not always great in the United States) for a variety of other beautiful citrus fruits. The yum goong salad on page 103 combines grilled shrimp and lychees for a stunningly good combination of flavors and textures.

No need to worry, Thai salads don't have to be devilishly spicy to have a personality. Good Thai cooks pull many levers to craft exciting, bold-flavored salads. Get ready for lots of fresh herbs. Mint, cilantro, sawtooth herb, and Vietnamese coriander add complexity and verve.

Other common Thai salad ingredients do double or even triple duty. For instance, in the laab recipes (pages 106 and 107), toasted rice powder (khao kua) not only adds crunch but also provides the much-needed body to unite the salad components. My aromatics-laced khao kua recipe on page 47 will amp up any laab with hints of galangal, lemongrass, and makrut lime.

The best Thai salads hit you on many levels, combining salt, acid, heat, and sweetness, and often contain a crunchy element for textural contrast too. Rooted in umami, many of the dressings and sauces get their salinity from nampla (fish sauce), gapi (shrimp paste), or pla ra (fermented fish). The bright acid element might be from lime or other citrus juices or more earthy tamarind liquid. The sweetness can come from fresh fruit or palm sugar. The crunch can turn up as fried garlic, shallots, nuts, or toasted coconut flakes. You can also pair complementary opposites, such as crisp fried fish cereal "clouds" and bright, spicy mango salad.

There are no rules about how to serve Thai "salads." Feel free to enjoy the recipes in this chapter however you want—as a one-dish light lunch, as part of a bigger dinner, or dressed up nicely as little bites for hors d'oeuvres.

Thai salads can take on so many beautiful guises. Learn the basics of som tum by making the green papaya salad on page 92 and you can som tum anything! The same goes with laab. Learn the rules, master the classics, and let loose your imagination.

ยำส้มโอ | Yum Som-O

Savory Citrus-Herb Salad

SERVES 6

In Thai, *yum som-o* means "pomelo salad," but I've long adapted this salad to use whatever citrus is currently in season. It never fails to please dinner-party guests. Use a mix of tart, sweet, and colorful citrus varieties for this gorgeous and easy salad. Feel free to play too: This recipe is a formula for crafting your own rainbow. For instance, substitute other kinds of basil or soft green herbs for the ones called for here. For a summery version, feature nectarines, plums, and other stone fruits in place of the citrus. This salad does not need to be overly spicy, so add as much (or as little) chili as you want.

DRESSING

60ml | ¼ cup lime juice

3 Tbsp fish sauce or Japanese white soy sauce (see Notes)

1 pinch of Thai palm sugar or light brown sugar

2 to 4 fresh Thai chilies, chopped (seeded if you like), plus more for garnish

Ready the dressing: In a small bowl, stir together the lime juice, fish sauce, sugar, and as much chili as you like. It is important to taste the sauce because the acidity of lime juice, saltiness of fish sauce, and sweetness of palm sugar vary. The ideal dressing tastes tart, salty, and just a little sweet, in that order. Avoid adding too much sugar now when using all sweet citrus in the salad.

SALAD AND GARNISH

2 small blood oranges

1 Cara Cara orange

1 navel orange

2 large or 4 small mandarin oranges, tangerines, or clementines

40g | 2 small shallots, thinly sliced (about ⅓ cup)

3 Tbsp toasted unsweetened dried coconut flakes (see page 56), gently crumbled

3 Tbsp fried shallots

2 Tbsp chopped salted or unsalted roasted peanuts (optional)

Leaves from a few mint, shiso, Thai basil, or lemon basil sprigs, or a combo

Prep the citrus: Using a knife or your fingers, peel the citrus by hand or with a sharp paring knife. Slice crosswise into rounds about ¼ inch (6mm) thick. Aim for a total of about 3 cups (710ml) prepped citrus. Remove any seeds that are present. Arrange the citrus beautifully—interspersing different colors and sizes—on a serving platter.

Assemble the salad and serve: Pour all the dressing over the citrus, then sprinkle on the sliced shallots, coconut, fried shallots, and peanuts (if using). Add the herbs, tearing the leaves as needed. Finish with some chili for extra fire. Serve immediately to avoid the salad becoming watery and diluted in flavor.

NOTES

Make the dressing up to 1 day ahead. Several hours before serving, peel and slice the citrus and refrigerate.

If you don't have fish sauce or white soy sauce, use 3 Tbsp of Fast Fake Fish Sauce (page 23).

ส้มตำไทย | Som Tum Thai

Green Papaya Salad

SERVES 4

Many people define som tum as a green papaya salad, but Thai cooks can som tum practically anything. The term *som* (ส้ม) means "sour flavor," and the term *tum* (ตำ) means "to pound with a pestle." Together, som tum denotes a particular tart-spicy-salty dish that's made by using a mortar and pestle to bruise and combine ingredients. The basic framework calls for crunchy, tart, or neutral-tasting produce enrobed in a tangy, garlicky, spicy dressing. Those main components are gently pounded and mixed with add-ins that lend umami, fruity, verdant, or nutty notes.

Below is a master recipe showcasing green papaya (sold at many Chinese and Southeast Asian grocers), followed by ideas for your experimentations. Up to 3 days ahead, prep the dressing, add-ins, and green papaya. Traditionally, all the ingredients are pounded together in a conical-shaped earthenware mortar with a wooden pestle. I assemble som tum Thai (photographed on pages 94 and 95 with "freestyle" variations) in a mixing bowl, so no special equipment is required.

DRESSING

3 to 8g | 2 to 5 fresh Thai chilies (red, yellow, or orange), to taste

7.5g | 2 medium or 3 small garlic cloves

1½ tsp firmly packed Thai palm sugar, plus more to taste

60ml | ¼ cup lime juice, plus more to taste

60ml | ¼ cup fish sauce or Fast Fake Fish sauce (page 23), plus more to taste

Make the dressing: Using a mortar and pestle, pound and flatten two chilies. Add the garlic to the chilies and pound to flatten. Push the mixture to the side, add the sugar, and pound gently to smoosh it. Use a spoon to scrape the chilies, garlic, and sugar into a measuring cup, then stir in the lime juice and fish sauce. Let the dressing rest briefly to bloom the flavors, then taste and add more chilies (pound before incorporating), sugar, lime juice, and fish sauce as needed to create a hot, tart, pungent, salty finish.

ADD-INS

30g | 3 long beans, or 4 or 5 pencil-thin green beans

80g | ½ cup firm cherry tomatoes, preferably unripe and tangy

5 to 10g | 1 to 2 Tbsp small dried shrimp (optional)

3 to 4 Tbsp neutral oil, such as rice bran (if frying the shrimp)

2 Tbsp roasted peanuts or cashews

Ready the add-ins: Trim the beans and cut into 2-inch (5cm) lengths. If the beans are woody or taste unpleasantly green "beany," blanch the cut pieces in boiling water until bright but still crisp, 30 to 45 seconds, then submerge them in an ice bath to halt the cooking, and drain well. Keep the green beans and cherry tomatoes handy.

If using dried shrimp, soak them in warm water for 2 minutes, drain, pat dry with a paper towel, and then pound in a mortar with a pestle to a fluffy, fine texture. Or for a delicate deliciousness that I prefer, after soaking and drying the shrimp, fry them in the oil in a small saucepan over medium-low heat until dark orange, about 2 minutes, then transfer to a plate and use the shrimp whole.

Add the peanuts to the mortar and pound lightly to crush slightly. Keep the peanuts and shrimp together.

PAPAYA AND ACCOMPANIMENT

One 675g | 1½-lb small green papaya

1 batch Khao Niew Neung (Microwave Sticky Rice, page 257; optional)

Cut the papaya: Using a sharp knife or vegetable peeler, thoroughly remove the thick skin of the papaya. Rinse the peeled papaya under cool running water and pat dry with paper towels. Trim the stem, cut the papaya lengthwise, and then use a spoon to scrape out the seeds. Use a mandoline or the knife to cut the papaya into pieces ⅛ inch (3mm) thick, making them as long and as wide as possible. Stack a few pieces at a time and cut into uneven matchsticks for a hand-crafted look. (See the Note for the old-school method.)

You need a generous 8 oz (250g, about 3 cups) of matchsticks for a single batch of salad. Put that amount into a big bowl. If you like, cut the rest of the papaya for a future salad and refrigerate in an airtight container for up to 3 days, or wrap the uncut papaya in plastic wrap and refrigerate for up to 1 week.

Assemble the salad and serve: Pour about half of the dressing (¼ cup | 60ml) onto the papaya. Using the pestle, gently pound and bruise the papaya, pausing now and then to scoop and flip the papaya with a spoon. Add the green beans and gently pound to bruise and release flavor. Add the tomatoes and pound to burst open.

Add the dried shrimp (if using), peanuts, and the remaining dressing. Gently pound and then scoop and flip to mix, repeating until all the elements are well combined and slightly softened. Assembling the salad should take only 1 to 2 minutes total. If you go into overtime with the pounding, the salad will be overly bruised. Transfer everything (yes, including the dressing) to a shallow bowl or deep plate. If desired, eat with sticky rice, dipping small balls of rice into the dressing.

NOTE

If you like, cut the green papaya shreds the old-school way. Holding the peeled, whole papaya with a folded dish towel (for safety), use a sharp knife to gently tap the top, making long, narrow cuts. Once the cuts total an area about 2 inches (5cm) wide, turn the knife 90 degrees and cut off uneven shreds of papaya. Repeat until you have enough for a salad.

VARIATION

ส้มตำลาว | Som Tum Lao

Issan-Style Som Tum

Make the classic green papaya version in the main recipe as directed, but omit the peanuts and use a fifty-fifty combo of fish sauce and funky pla ra (fermented fish). Employ extra chilies for true Isaan soul.

FREESTYLE SOM TUM!

Green papaya som tum (pictured at center) is iconic but not your only option. Keeping the dressing and add-ins constant, simply substitute crunchy vegetables or fruits for the green papaya in the master recipe on page 92. For instance, I love combining Piel de Sapo and other crisp melons with Japanese cucumber. Consider color to make pretty salads. Avoid mushy produce because it won't stand up to the dressing or pounding. Be artful with cutting up the fruits and vegetables to ensure your som tum has movement and grace. Here are some ideas:

Carrot Som Tum: generous 8 oz (250g) peeled young rainbow carrots, shaved with a vegetable peeler

Apple and Asian Pear Som Tum: 150g (5 oz) unpeeled tart apple + 120g (4 oz) unpeeled Asian pear, cut as matchsticks

Kohlrabi and Apple Som Tum: 150g (5 oz) peeled kohlrabi + 120g (4 oz) unpeeled tart apple, cut as matchsticks

Melon and Cucumber Som Tum: 150g (5 oz) seeded, peeled crisp melon + 120g (4 oz) seeded, unpeeled cucumber, very thinly sliced with a knife or shaved with a vegetable peeler

ยำกะทิหอยเชลล์ | Yum Gati Hoy Shell

Seared Scallops with Coconut–Chili Jam Sauce

SERVES 4

Easy and delicious, this exquisite starter relies on excellent chili jam, such as my grandmother's version on page 44. You already have it in the fridge, don't you? I hope so because the jam enables you to pull this one off quickly. Namprik pao defines yam gati's gently spicy-sweet coconut sauce, which involves stirring only four ingredients together! Just sear some large sea scallops and assemble the dish to show off your Michelin-star-chef plating skills.

SAUCE

60ml | ¼ cup coconut milk

40g | 2 Tbsp Namprik Pao (Grandmother's Chili Jam, page 44), plus some of the oil for garnish

1 tsp fish sauce

2 tsp lime juice

30g | 1 medium shallot

1 tsp lime juice

225g | 8 large sea scallops

Fine sea salt

2 to 3 tsp neutral oil, such as rice bran

2 to 4 Tbsp chopped or hand-torn mixed fresh herbs (such as basil, cilantro, mint, and chives)

3 to 4 Tbsp fried shallots, toasted unsweetened dried coconut flakes (see page 56), or a combo

Sliced fresh Thai chilies, for serving (optional)

Make the sauce: Put the coconut milk into a small microwave-safe bowl and microwave on high power for 15 to 30 seconds to warm. Remove from the microwave and stir in the chili jam. Season with the fish sauce for salinity and the lime juice for brightness. Use soon or refrigerate for up to 5 days (return to room temperature or slightly warm before using).

Mellow the shallot: Cut the shallot into superthin rounds. Separate the rounds into individual rings, put them into a small bowl, sprinkle with the lime juice, and toss to mix evenly. Let sit until serving.

Sear the scallops: Pat the scallops dry with paper towels, then season lightly on both sides with salt. Heat a medium cast-iron or carbon-steel skillet over high heat until smoking hot. Lower the heat to medium, add 2 tsp of the oil, and swirl the pan to coat the bottom. Add the scallops and let sear on the underside until crisp and golden brown, 1 to 2 minutes, depending on their size. If the pan looks dry, add the remaining 1 tsp oil before flipping and searing on the second side until crisp and golden brown, 1 to 2 minutes. The scallops should wobble slightly when pressed with a fingertip to indicate slight rawness in the center. (Cook longer if you prefer your seafood cooked through.) Transfer the cooked scallops to a plate.

Assemble and serve: Use a spoon to smear some of the sauce on a serving platter, then scatter some of the raw shallots over the sauce and arrange the scallops on top. Drizzle on a little more sauce, add the remaining raw shallot, then artfully add the herb salad. Sprinkle on the fried shallots and/or coconut, drizzle about 1 tsp oil from the namprik pao around the perimeter of the platter, and then top the scallops with a scattering of chilies (if using). Serve the remaining coconut-chili jam sauce on the side.

ยำมะเขือยาว | Yum Makeua

Burnt Eggplant Salad

SERVES 4

This plush salad is among my favorite ways to show off eggplant's sweet flesh, which shines with a tart-salty dressing and fried garlic and shallots, dried shrimp, herbs, coconut, and chilies. Thai cooks typically grill eggplant, but if you don't have a charcoal fire going, here's a simpler home method: Partly char the small, meaty eggplants to impart light smokiness and then microwave them to complete the cooking. You'll be eating this splendid salad a lot sooner.

500g | 4 or 5 small Japanese or Fairy Tale eggplants (see Note)

2 Tbsp small dried shrimp (optional)

3 to 4 Tbsp neutral oil, such as rice bran

2 Tbsp fish sauce, Japanese white soy sauce, or Fast Fake Fish Sauce (page 23)

2 Tbsp lime juice

¼ tsp firmly packed Thai palm sugar

120ml | ½ cup chopped or hand-torn mixed fresh herbs (such as basil, cilantro, mint, shiso, and green onion)

2 Tbsp fried garlic chips, homemade (page 56) or purchased

3 Tbsp fried shallots, or 1½ Tbsp toasted unsweetened dried coconut flakes (see page 56) plus 2 Tbsp fried shallots

3 fresh Thai chilies, chopped, or 1 small fresh Fresno chili, seeded and thinly sliced

Cook the eggplants: Tear off the green flaps at the stem end of each eggplant. Over a medium-high flame on a gas stovetop, char an eggplant, rotating it frequently, until it is "kissed" with smoke, the flesh is only slightly cooked, and the skin is blackened or dark brown here and there, 1 to 2 minutes, depending on the size. Transfer the still-firm eggplant to a microwave-safe plate and repeat with the remaining eggplants. Cover the eggplants with a vented microwave splatter guard and microwave on high power until slightly softened, 2 to 3 minutes. (Alternatively, prepare a charcoal or gas grill for direct-heat cooking over a medium-hot fire. Place the eggplants on the grill rack and grill, turning as needed, until charred evenly on the outside and the flesh is soft and unctuous all the way through, 6 to 10 minutes.) Let the eggplants sit, covered, to loosen the skin and further soften, about 5 minutes. Remove and discard the skin, leaving the stems intact.

Fry the shrimp: Soak the dried shrimp in warm water for 2 minutes, drain, and pat dry with a paper towel. In a small saucepan, heat the oil (it should generously cover the bottom) and dried shrimp over medium-low heat. Gently fry the shrimp until they are dark orange, 1 to 2 minutes.

Marinate, assemble, and serve: In a small bowl, stir together the fish sauce, lime juice, and palm sugar. Cut each eggplant lengthwise into slices about ½ inch (1.25cm) thick, stopping just short of the stem so the slices remain attached at the stem. Place the eggplants on a serving plate, fanning out the cut slices to expose the inner flesh. Spoon about 3 Tbsp of the dressing onto the eggplants. Let marinate for a few minutes, then pour on the remaining dressing. Top with the herbs, fried garlic, dried shrimp, fried shallots, and chilies. Enjoy immediately.

NOTES

Here's a swap tip: Use two small Graffiti (striped), Italian, or globe eggplants, char each for about 4 minutes, and then microwave for 3 to 4 minutes.

For a more substantial salad, add a hard-boiled egg, cut into wedges, to the plate.

ยำปลาดุกฟู | Yum Pla Duk Foo

Fish Cereal with Green Mango Salad

SERVES 4

Excitingly crunchy and refreshing, this combo of crispy fried fish and spicy tart salad is nonpareil Thai food. Once you have the fish cereal around, you can whip up this impressive snack in no time.

---

1 batch Pla Duk Foo (Fish Cereal, page 75)

60ml | ¼ cup lime juice, plus more to taste

2 Tbsp fish sauce, plus more to taste

¼ tsp firmly packed Thai palm sugar, plus more to taste

1 or 2 fresh Thai chilies, thinly sliced

30g | 1 medium shallot, thinly sliced

120g | 4 oz peeled green mango, unpeeled tart apple, or a combo, cut into matchsticks or thinly sliced (about 1½ cups | 360ml)

2 to 3 Tbsp whole roasted cashews

3 fresh red Thai chilies, lightly smashed, for garnish (optional)

Cilantro sprigs, for garnish (optional)

Ready the fish cereal: Make the fish cereal, or if already on hand, re-crisp as directed in the recipe, then let cool.

Make the salad: In a medium bowl, combine the lime juice, fish sauce, sugar, and sliced Thai chilies and stir to dissolve the sugar. Taste and verify a tart, salty, hot flavor. Add a squeeze of lime, a touch of fish sauce, or a pinch of sugar if needed. Add the shallot, stirring to separate the slices into rings. Add the mango and cashews and toss to mix evenly.

Assemble and serve: Arrange the fish cereal on a serving plate and top with the salad. Or offer the salad in a separate bowl for diners to serve themselves. You can also make a bed of the salad on a serving plate and arrange the fish cereal on top. For extra drama and flavor, finish with the smashed chilies and cilantro sprigs, if using. To eat, mix together the salad and fish, breaking the cereal into small bits like croutons from the sea, then dive in!

ยำกุ้งใส่ลิ้นจี่ | Yum Goong Sai Linchee

Grilled Shrimp and Lychee Salad

SERVES 4

Central Thai in flavor, this uncommonly delicious and supremely easy salad combines gently cooked shrimp, floral lychee, zippy herbs, and rich cashews—all harmoniously united by a mildly spicy, tangy, salty dressing. Feature fresh lychees when they are in season but canned lychees, drained of their syrup, work very well for this salad. Use fresh longans, when available, for a different rendition. Very large shrimp, sometimes labeled as "colossal," are great for this salad.

---

2 fresh Thai chilies, plus more to taste

10g | 3 garlic cloves

½ tsp firmly packed Thai palm sugar, plus more to taste

3 Tbsp lime juice, divided, plus more to taste

1½ Tbsp fish sauce, plus more to taste

500g | 8 very large head-on shrimp, or 360g | 12 very large head-off shrimp

15g | 3 Tbsp thinly sliced shallots

150g | 5 oz pitted, peeled lychees (12 to 16)

Mounded 1 Tbsp super-thinly sliced lemongrass (see page 30)

2 Tbsp lightly packed fresh cilantro leaves, plus more for garnish

2 Tbsp lightly packed fresh mint leaves, hand torn if big, plus more for garnish

30g | 3 Tbsp roasted cashews, divided

1 Japanese or ½ English cucumber, sliced, for serving

Little Gem or radicchio leaves, for serving

Make the dressing: Use a mortar and pestle to pound and flatten the chilies. Add the garlic and pound to small pieces, incorporating the chilies into the mixture. Push the mixture to the side, add the sugar, then gently pound to smoosh. Use a spoon to scrape into a small bowl, then stir in 2 Tbsp of the lime juice and the fish sauce. Briefly rest, then taste to verify a tangy, salty, moderately spicy, and slightly pungent dressing. Sweetness should be barely detectable (the lychees have sweetness, so don't go crazy now). If needed, add extra pounded chili, sugar by the pinch, or lime juice or fish sauce by the 1 tsp.

Gently grill the shrimp: Preheat an outdoor grill to medium or set a heavy skillet or cast-iron stovetop grill pan over medium heat. When hot, cook the shrimp on the grill (or skillet) to your preferred doneness. The salad is best with barely done, succulent shrimp that are cooked for 3 to 6 minutes (head-on shrimp grilled outdoors take the longest). If you prefer fully cooked seafood, cook the shrimp longer. Let cool for at least 5 minutes, or until manageable. Peel and devein the shrimp, then cut each in half (hold your knife at a steep angle to yield artful pieces).

Prep the shallots and fruit: Separate the shallots into rings, dropping them into a medium bowl. Add the remaining 1 Tbsp lime juice and toss. Let sit for 1 to 2 minutes to mellow, then pour off the lime juice. Tear the lychees in half, dropping them into the bowl with the shallots. Add the lemongrass, separating it into individual rings.

Assemble and serve: Add the shrimp to the bowl with the shallots and lychees. Pour over the dressing and toss to combine.

Put 2 Tbsp of the cashews in the mortar and very gently pound to slightly crush. Scrape into the salad. Add the cilantro and mint leaves. Toss the salad well.

Mound the salad on a plate, including all the dressing. Garnish with the remaining 1 Tbsp cashews and extra cilantro and mint leaves. Serve with the cucumber and lettuce. Invite diners to enjoy the salad with the vegetables as refreshing chasers, or to encase the salad and cucumber in the leaves to eat as wraps.

HOW TO LAAB

Classically, laab (ลาบ) refers to robustly seasoned raw or cooked meat "salads" from the Lao-influenced northeast (Isaan) and north of Thailand. Typically hand-chopped or ground, the meat-heavy dish was once reserved for special occasions, but nowadays laab can be enjoyed any time. You can laab practically anything so long as you know the basics.

Flavor profile: The main laab "salad" should be stunningly bold, with plenty of fire, aromatics, and herbs, particularly sawtooth herb. The main feature is gently cooked to retain its succulence. Alliums, both fresh and fried, play a major role in balancing flavors, and spices sometimes go beyond chilies.

Accompaniments: What you serve laab with depends on what's handy and what you like. As you compose those add-ons, think of flavor and visual appeal. Along with vegetables, the sticky rice mellows laab's signature chili heat. The vegetables refresh the palate while adding zippy, bitter, or vegetal notes. Prepare the accompaniments before tackling the laab so it's all ready to serve when the laab is done.

If you opt to serve all the vegetables suggested in the laab family of recipes on pages 106 to 112, consider these amounts:

1 small head lettuce (any kind), leaves separated

1 or 2 handfuls herb sprigs (use what you put into the laab)

8 to 12 mild radicchio leaves or similarly bitter leafy green

240ml | 1 cup thickly sliced cucumber

120ml | ½ cup thinly sliced radish

12 green beans or 4 long beans, cut into finger lengths (blanch in boiling salted water for 30 to 45 seconds if they taste too "beany" or are mature)

Eating tips: Thai people typically pinch up some of the rice, press it onto the laab salad to retrieve tasty bits, and then eat the morsel with vegetables and herbs. That approach takes practice and can get messy. I prefer to load up my spoon with laab, chase it with a little rice, then use my fingers to pick up some vegetables and/or herbs to nibble on as a cooling refresher. You can fashion laab lettuce wraps (use supple varieties) with the seasoned salad, a bit of rice, and other vegetables, like many diners at my restaurants do.

ลาบอีสาน | Laab Isaan

Any Meat Laab Isaan

SERVES 4

Salty, spicy, tangy, and herbaceous Isaan laab salads vary widely. Some are complex and require uncommon ingredients, but for a splendid quotidian experience, use this simple plug-and-play recipe that works with any kind of ground meat. The seasonings and vegetables are the most important components, particularly two Thai larder ingredients: Khao Kua (Isaan Fragrant Rice Powder, page 47) and Prik Pon (Toasted Chili Flakes, page 46). My Isaan rice powder adds nuttiness while thickening the mixture, and the chili flakes lend aromatic heat and a vibrant reddish-orange hue. A generous measure of shallots flavors the meat with sweet pungency. Alter the accompaniments as you wish. Photographed on page 105, this blueprint recipe is my go-to laab formula, so if you are making it for the first time, follow the recipe to achieve my intended flavors. But after that, feel free to have fun with the recipe.

For this and other laab and laab-ish salads in this chapter, ready the accompaniments before prepping the main feature so you'll be ready to eat after you finish seasoning things.

450g | 1 lb ground pork, chicken, or beef (see Note)

2½ Tbsp fish sauce, plus more to taste

120g | 1¼ cups thinly sliced shallots

30g | 3 Tbsp Khao Kua (Isaan Fragrant Rice Powder, page 47), plus more for garnish

10g | 2 Tbsp Prik Pon (Toasted Chili Flakes, page 46), plus more to taste

1 tsp firmly packed Thai palm sugar

60ml | ¼ cup lime juice, plus more to taste

25g | ¼ cup chopped green onions, plus more to taste

20g | ½ cup coarsely chopped fresh mint and cilantro, plus more to taste

1 to 2 Tbsp coarsely chopped fresh sawtooth herb, Vietnamese coriander, or a combo (optional)

Cook and season the meat: In a cold medium saucepan, combine the meat and fish sauce. Set the pan over medium heat and cook, stirring, until the meat is just cooked, 4 to 6 minutes. Add half of the shallots and all of the khao kua, prik pon, and sugar and stir until the sugar dissolves, about 45 seconds. Add the remaining shallots and cook briefly, stirring, just until the shallot wilts, about 30 seconds longer, then slide the pan to a cool burner. The mixture will have thickened from the rice powder and turned orange-red from the chili flakes.

While the meat is still warm, stir in the lime juice, green onions, cilantro and mint, and 1 Tbsp of the sawtooth herb (if using). Taste and boost the seasonings if needed to craft a hot (prik pon), savory (fish sauce), tart (lime juice), and herby (green onions and herbs) finish.

ACCOMPANIMENTS

1 batch Khao Niew Neung (Microwave Sticky Rice, page 257; optional)

Vegetables, such as lettuce leaves, radicchio leaves, fresh herbs (cilantro, mint, sawtooth herb), thickly sliced cucumber, thinly sliced radishes, and green or long beans (see page 104 for tips)

Ready the accompaniments and serve: Prep the accompaniments of your choosing, then place them at the table. Pile your gorgeous laab onto a plate or into a shallow bowl. For extra drama and flavor, garnish with khao kua, prik pon, and herbs. Enjoy with the accompaniments.

NOTE

For a laab with varied textures, cut boneless chicken, pork, or beef into 1-inch (2.5cm) cubes. Arrange in a single layer on a parchment paper–lined sheet pan and freeze until partially frozen, 15 to 20 minutes (to test, press on a few pieces; they should feel firm). Working in batches, pulse in a food processor to a minced, irregular texture. Use right away, or cover and refrigerate overnight.

ลาบมังสวิรัติ | Laab Jae

Tofu Laab Isaan

SERVES 4

Tofu is a great protein option for laab. Use super-firm tofu because it stands up well to the bold seasonings, and the resulting laab looks like its meaty kin on page 106. Sold in vacuum-sealed packages at many markets, super-firm tofu doesn't shrink like meat does, so you need 8 oz (225g) per recipe. Use the leftover tofu for the pad kee mao (drunken noodles) on page 261.

225g | 8 oz super-firm tofu

4 tsp Thai thin soy sauce

Fine sea salt

1 Tbsp neutral oil, such as rice bran

65g | scant ⅔ cup thinly sliced shallots

15g | 1½ Tbsp Khao Kua (Isaan Fragrant Rice Powder, page 47), plus more for garnish

5g | 1 Tbsp Prik Pon (Toasted Chili Flakes, page 46), plus more to taste

½ tsp firmly packed Thai palm sugar

1 Tbsp water

2 Tbsp lime juice, plus more to taste

13g | 2 Tbsp chopped green onions, plus more to taste

10g | ¼ cup coarsely chopped fresh mint, cilantro, or a combo, plus more to taste

1 to 2 Tbsp coarsely chopped fresh sawtooth herb or Vietnamese coriander leaves, or a combo (optional)

Cook and season the tofu: Crumble the tofu into chunks and bits resembling coarsely ground meat, dropping them into a medium bowl. Season with the soy sauce, ¼ tsp salt, and half of the oil. Heat a medium skillet (nonstick or well-seasoned carbon steel or cast iron) over medium heat. When the pan is hot, add the remaining oil and swirl the pan to coat the bottom. Add the tofu and cook, stirring occasionally, until gently sizzling and heated through, 3 to 4 minutes. Add half of the shallots and all of the khao kua, prik pon, palm sugar, and water and stir until the sugar dissolves, about 45 seconds. Add the remaining shallots and cook briefly, stirring, just until the shallots wilt, about 30 seconds longer, then slide the skillet to a cool burner. The mixture will have thickened from the rice powder and darkened a tad from the chili flakes. (If cooking in a cast-iron or carbon-steel pan, transfer the contents to a bowl to finish.)

Turn off the heat, then stir in the lime juice, green onions, and all the herbs. Taste and boost the seasonings if needed to craft a hot (prik pon), savory (salt), tart (lime juice), and herby (green onions and any herbs) finish.

ACCOMPANIMENTS

1 batch Khao Niew Neung (Microwave Sticky Rice, page 257; optional)

Vegetables, such as lettuce leaves, radicchio leaves, fresh herbs (cilantro, mint, sawtooth herb), thickly sliced cucumber, thinly sliced radishes, and green or long beans (see page 104 for tips)

Ready the accompaniments and serve: Prep all the accompaniments of your choosing and place them at the table. Pile the laab onto a plate or into a shallow bowl. For extra drama and flavor, garnish with khao kua, prik pon, and herbs. Enjoy with all the accompaniments.

เห่าดง | Hao Dong

Hissing Cobra

SERVES 4

Hissing cobra salad gets its name from the bracing heat that will make you hiss like a menacing cobra. The ingredients are laab-like, but because the beef is thinly sliced (not ground), the eating experience is distinctly different. Traditionalists swish the meat in boiling water to briefly cook it. But for beefiness that stands up better to the seasonings, I quickly sear presliced well-marbled beef steak sold at Asian markets for shabu shabu, sukiyaki, bulgogi, or hot pots (if possible, buy prime or Wagyu). Hissing cobra celebrates holy basil (bai gaprao), whose intriguing earthy flavors shine in this dish. However, that herb has a fleeting season, so swap in mint, Thai basil, or a combo of both so you can hiss anytime.

300g | 10 oz very thinly sliced beef chuck, rib eye, or New York strip steak (see headnote)

55ml | 3½ Tbsp lime juice, plus more to taste

2 Tbsp plus 2 tsp fish sauce, plus more to taste

Rounded ¼ tsp firmly packed Thai palm sugar

50g | ½ cup thinly sliced shallots

15g | 2 Tbsp roughly chopped green onion

7g | 1½ Tbsp Prik Pon (Toasted Chili Flakes, page 46), plus more to taste

20g | 2 Tbsp Khao Kua (Isaan Fragrant Rice Powder, page 47), plus more for garnish

30g | 1½ cups fresh holy basil leaves, plus small handful for garnish

Form beef mountains: Peel apart the beef slices. Then use a four-finger pinching motion to pick up a slice from its center and place it on a plate as a mini mountain (see photo). That shape enables you to sear the beef quickly without overcooking.

Sear and mix: In a large bowl, combine the lime juice, fish sauce, sugar, and shallots and stir to dissolve the sugar. Set the bowl near the stove along with the green onions, prik pon, khao kua, and basil.

Set a large, well-seasoned cast-iron or carbon-steel skillet over high heat. When the skillet is ripping hot, working in batches and using tongs, sear the beef, turning each slice once, until slightly caramelized and browned on both sides, 1 to 2 minutes total. As each batch is ready, transfer it to the bowl with the seasoning mixture.

Gently mix the warm beef with the seasoning mixture, then add the green onions, prik pon, khao kua, and basil and mix well. Wait for a minute for the chili heat to bloom, then taste and add prik pon by the ½ tsp as needed. You want spiciness but also a balance of salty and tart flavors with plenty of herbal punch from the holy basil. Adjust with fish sauce or lime juice by the ½ tsp, or holy basil by the small handful.

ACCOMPANIMENTS

1 batch Khao Niew Neung (Microwave Sticky Rice, page 257; optional)

Vegetables, such as lettuce leaves, radicchio leaves, fresh herbs (cilantro, mint, sawtooth herb), thickly sliced cucumber, thinly sliced radishes, and green or long beans (see page 104 for tips)

Ready the accompaniments and serve: Prep the accompaniments of your choosing, then place them at the table. Pile the hissing cobra onto a plate or into a shallow bowl. Garnish with extra khao kua and basil. Serve with the accompaniments of your choosing.

ตำบ่าหนุนปลอม | Laab Meung Jae

Not-Quite-Jackfruit Laab

SERVES 4

Many people in Northern Thailand adore the spicy salad called tum baanoon that features young, green jackfruit. It's very good when made with fresh jackfruit (rather than using the canned or frozen variety). Looking for a substitute in the United States that could take the heat, spices, aromatics, and herbs, I landed on an excellent option: artichoke hearts! They mimic the texture of fresh immature jackfruit and quickly absorb seasonings to create a sensational laab that's just as good—if not better—than the original. This Chiang Mai-inspired laab (see top of opposite page) doesn't want lime juice. It's lively and bright from the prik laab spice blend, which helps amplify artichoke's natural umami. If you want a Northern Thai touch, include pork cracklings as an accompaniment.

One 360g | 12-oz package frozen artichoke hearts, thawed

2 Tbsp neutral oil, such as rice bran

60g | good ½ cup thinly sliced shallots

15g | 2 Tbsp super-thinly sliced lemongrass

2 Tbsp Prik Laab (Northern Thai Chili-Spice Blend, page 49), plus more to taste

2 Tbsp fish sauce or Thai thin soy sauce, plus more to taste

Fine sea salt

35g | ⅓ cup chopped green onions

80ml | ⅓ cup coarsely chopped cilantro sprigs

80ml | ⅓ cup hand-torn fresh mint leaves

2 or 3 makrut lime leaves, finely slivered (see page 31)

60ml | ¼ cup fried shallots

2 Tbsp fried garlic chips, homemade (page 56) or purchased

2 dried puya chilies, fried (optional; see Note)

Prep the artichoke hearts: Halve each artichoke heart lengthwise. Each piece will be about ½ inch (1.25cm) thick.

Cook and season the laab: In a medium skillet over medium-low heat, combine the oil, half of the sliced shallots, and all of the lemongrass and prik laab. When gently sizzling and perfumy, turn down the heat to low, add the artichoke hearts and the remaining sliced shallots, and mix well. Season with the fish sauce and a big pinch of salt, then remove from the heat. Let rest for a few minutes, then taste to verify a slightly edgy, hot, savory flavor. If needed, add prik laab and salt by the pinch and fish sauce by the ½ tsp.

Mix in the green onions, cilantro, mint, and lime leaves. Work in most of the fried shallots and garlic chips (lightly crumble big chips), reserving some of each type of allium for garnish.

ACCOMPANIMENTS

1 batch Khao Niew Neung (Microwave Sticky Rice, page 257; optional)

Pork cracklings (chicharrones) or vegan pork rinds

Vegetables, such as lettuce leaves, radicchio leaves, fresh herbs (cilantro, mint, sawtooth herb), thickly sliced cucumber, thinly sliced radishes, and green or long beans (see page 104 for tips)

Ready the accompaniments and serve: Prep the accompaniments of your choosing and place them at the table. Pile the laab onto a plate or into a shallow bowl. Garnish with the remaining fried shallots and garlic chips. For dramatic effect, dust with prik laab and crown with the fried chilies, if using. (Or for extra-toasty, rich heat, crumble the fried chilies over the top.) Enjoy with the accompaniments.

NOTE

If making the fried garlic chips from scratch for this recipe, use the same oil to fry the whole puya chilies.

น้ำตกมังสวิรัติ | Nam Tok Jae

Nam Tok Beans

SERVES 4

Thai dishes can have quirky names, and sometimes cooks (like me!) deliciously add to the confusion. For instance, the food term *nam tok* (waterfall) refers to an Isaan meat salad that involves searing the meat just until its juices start dripping off, signaling that it's ready to be pulled off the heat. The barely cooked meat is sliced and tossed with the same seasonings as the main laab recipe on page 106.

When I opened Kin Khao, I wanted an interesting non-tofu vegetarian salad and developed this one (photographed on the bottom of page 111) using excellent beans from my friend Steve Sando of Rancho Gordo in Napa Valley. Nam tok beans was a hit and remains on the menu. At the restaurant, we flash-fry the beans so they blister and soak up the seasonings. Here's a small-batch home version for you. You can use any firm, largish cooked beans, such as cannellini or butter beans.

1 Tbsp neutral oil, such as rice bran

240ml | 1 cup well-drained cooked large beans, spread on a plate to air-dry

70ml | 4½ Tbsp lime juice, plus more to taste

2 Tbsp Thai thin soy sauce

⅛ tsp fine sea salt, plus more to taste

30g | 1 medium shallot, sliced paper-thin

10g | 1 Tbsp Khao Kua (Isaan Fragrant Rice Powder, page 47)

5g | 1 Tbsp Prik Pon (Toasted Chili Flakes, page 46), plus more to taste

18g | 3 Tbsp chopped green onions, plus more to taste

15g | 6 Tbsp coarsely chopped fresh mint or cilantro, or a combo, plus more to taste

1½ Tbsp coarsely chopped fresh sawtooth herb or Vietnamese coriander leaves, or a combo (optional)

Blister the beans: Set a medium skillet (stainless steel, carbon steel, or cast iron) over high heat. When the pan is hot, add the oil and swirl the pan to coat the bottom, then dump in the beans, spreading them out in an even layer. Let them sear, undisturbed, until toasted and slightly crunchy and blistery, about 1½ minutes. Shake the pan to flip the beans and then sear the beans, undisturbed, until blistered on the second side, about 30 seconds. Remove from the heat.

Season the beans: While the beans are still warm, in a large bowl, stir together the lime juice, soy sauce, and salt. Add the beans and shallot and toss to mix well. Add the khao kua, prik pon, green onions, and all the chopped herbs and mix well. Taste and boost the seasonings if needed to craft a hot (prik pon), savory (salt), tart (lime juice), and herby (green onions and herbs) finish.

ACCOMPANIMENTS

1 batch Khao Niew Neung (Microwave Sticky Rice, page 257; optional)

Vegetables, such as lettuce leaves, radicchio leaves, fresh herbs (cilantro, mint, sawtooth herb), thickly sliced cucumber, thinly sliced radishes, and green or long beans (see page 104 for tips)

Ready the accompaniments and serve: Prep the accompaniments of your choosing and place them at the table. Pile the nam tok beans onto a plate or into a shallow bowl. For extra drama and flavor, garnish with extra prik pon and herbs and enjoy with the accompaniments.

NOTE

To air-dry the beans, pat excess moisture off with paper towel, then spread them out on a plate or small sheet pan. Leave to dry, uncovered, for about 30 minutes.

อาจาด | Ajaad

Cucumber, Pepper, and Shallot Pickle

MAKES ABOUT 3 CUPS (750ML)

My version of Thai ajaad is a tangy, bright pickle that uplifts other foods. The shallots mellow in the vinegar and turn magenta. The peppers add color and fruity chili sweetness.

To craft extra beautiful ajaad, create artful pieces of cucumber. For instance, I use a Thai fruit carving knife to cut exaggerated triangular pieces. This handsome, easy flash pickle requires steeping the vegetables for about an hour, though you can let them sit up to overnight. Serve it with the curry puffs on page 81 and other rich foods. As photographed on page 216, ajaad pairs especially well with the Muslim-influenced golae grilled lamb, chicken, and tofu. It can be a salad-like side dish to enjoy with curries and rice dishes too. Choose mini sweet peppers of different colors for extra cheer.

480ml | 2 cups unseasoned rice vinegar

3 Tbsp granulated sugar, plus more to taste

1 Tbsp fish sauce

300 to 400g | 1 English or 4 Persian cucumbers

120g | 4 sweet mini peppers

50g | 2 medium-small shallots

Make the brine: In a small saucepan, combine the vinegar, sugar, and fish sauce and warm over medium heat, stirring, until the sugar dissolves, 1 to 2 minutes. Remove from the heat and let cool to room temperature. Taste and add sugar if needed to yield a pleasant tart-sweet edge.

Prep the vegetables: Meanwhile, halve the cucumber lengthwise and scoop (or cut) out the seeds. Cut each half on the diagonal into slices about 3 inches (7.5cm) long and a good ¼ inch (6mm) thick. Put the cucumber slices into a medium bowl.

Trim off the stem end of each pepper, then halve lengthwise and scoop out the seeds and membranes. Cut into long spears to match the cucumber pieces. Add to the bowl holding the cucumber.

Halve the shallots lengthwise, then cut the halves lengthwise into wedges each about ½ inch (1.25cm) wide. Separate the wedges into layers as you drop them into the bowl with the cucumber and peppers.

Pickle and serve: Pour the cooled brine over the vegetables. They should be just covered. Let sit for 1 hour, or cover and refrigerate overnight. Transfer to a serving bowl and enjoy.

WHY SEED "SEEDLESS" CUCUMBERS?

We like to seed cucumbers to rid them of their watery core, which can dilute flavors. English and Persian cucumbers are technically described as "nearly seedless" because of their relatively small seeds. However, their "seedy" centers are always moisture laden. Scoop or cut out the centers to make food with bigger flavor.

แกงโฮ๊ะ
ตำขนุนอ่อน
ถุงละ 50-100 บาท
น้ำพริกมะขามสด
(ไม่ใส่หมู)
ขีดละ 40 บาท
แกงฮังเลหมู
70-100-140 บาท
น้ำพริกอ่อง
ขีดละ 50 บาท

4 น้ำพริกและเครื่องจิ้ม

Relishes

The Beauty of Funk

"กินข้าวกับน้ำพริกสิจ๊ะ ถึงได้สะได้สวย" claimed a Thai country song from the 1950s. The phrase roughly translates to "I eat namprik; therefore, I am beautiful!"

While I can't verify the causality between namprik and beauty, there is no denying the prominence of namprik relishes in Thai cuisine. If you look in the pantry or fridge of any Thai home, in Thailand or abroad, I'll bet money that you'll find all kinds of intensely flavored jarred namprik at the ready for mixing into rice for a quick meal, smearing on a piece of protein like the simple steak on page 128, or eating between bites of crisp vegetables or even tart fruits. If you are lucky enough to be invited to a home-cooked dinner in Thailand, anywhere up and down the country, you'll find *at least* one bowl of namprik on the table too.

Namprik is a diverse, deeply rooted Thai traditional food that's enjoyed by people at all levels of society. The first published Thai cookbook, *Mae Krua Hua Pa* (แม่ครัวหัวป่าก์), written in the late nineteenth century by the aristocrat Plian Phasakorawong, included over sixty namprik recipes. Even an ex-prime minister of Thailand has penned a namprik cookbook.

But as important as namprik is in Thai culinary culture, it has yet to be well known outside of Thailand. You are unlikely to find it at most neighborhood Thai restaurants in the West.

Why is namprik obscure? The problem might just be in the name itself. The generally accepted translation of *namprik* is "relish," and that's the term I use on my restaurant menus and in this book. While the word *relish* is too simplistic to fully capture the importance of namprik, for lack of a better term, we will make do with it. Like relishes, nampriks are often served as a condiment, sauce, or dip.

The characteristically strong flavors and pungency of nampriks are probably another reason why most Thai restaurants in the West avoid putting them on menus. The first time I put one on the menu at Kin Khao, I felt compelled to put a "Not Thai Food for Beginners" warning under it. Curious diners tried it and embraced it, so I now always have a namprik at all my restaurants.

The basic components of a namprik are sharp alliums (garlic and shallots), a funky umami base (most often fermented shrimp paste, but it can also be dried or smoked fish or shrimp, all of which provide much-needed salinity to the dish), heat from fresh or dried chilies and sometimes other spices, and differing levels of acidity from citrus, tamarind, or other tart fruits or leaves. The cook needs to work strategically to coax out and layer the flavors of this wonderful amalgam of ingredients. (But don't worry, that's why I'm here!)

There are two main types of namprik: namprik tum and namprik pad. Namprik tum (น้ำพริกตำ, literally "pounded namprik") is a fresh namprik that involves pounding ingredients together. Gapi (fermented shrimp paste) may be cooked or heated ahead of pounding, but there's usually no further cooking once all the ingredients are mixed. A pounded namprik, like the stalwart namprik gapi on page 119, is meant to be eaten the day it's made.

Namprik pad (น้ำพริกผัด, which means "fried" or "cooked namprik"), in contrast, is meant for long keeping. It usually features dried or preserved ingredients plus fresh alliums that are cooked into a tight paste that can be stored for months. I've soothed many midnight hankerings while studying for grad-school exams with little more than hard-boiled eggs mixed with rice and salted-egg namprik kai kem (page 130).

But of course, us Thais are not always strict rule followers. There are also some in between nampriks, such as namprik ong, the mildly spicy, umami-intense tomato relish on page 123, and namprik noom, the smoky charred chili relish from Northern Thailand on page 124. They're crafted to last a week or so (if you can control yourself).

Remember that nampriks are strongly flavored because they are not something you eat alone by the spoonful. Just a bit will do to enhance other foods. So don't be shy when you season your namprik. You can always cool your palate down with side accompaniments at the table. Maybe try a Thai diet of namprik with dinner for a spell because, who knows, that country song could be true!

กะปิดี | Gapi Dee

Good Gapi

MAKES AT LEAST ½ CUP (120ML)

Before making namprik relishes, know that they are only as good as the gapi (fermented shrimp paste) that's in them. It's important to get stellar stuff, which is mauvy red and creamy, tastes bright, and has a briny, salty punch. Essentially, it's concentrated umami. Artisanal, luxe-tasting gapi dee (literally, "good shrimp paste") is hard to source outside of Thailand, so here's my work-around: Combine store-bought shrimp paste with koey (เคย), tiny shrimp in salt brine.

Because koey isn't widely sold outside of Thailand, I use a similar product called saeujeot, which is easily sourced at Korean markets because it's a key ingredient for making kimchi (see Note). The shrimp softens the rough edges of commercial gapi while amplifying its natural umami goodness. I use this good gapi for the namprik at my restaurants, at home, and in this book. It's suggested for some non-namprik recipes too. One batch keeps well for many memorable foods and meals.

One 500g | 1.1-lb jar Korean salted shrimp (see Note)

50 to 75g | 1.7 to 2.5 oz gapi (Thai shrimp paste; see buying tips on page 22)

Prep the salted shrimp: To mellow the salted shrimp's intense flavor, dump them into a fine-mesh strainer and rinse under cool running water, stirring and folding the shrimp with a silicone spatula, for about 20 seconds.

To remove as much liquid from the shrimp as possible, put on a nitrile glove, grab a small handful of the shrimp, and *very firmly* squeeze out the liquid. Aim for a very compact, dryish mass. You'll know you have squeezed enough when no more liquid releases. Repeat, always working with a small handful, until all the shrimp are free of liquid. Alternatively, wring out the shrimp in a piece of muslin or a triple layer of cheesecloth. As a last resort, use the spatula to very firmly press against the shrimp in the strainer, repeatedly folding the shrimp over, until no more liquid releases.

Weigh the shrimp. They should weigh 50 to 75g (1.7 to 2.5 oz). What you net depends on the brand of the shrimp and how firm and fresh they were before you began working with them. The ratio of liquid to solids also impacts the net quantity (you may have more than what we get), so jot down the net weight of the shrimp now! Transfer the shrimp to a mortar, then use the pestle to pound the shrimp a bit to mush them up a little more.

Mix in the gapi: Weigh out the same amount of gapi as you have of the squeezed salted shrimp, and then add it to the mortar. Resume pounding until a soft paste forms, about 1 minute. The finished gapi dee will be slightly coarsely textured because of the shrimp. Use immediately or scrape into a jar, cap, and refrigerate indefinitely.

NOTE

At Korean markets, look for jars of saeujeot labeled "salted shrimp" in the cold cases near pickled ginger or kimchi. Quite often, the saeujeot came from Thailand so inspect the label to see. The shrimp can leave a strong flavor, so soak and wash equipment soon after using it.

น้ำพริกกะปิ | Namprik Gapi

Standard-but-Not-Ordinary Shrimp Paste Relish

MAKES ⅔ TO 1 CUP (160 TO 240ML), TO SERVE 4 TO 6

In Thailand, namprik gapi is often described as the standard shrimp paste relish. But that moniker and the simplicity of the relish belie its true complexity. Making namprik gapi involves using a Thai granite mortar and pestle to carefully layer the texture, color, and flavor of all the components. My recipe will enable you to prepare this iconic relish like a true Thai cook.

Namprik gapi (photographed on page 121) is often eaten with lots of plain rice plus raw vegetables and tart fruits and sometimes fried fish. Make the relish spicier and stronger tasting than what you think is in your comfort zone. That's the standard of namprik gapi; go big or go home! However you enjoy namprik gapi, note that it's garlicky, so enjoy it with your partner for domestic harmony. If you have leftovers or want a tamer namprik gapi experience, make the fried rice or soup on pages 259 and 198.

50g | 2½ Tbsp packed Gapi Dee (Good Gapi, page 118)

12g | 2 Tbsp small dried shrimp

Coarse sea salt

40g | ¼ cup garlic cloves

5 to 10g | 5 to 10 fresh Thai chilies, to taste

10g | 1½ tsp firmly packed Thai palm sugar, plus more to taste

10 pea eggplants, or 3 golf-ball-size Thai eggplants (omit if using relish for fried rice and soup recipes)

60ml | ¼ cup lime juice, plus more to taste

Fish sauce, for finishing (optional)

Toast the gapi: Put the gapi dee in the center of a 5-inch (12.5cm) square of aluminum foil (if handy, line the foil first with a piece of banana leaf), then use the back of a spoon to press the paste into a disk 3 inches (7.5cm) wide. Fold the foil inward to completely encase the disk. Place the foil packet in a toaster oven and broil until you can smell the aroma of toasted shrimp shells through the foil, 6 to 8 minutes. (Alternatively, set the foil packet over a high flame on a gas stovetop or over a hot fire on a charcoal or gas grill, flipping the packet once or twice, until you can smell the aroma of toasted shrimp shells, 3 to 5 minutes.) Let cool briefly, unwrap, and set aside.

Make shrimp floss: In a small bowl, soak the dried shrimp in hot water to cover to soften, 3 to 5 minutes. Drain and pat dry with a paper towel, then transfer the shrimp to a mortar. Start pounding the shrimp with a pestle, aiming it slightly off-center up the side of the mortar. After the shrimp start breaking up, add a pinch of salt to create friction and keep efficiently pounding (see page 37 for tips) until the shrimp are transformed into tiny, flossy shreds. (To save time and effort—and if you don't mind extra dishwashing—use an electric grinder or small chopper.)

Add the aromatics: Add the toasted gapi and pound to incorporate. Use a spoon to scrape, gather, and bank the mixture to the side of the mortar.

Drop in half of the garlic and continue pounding (still aiming slightly off-center) to crush, yielding a coarse mixture. Add the chilies to the center of the mortar and pound briefly to crush into biggish pieces, about 10 seconds. Push the mixture back to the center, then gently pound to mix.

Season the relish: Add the sugar to the side of the mortar, mash with the pestle, and then work into the mixture. Use the spoon to scrape, gather, and identify large chili pieces. Pound them into smaller pieces, then stir back into the mixture.

Add the remaining garlic and pound to crush, aiming for larger pieces than earlier. (Resist pounding too small, or the garlic will become acrid and lose its chunky texture!) Scrape and bank the mixture to the side of the mortar. If using the pea eggplants, drop them into the mortar and pound gently to smash open, then stir into the relish to combine. If using Thai eggplants, quarter then cut out and discard most of the bitter, seedy center. Cut the eggplant into irregular pieces and then just stir into the relish.

CONTINUED

Add the lime juice and use the pestle to mix in well. Taste for a good salty-tangy balance with a good kick of spicy heat and a touch of sweetness at the end. If needed, curb the heat by stirring in lime juice by the 1½ tsp. To mellow sharp fermented brininess, stir in sugar by the ½ tsp. Keep tasting by the pinch and adjusting with lime juice (acidity) and sugar (sweetness). If you want to round out the umami flavor, add fish sauce by the ½ tsp, then retaste and add a smidgen of lime juice if needed.

ACCOMPANIMENTS

1 batch Khao Suay (Basic Jasmine Rice, page 256; optional)

Assorted raw vegetables and tart fruits, edible blooms, slightly bitter leaves suitable for a crudités platter, or a combo (optional)

Prep the accompaniments and serve: Cook the rice, if including. Cut the vegetables and fruits into bite-size pieces, and place at the table. Transfer the namprik gapi to a bowl and enjoy with the accompaniments.

NOTES

To enjoy namprik gapi with blanched vegetables and creamy coconut milk, prepare the relish with less lime juice (use 3 to 4 Tbsp) so it better harmonizes with the richness of the coconut milk. Blanch vegetables such as green beans, Romanesco broccoli, and cabbage to a toothsome tenderness, drain, immerse in an ice bath to arrest the cooking, and then drain well and arrange on a plate. Collect ¼ cup (60ml) thick coconut milk from the top of an unshaken can of coconut milk, season it with a pinch of fine sea salt, warm it gently to loosen and activate the flavors, and then pour evenly over the vegetables. Serve the vegetables with the relish and rice.

If you are worried about the garlic being too pungent, start with a little less than the full amount. Taste and if the finished relish is too mild, separately pound the balance of the garlic and stir it into the relish.

น้ำพริกอ่อง | Namprik Ong

Pork and Tomato Relish

SERVES 4

Mildly spicy, deeply umami, and very easy to eat, namprik ong is a gateway Thai relish. It's at home in Northern Thailand, but I think it should be the new hot Super Bowl dip, served with lots of raw vegetables and chicharrones (fried pork rinds), as photographed here on the top left. Add sticky rice if you want a carb component. Pork is the traditional protein, but ground chicken works, too, as does tofu (see the Variation). If you have Northern curry paste already in your larder, then this namprik comes together easily and quickly.

- 1 Tbsp neutral oil, such as rice bran
- 300g | 10 oz ground pork
- 60g | ¼ cup Prik Gaeng Mueng (Northern Curry Paste, page 184)
- 150g | 1 medium tomato, coarsely chopped
- 80ml | ⅓ cup water
- 3 Tbsp fish sauce
- ½ tsp firmly packed Thai palm sugar
- 120g | ¾ cup cherry tomatoes, halved
- ½ to 1 tsp sherry vinegar or unseasoned rice vinegar (optional)

Cook the meat: Set a medium saucepan over medium-high heat. When the pan is hot, add the oil and swirl the pan to coat the bottom. Add the pork and curry paste and stir and poke to break up the meat and coat the resulting nubs with the paste.

Phase in the tomatoes: Lower the heat to medium, add the chopped tomato, and stir and poke to smoosh the tomato further. When it starts collapsing, 1 to 2 minutes, add the water, let the mixture come to a simmer, and season with the fish sauce and the sugar, stirring to dissolve the sugar.

Now add the cherry tomato halves and simmer until they soften slightly, 2 to 3 minutes. Turn off the heat and let rest for 5 minutes to settle the flavors. Taste the relish. If a little acidity is needed, stir in the vinegar to taste. Cover the relish to keep warm.

ACCOMPANIMENTS

- 1 batch Khao Niew Neung (Microwave Sticky Rice, page 257; optional)
- Chicharrones (optional)
- Vegetables, such as cucumber, radicchio, radishes, endive, and fresh herbs (mint, cilantro, dill, sawtooth herb, Vietnamese coriander, and green onions) (optional)

Ready accompaniments and serve: Prepare the accompaniments of your choice, cutting the vegetables into bite-size pieces, as needed. Place everything at the table. Transfer the warm namprik ong to a bowl and enjoy with the accompaniments.

VARIATION

น้ำพริกอ่องเต้าหู้ | Namprik Ong Jae

Vegan Namprik Ong

Instead of the pork, use 8 oz (225g) super-firm tofu, crumbled into pieces no bigger than ½ inch (1.25cm). Heat the pan and oil, add the curry paste and stir to break it up, and then dump in the crumbled tofu, stirring to coat well. Phase in the tomatoes, replacing the fish sauce with Thai thin soy sauce or Fast Fake Fish Sauce (page 23), and finish as directed.

น้ำพริกหนุ่ม | Namprik Noom

Charred Chili Pepper Relish

SERVES 6

Traditionally, namprik noom (literally "young pepper relish") features immature, medium-spicy green chilies. Because they are hard to find, I mimic the flavor by combining hot and sweet chilies of varying colors and flavors; the result is photographed on the lower left of page 122. Serve this relish of smoky chilies, alliums, and toasted tua nao (dried fermented soybeans) with grilled sausages, sticky rice, and raw vegetables to enjoy Northern Thai country funk at its best. Or tuck a bit into a sandwich or quesadilla. Tua nao lends earthy distinction but is difficult to source outside of Thailand. When in the United States, I dehydrate hatcho miso (see page 22) to use in its place.

- 7g | 1 tsp hatcho miso, or 5g | 1 by 2-inch piece tua nao (dried fermented soybeans)
- 2 Tbsp fish sauce, or 4 tsp Thai thin soy sauce plus ⅛ tsp fine sea salt
- 180g | 6 oz spicy green chilies, such as serrano or jalapeño
- 250g | generous 8 oz mild chilies (any color but green), such as Jimmy Nardello or mini sweet
- 100g | 2 medium-large shallots, unpeeled
- 20g | 4 large garlic cloves, unpeeled
- 2 tsp lime juice (optional)

Make quick tua nao: If using premade tua nao, skip to toasting. When starting from miso, shape it into a ball, then flatten into a patty ¼ inch (6mm) thick and place between two small pieces of parchment paper roughly the size of a greeting card. Use a rolling pin to roll the miso into a very thin disk about 2½ inches (6.25cm) wide. Remove the top parchment.

To dehydrate the miso (still on the parchment), microwave it on medium-low power, turning the disk over every 20 to 30 seconds, until barely damp and bubbles have formed here and there, about 1½ minutes. If there are still soft spots, lower the power a notch and microwave in 30-second bursts until dryish. (Without a microwave, see the Northern curry paste recipe Note on page 185 for an oven method.) Let cool completely.

Toast the tua nao and mix the seasoning liquid: Select a vegetable grill pan or perforated skillet (or a cast-iron or carbon-steel skillet) to toast the tua nao. Apply medium heat, turning the tua nao often, until it is fragrant and blisters have formed here and there, 30 to 45 seconds if using a grill pan or perforated skillet (or up to 10 minutes if using a cast-iron or carbon-steel skillet). The toasting time depends on your pan and heat source, so watch the tua nao closely to avoid burning. Remove from the heat, let cool completely, and then transfer to a mortar and pound with a pestle to a powder resembling ground coffee. Scrape into a medium bowl, add the fish sauce, and stir to yield a seasoning liquid.

Char the vegetables: Reheat the pan used to toast the tua nao over medium-high to high heat. In batches, char the serranos, sweet peppers, and shallots, turning often, until mostly blackened but only partially cooked, 4 to 8 minutes if using the grill pan or perforated skillet (6 to 10 minutes if using a cast-iron or carbon-steel skillet). Char the garlic in a coolish area of the pan until softened but not totally blackened, 2 to 3 minutes. Transfer the charred vegetables to a bowl, cover with a dish towel or plate, and let sit for at least 5 minutes to sweat and loosen the skin.

Peel and mix the vegetables: Wearing gloves, peel and scrape the charred skin off the chilies and sweet peppers. Seed the chilies and sweet peppers as you work (some stubborn lingering seeds are fine). Hand tear or use a knife tip to render the chilies and sweet peppers into irregular skinny strips about the length of your index finger. Add to the bowl of seasoning liquid.

Slip off the charred skin from the shallots (lingering blackened bits are OK), chop coarsely, and add to the chili mixture. Peel the garlic, use a knife (or the mortar and pestle) to mash the cloves, and then add to the chili mixture. Mix all the ingredients together well. For tang or to curb the heat slightly, add the lime juice. Transfer to a bowl if serving soon or into a storage container to keep refrigerated for up to 1 week.

ACCOMPANIMENTS

Sai ua or other grilled sausages (optional)

1 batch Khao Niew Neung (Microwave Sticky Rice, page 257; optional)

Crisp vegetables, such as cucumber, radishes, jicama, Little Gem lettuce leaves, and Belgian endive (optional)

Ready the accompaniments and serve: Prepare the accompaniments of your choice. As needed, slice the grilled sausages for easier serving and cut the vegetables into bite-size pieces. Enjoy the relish at room temperature with all the accompaniments.

NOTE

For easier charring, choose relatively straight peppers with few twists and wrinkles. Charring on an outdoor grill works well as long as the garlic doesn't fall through the grate.

น้ำพริกหมากมาด | Namprik Makmaad

Heaven or Hell Prickly Ash Relish

MAKES 1 CUP (240ML)

This piquant, tingly namprik resulted from my researching old recipes for namprik pad (cooked Thai relishes). I found many instances of a special namprik pad featuring a copious amount of Thai prickly ash (*Zanthoxylum limonella*, also called Thai makwaen and Vietnamese mắc khén), an asterisk-shaped relative of Sichuan peppercorns. Reading about this hot, tingly, umami-rich relish led me to create this recipe, which I call namprik makmaad, using the Central Thai name for the spice.

This excellent relish is a particular favorite of mine. I hope its piquancy enchants you without tormenting your taste buds too much. To craft a tamer but equally zingy version, check the Notes. Serve namprik makmaad with grilled steak, as photographed here; the variation on page 128 offers an easy recipe.

---

60 ml | ¼ cup neutral oil, such as rice bran, divided

50g | 1.7 oz dried yellow croaker fish flesh (see Notes)

75g | 2½ oz shallots, halved

50g | ⅓ cup garlic cloves

25g | 0.9 oz seeded dried prik chee fa or puya chilies, roughly chopped or snipped

5g | scant 0.2 oz seeded dried prik jinda or árbol chilies

10g | 3 Tbsp Sichuan peppercorns, or ¼ cup makwaen (see Notes)

30g | 1½ Tbsp firmly packed Thai palm sugar

3 Tbsp Nam Makam (Tamarind Liquid, page 52)

2 to 4 Tbsp fish sauce, to taste

Fry the fish and aromatics: Set a large wok over medium heat and add about half of the oil. When the oil is barely shimmering, add the fish and fry gently until the edges crisp up and the fish turns golden but not quite brown, at least 2 minutes. (The timing depends on the type of fish used and whether it was soaked during prep.) Scoop the fish into a small heatproof bowl, leaving most of the oil in the pan.

With the wok still over medium heat, add the shallots and garlic and cook, stirring often, until slightly softened, richly browned here and there, and almost cooked through, 4 to 5 minutes. Add all of the chilies and peppercorns and stir a few times to mix well. Return the fish to the wok and continue stirring until you can smell the fragrant chilies and peppercorns, 1 to 2 minutes. Turn off the heat. Transfer the mixture to a medium bowl and let cool briefly.

Make a smooth paste: You can either pound the mixture in a mortar or use a food processor or blender. Whichever method you choose, aim for a fine, smoothish paste with some visible bits of peppercorn and chili.

Recook and fine-tune: Scrape the paste into the wok, set over medium-low heat, and stir in the remaining oil. Add the sugar and tamarind and stir to blend. The mixture will look dull but keep stirring, scraping the sides of the wok to avoid burnt spots, until the mixture starts developing a nice sheen, 2 to 3 minutes. Lower the heat if needed to prevent scorching.

Taste a little bit. You'll likely need to add some fish sauce, 1 Tbsp at a time. (I didn't have you add it earlier because how much you need depends on the saltiness of your fish, and it's easier to add salt than to take it away.)

Add more tamarind and sugar by the 1 tsp if you think it needs extra tang and sweetness. After each addition, stir well and keep cooking for a minute or so to return the sheen to the paste, which should eventually become a lava-like mound. When satisfied with the taste, turn off the heat and transfer the finished namprik pad to a heatproof bowl or glass jar. Let cool, uncovered, before serving or capping tightly and storing. It will keep in a cupboard for about 1 week or in the fridge for at least 6 months—if you have that kind of self-control.

CONTINUED

NOTES

Use all red Sichuan peppercorns or a fifty-fifty blend of red and green ones. Burlap & Barrel is a reliable stateside source for makwaen, which is sourced from Vietnam and labeled "mắc khén."

Dried yellow croaker is typically sold in plastic packaging near the dried shrimp at Chinese and Vietnamese markets. Look for clean-looking headless fish or cut sections, and check best-buy dates for freshness. If you can easily remove the skin and pick the flesh off the bones, do so. If the fish proves stubborn, soak it in warm water to cover for 5 to 10 minutes, then drain, pat off excess moisture with a paper towel, and let the softened fish dry for a few minutes before discarding the skin and removing the flesh from the bones. Start with about 2.8oz (80g) of fish to yield the 1.7 oz (50g) of flesh needed for the recipe. Don't obsess about removing all of the little bones. They're just extra calcium.

This namprik can be made with many different types of dried fish, even smoked whitefish (pat away moisture well and use about 2 oz | 60g total). Initial frying time will vary depending on the type of fish, but experiment to make my recipe yours!

For a less spicy namprik, use 1 oz (30g) dried prik chee fa (or puya) chilies and skip the prik jinda (or árbol) chilies. Or employ 1 oz (30g) dried guajillo or New Mexico chilies for an even milder version.

VARIATION

เนื้อย่างกับน้ำพริกหมากมาด | Namprik Makmaad Neua Yang
Namprik Makmaad and Grilled Steak

A dab of the vibrant namprik makmaad elevates a juicy steak any day. Choose a fast-cooking cut, like skirt or bavette. (It's also great with flanken short ribs.) Because the relish is so boldly flavored, season the beef simply. Rub it with fish sauce (2 Tbsp per lb | 450g), then chill in the fridge, uncovered, for 1 to 2 hours before grilling. Serve with namprik makmaad for an easy, knockout Thai main dish.

น้ำพริกไข่เค็ม | Namprik Kai Kem

Spicy Salted Duck Egg Relish

MAKES ABOUT 1½ CUPS (360ML)

Spicy, salty, and slightly sweet, this crimson keeper falls into the namprik pad, or cooked relish, category. It's loaded with umami richness, thanks to unctuous salted duck egg yolks. Pair versatile namprik kai kem with grilled meat or seafood. Serve it with sliced crunchy vegetables (such as cucumbers, radishes, and sweet peppers) or tart fruits (such as unripe plums, tart apples, and green mangoes) for a quick snack. Showcase it in the uncommonly delicious fried rice on page 258. Simply eaten with rice, the relish has saved my life on many a hungry night! Make a double batch like I always do. It's so easy and keeps in the fridge for weeks or possibly months, though I can't really say for sure because I've always devoured mine long before that.

30g | 1 oz seeded dried prik chee fa or puya chilies

60ml | 4 Tbsp neutral oil, such as rice bran, divided

60g | 2 medium shallots, halved

60g | mounded ⅓ cup garlic cloves (from 2 small heads)

120ml | ½ cup water

90ml | brimming ⅓ cup Nam Makam (Tamarind Liquid, page 52), plus more to taste

30g | 1½ Tbsp firmly packed Thai palm sugar, plus more to taste

30g | 1½ Tbsp packed Gapi Dee (Good Gapi, page 118)

75g | 4 cooked salted duck egg yolks, crumbled or mashed (see tips on page 131)

1 Tbsp fish sauce, plus more to taste

Soak and snip the chilies: If you want to lessen the chili heat but retain the fruity nature, soak the chilies in cold water to cover for about 1 minute, then drain and pat lightly with a paper towel to remove most of the moisture. Whether or not you soaked the chilies, snip or chop them into coarse pieces.

Make the spicy base: Heat a large wok over medium heat. When the pan is hot, add 1 Tbsp of the oil (reserve the rest for later) and swirl the pan to coat with the oil. Add the shallots and garlic and cook, stirring frequently, until fragrant and beginning to pick up a bit of color and caramelize, 3 to 4 minutes. Be careful not to burn them. Add the chilies and cook, stirring, until fragrant, about 1 minute. Remove the wok from the heat.

Transfer the toasted chilies and alliums to a mortar or food processor. Pound or process to a nearly fine paste. This is a chunky relish, so there's no need to aim for smithereens.

Scrape the paste into a medium bowl. Pour the water into the mortar or food processor, stir or whirl to dislodge all the lingering good stuff, and then add the water to the chili-allium bowl. Add the tamarind and sugar and stir to mix.

Cook the namprik: Reheat the wok over medium heat. When the pan is hot (to test, flick in a few drops of water; they should sizzle and evaporate within seconds), add the remaining 3 Tbsp oil and gapi, then, using a silicone or wooden spatula, break up the paste and cook until it begins to sizzle. Add the spicy base and cook, stirring, until the sugar dissolves, then stir in the salted egg yolks.

Continue cooking, stirring and scraping the wok bottom constantly to prevent burnt spots. The muddy, dull mixture will eventually turn ruddy and beautiful. As the liquid evaporates, the mixture will thicken and become viscous. Visible speckles of egg yolk are usual. After about 5 minutes, a bit of oil will have separated from the mass, giving the crimson mixture a nice sheen. As you push the spatula along the wok bottom, the namprik should part and then slowly come together (like Charlton Heston parting the Red Sea in *The Ten Commandments*).

Taste and fine-tune: Turn the heat down to low and taste. In order of sensations, you'll want this to be spicy, salty, and a little sweet, with a touch of acidity to cut through the richness. Add the fish sauce a little at a time for salinity. You may not need the whole 1 Tbsp or you may need a bit more. (I didn't have you add it earlier because the saltiness of the shrimp paste and salted eggs can vary, and I don't want to risk oversalting from the get-go.) If a touch of acid or sweetness is needed, add tamarind or sugar by the 1½ tsp. Continue cooking the relish for a couple of minutes after each addition before tasting again.

When the seasoning is right, turn off the heat and transfer the finished namprik kai kem to a heatproof bowl or glass jar. Let cool, uncovered, before serving or capping tightly and storing. It will keep in the refrigerator for up to 6 months.

SALTED DUCK EGG TIPS

Cooked salted duck eggs are sold at Chinese and Southeast Asian markets, typically unrefrigerated; avoid buying salted yolks separately. Check best-by dates before buying. To prep, use the spine of a knife blade to crack the egg, then halve it with the cutting edge and scoop out the yolk from each half with a spoon. Some people enjoy the leftover cooked whites with plain rice and in rice porridge.

70-140 บาท
ปูหลน
มัสมั่นไก่
ถุงละ 100
เต้าเจี้ยว
แกงเขียวหวาน
ไก่ยอดมะพร้าว
ถุงละ 70-140 บาท
แกงเขียวหวานเนื้อมะเขือ
ถุงละ 100-200 บาท
แกงคั่วหน่อไม้ดองไก่
ถุงละ 70-140 บาท
ต้มข่าไก่
แกงเขียวหวานปลากราย
ถุงละ 70-140 บาท
ถุงละ 60-120 บาท

5

ชามแกง

Curries

คั้นกะทิสด

1300
1100

Sassy, Saucy Head Turners

If there is one thing I can teach you, it's how to make your own Thai curry paste. Understandably, many otherwise competent cooks find it daunting—so many ingredients, so much prep work, so much time. But let me tell you, it's so worth it! In fact, you'll lift your Thai food game to an entirely new level with freshly made, well-crafted curry paste.

In the Thai culinary tradition, dishes called gaeng (แกง) always start with a paste. Gaeng can be made with or without coconut milk and can be soupy, saucy, or even dryish, but they all start with pounding ingredients into a bold-flavored, heady paste. So the key to good gaeng (curry) is in the paste itself.

When you make a fresh paste, you gain a better understanding of the flavors and the aromatic profile of what you're cooking, which gives you greater control of the final dish. In contrast, if you use a store-bought paste, your only decision is how much of it you should put into your curry. For example, if you're sensitive to spice, you might use a smaller amount than the recipe calls for. But by doing that, you end up muting not just the chili heat but also many other flavors and aromas, resulting in what could very well turn into a bland, tasteless dish.

When you eat Thai curry prepared from homemade paste, it's like seeing the cuisine through a kaleidoscope. It's brighter, more colorful, more nuanced, and all around more beautiful. It's when you make your own curry pastes that you truly experience the great range of Thai curries.

Despite what most Thai restaurant menus suggest, Thai curry is much more than just red, yellow, and green curries. Naming curries by their color is not totally wrong. (Red and green curry pastes are among the many recipes in this chapter!) But color doesn't tell you enough about the flavor. Calling a dish a red curry, for example, is like using the word *salsa* for all Mexican sauces. It's not informative.

The main components of a curry paste are alliums, dried or fresh chilies, fresh aromatics like lemongrass, dried spices, and a rich source of umami, often gapi (fermented shrimp paste). The composition of ingredients and how they are treated are what make one curry paste different from another.

For instance, Massaman Curry Paste (Prik Gaeng Massaman, page 154) and Red Curry Paste (Prik Gaeng Ped, page 144) employ similar ingredients, but they are put together differently. For smoky, nutty massaman curry, paste ingredients are initially burnt or fried before they're blended with dry spices. On the other hand, for the fresher and spicier prik gaeng ped, all the ingredients except the dry spices are kept raw.

Because curries are elemental in Thai cuisine, this chapter is a mini book within this book. It begins with a primer on Thai curries that covers equipment, ingredients, techniques, and some tips and tricks that I've amassed over the years. The recipes that follow will not only guide you through the ingredients and how to treat each one but will also teach you how to dial up or down the Scoville scale without losing the soul of the curry paste you're making. And rest assured, pounding with a mortar and pestle is not required. You can totally make wonderful pastes with machines.

So sharpen your knife, pull out the good blender or food processor, turn on your favorite podcast or blast your happiest music, and begin gathering and chopping curry paste ingredients. You can make your pastes in large quantities and either save them for future use or share them with your friends and neighbors and become the most popular person in town!

Once you have your homemade curry paste, follow my recipes to make some of my favorite classic curries. (And because curries are endlessly adaptable, feel free to have some fun and create your own.) Additionally, some of the curry pastes in this chapter are used elsewhere in this book for seasoning fried fish cakes (page 72), roast fish (page 223), steamed curry mousse (page 225), and fried rice (page 258).

Thai Curry Primer

BASIC EQUIPMENT

Nothing fancy is required, but choose wisely for a superb Thai curry life.

For making curry pastes, reach for a machine. Undoubtedly, curry paste made entirely with a mortar and pestle is superior to a machine-made paste because pounding releases natural flavor better than chopping (if you want to give pounding a try, see the sidebar for a quick how-to). But machine-assisted, freshly made paste will be infinitely better than anything you get from a can or jar. Machines are what I and many Thai cooks often use!

- **Food processor:** A small to medium (7- to 11-cup | 1.7 to 2.6L capacity) processor works well for single or double batches of curry paste. Larger (over 12-cup | 3L capacity) processors are better for double batches or more.
- **Blender:** Most countertop blenders are best for a double batch or more of curry paste. For single batches, use an Indian mixer blender or a Vitamix 5200 blender with its classic slender jar. Immersion and bullet-style blenders do not grind Thai curry paste well.
- **Food chopper:** A small food chopper with a quad-blade design, such as the Ninja Express Chop, functions like a hybrid processor-blender and can handle single batches of curry paste. A standard food chopper (mini food processor) does not grind paste ingredients fine enough, though it may work for curry pastes made with coarse gochugaru (Korean chili powder).
- **Electric grinder or mortar and pestle:** To grind large amounts of spices, use an electric grinder (a spice grinder or coffee grinder dedicated to spices). Reach for a Thai granite mortar and pestle for grinding small amounts.

To char and toast certain curry paste ingredients, use a large **wok, saucier, braiser,** or a similarly shaped vessel. Such a pan effectively contains bulky ingredients, conducts heat broadly, and allows for easy stirring.

When making and blooming curry pastes, a silicone spatula efficiently stirs and scrapes the paste. Dedicate a special one to the cause if you plan on making curry often. You don't want to use your curry spatula to stir your next batch of ice cream custard!

For cooking curries, choose a roomy, wide vessel. They are traditionally prepared in a thick-walled, wok-like pan with no side corners and a curved bottom to prevent curry paste from sticking as it fries and blooms. Simmer your curries in a **wok, saucier, braiser,** or similar pan. I regularly use a Dutch oven too.

HAND POUNDING CURRY PASTE

To practice old-fashioned, unplugged cooking while toning your arms, make curry paste using a krok (Thai granite mortar and pestle). Hand pounding is easiest for half batches of my paste recipes.

In general, pound each solid ingredient individually (the order doesn't matter). Work on a small amount at a time, scraping the resulting fine mixture into a bowl as you progress down the list of ingredients. After pounding the solid ingredients, return them all to the mortar, add any soft ingredients, and then pound everything into a blended paste. There's no need to add coconut oil or water to help emulsify the mixture. Krok pointers are on page 37, in case you need an extra assist.

CORE INGREDIENTS

What and why are certain ingredients used for Thai curry? (Look for sourcing tips starting on page 17.)

Chilies contribute flavor, color, body, and heat. You'll use a lot of them because that's the Thai way.

- **Dried chilies** add luscious crimson color and fruity heat. You'll mostly use medium-hot prik chee fa or puya chilies and occasionally use hot prik jinda or árbol chilies. Recipes offer specific chili swaps to adjust heat to your liking. General tips for fine-tuning chili heat are on page 138.
- **Fresh chilies** lend verdant, bracing flavor to green curry paste (page 162). Occasionally whole chilies are added to finish a curry—they add bling, yes, but are also for diners who want a little extra fire to eat!
- **All chilies are seeded** for curry pastes. Seed a bunch of dried chilies in advance to speed up making your curry pastes (see page 20 for pointers). To skip seeding chilies, use coarse gochugaru (Korean chili powder). Note that this shortcut only works for red gaeng ped, southern gaeng tai, and sour gaeng som on pages 144, 168, and 179. You may have to add prik pon (page 46) to up the heat, so remember to finesse your flavor toward the end of cooking.

Fresh aromatics add flavor notes to build a curry's character.

- **Garlic** works with chilies to anchor curry paste with its strong aroma and flavor.
- **Shallot** starts out acrid but reveals caramelly sweetness when bloomed in the pastes.
- **Lemongrass** adds important floral, citrusy qualities to curries. (See lemongrass prep tips on page 30.)
- **Galangal** lends pungent warmth. When fresh or frozen is unavailable, use galangal powder, subbing half the amount of fresh by volume.
- **Makrut lime rind** (the peel plus some white pith) peps up pastes with citrusy brightness. Regular lime is an OK substitute in a pinch.
- **Cilantro roots (or stems)** inject a low-key but crucial coriander edge.
- **Turmeric** imparts vibrant color and earthy flavor to certain curries. Use fresh when available.
- **Grachai (fingerroot)** adds unique menthol-like back notes.
- **Ginger** is occasionally used for sweet heat. Resist using it as a galangal or grachai substitute.

Dry spices ranging from star anise, ground turmeric, and mace to cumin, black pepper, and cardamom help define a curry's personality. It's not all chili driven.

Salty seasonings anchor and amplify each curry's savory, umami backbone.

- **Gapi (Thai shrimp paste)** contributes umami gravitas.
- **Fish sauce** may boost and balance flavor in various phases of the cooking process. **Thai thin soy sauce** is a good substitute in vegetarian curries.
- **Dried shrimp, smoked fish,** and miso-like **tua nao** (fermented dried soybeans) may also be used for umami notes.

Fat, sour, and sweet ingredients help to reveal and balance the curry's flavor.

- **Coconut oil and coconut milk** enrich and mellow the paste's rough edges while adding delicate sweetness as the paste blooms and the milk cracks (see page 142). When a curry recipe requires coconut cream or "thick" coconut milk, simply spoon it from the top of an *unshaken* can or box of coconut milk (commercial coconut cream tastes oddly soapy). What remains is the thinner milk, which the curry recipe may incorporate further down the line. If a curry calls for "800ml to 1L | 3½ to 4¼ cups coconut milk," use as much as you like for a rich sauce. I often empty out one big box!
- **Tamarind liquid** balances curry pastes with its fruity, earthy tang. Homemade (page 52) rules.
- **Thai palm sugar** softens with a touch of sweetness. Only a bit is needed when a curry is well crafted. Curry is not candy sweet.

More DIY Curry Paste Tips

When you make Thai curry pastes from scratch, you get to pull the levers to dial in flavors to please your palate. These extra pointers will further guide your journey.

HOMEMADE CURRY PASTE CONSIDERATIONS

From-scratch pastes are more vibrant and soulful than commercially produced ones. Keep a few things in mind so the project is not daunting.

Batch sizes: Making a single batch of paste takes nearly as much time as making a double batch, so why not do a double and freeze the extra? Multiuse curry pastes in this book have scalable recipes to encourage you!

My makeshift tamper: Lemongrass is always around a Thai kitchen, so when the Vitamix tamper isn't handy (or it's not long enough to reach ingredients), I bind together two or three firm stalks and use that to push and move ingredients toward the blade. Extra lemongrass will get blended into the paste to add extra flavor. Partially used stalks devoid of their bulbous bottom make perfect tampers.

Homemade versus commercial curry paste texture: Your homemade curry paste will have greater texture, character, and nuance than the commercial stuff. Grind ingredients finely in a processor or blender but don't aim to mimic ultrasmooth commercial curry paste. Flecks of chili, tiny bits of spices, and strands of lemongrass in curry paste are normal and akin to what you'd find in a hand-pounded paste. You can follow up the machine grinding with a good pounding in a Thai krok (see page 34), though I think that's too fussy.

TURNING THAI CURRY HEAT UP OR DOWN

Chili heat varies by type and harvest weather conditions, so know your ingredients and tolerance. Here are some strategies to consider.

I can't stand much chili heat! Make milder pastes. Some recipes are characteristically mild, while others suggest ways to tweak the chili blend for milder results that still thrill. If there isn't a heat tweak, swap in a milder dried chili, such as guajillo, New Mexico, or California. Use the weight amounts to ensure enough material in the paste.

Yikes! My paste is too hot! Make another batch of paste but omit the chilies. Mix the second batch into the overly hot paste to tone things down. We do this at my restaurants when the chilies are hotter than expected.

Meh! This curry is too polite! If you feel that your curry needs more heat to be more exciting, you can tweak it depending on how it was made. If the curry paste was prepared with dried chilies, add Prik Pon (Toasted Chili Flakes, page 46) by the ½ to 1 tsp, briefly simmering and curing before re-tasting; or add lightly smashed fresh chilies to the pot for diners to eat at will.

If the curry paste featured fresh chilies, such as green or rawang curry paste, don't use prik pon. Toss some lightly smashed fresh chilies into the curry before serving to allow them to release their heat.

พริกยอดสนแห้ง
Dried Chili
รสชาติเผ็ดกลาง หอมมาก เหมาะคั่วทำพริกป่น
Medium spicy, very fragrant
Popularly roasted to make chili powder.
(100 grams)
45
(1 Kg.)
450

From left to right:
Sour Curry Paste (page 179),
Golae Curry Paste (page 212),
Rawang Curry Paste (page 163),
Northern Curry Paste (page 184)

Clockwise from left:
Green Curry Paste (page 162), Massaman Curry Paste (page 154), Red Curry Paste (page 144), Southern Curry Paste (page 168), and Panang Curry Paste (pages 150 and 153).

Technical Know-How

Wonder why and how to do certain curry things? These pro tips are for you.

Seeding chilies means removing both the seeds and the fleshy parts that hold them in place. Check out page 20 for pointers. Thoroughly seed the chilies *before* measuring quantities for recipes.

Soaking dried chilies not only removes lingering surface dirt but also gently hydrates them for easier grinding. Dried chilies are traditionally soaked until pliable and then pounded by hand. You do not typically need a long soak when using a machine to make curry paste.

To help curry paste ingredients move along during grinding, add moisture wisely. Use Kee Lo (Cracked Coconut Milk, page 53) or coconut oil for pastes that will be cooked in coconut milk so they'll fry well in the pot later. Add water when the paste will be cooked in water.

Blooming curry paste yields stellar Thai curry. The process coaxes elegant, complex flavors from the paste, allowing oil-soluble components to fully express their sexiness. Depending on how much fat the paste contains, you'll first briefly fry the paste in coconut milk, coconut oil, or, better yet, Kee Lo (Cracked Coconut Milk, page 53). The initial blooming takes the paste from raw and acrid to enticingly perfumy.

To bloom the paste more, Thai cooks gradually add coconut milk and simmer vigorously to force its oil to break and separate, or "crack," and gently fry the paste. That cooking phase sets the foundation for a more complex-tasting curry. During this process (see photos on next page), any separated oil becomes stained by the paste and the coconut milk turns delicately sweet. Expect the paste to sizzle and resemble lava as it initially blooms. (Adjust the heat up or down and scrape the pan wall and bottom as needed to prevent scorching.) Sometimes you can splash in water and boil the mixture hard to force the cracking. Be patient, however, and if the milk doesn't crack (because it has too much emulsifier, for instance), it's not the end of the world. Just move on and try again with the next curry.

Using kee lo (page 53) guarantees a curry with a wondrous, slightly sweet roundness. Yes, you can theoretically use virgin coconut oil, but when a recipe specifies kee lo, use it for superior results.

Skimming fat is up to you. The oil layer that hopefully gathers is flavorful and aromatic (it's basically a chili oil!). Leave some in the pan, or your curry will be too tame and taste flat. Save any fat for fried rice, stir-fried vegetables, refried beans, or fried potatoes.

Finessing curry flavor is always required. You'll practice balancing the heat, saltiness, and sweet to tailor the curry's flavor profile to your preferences. Each recipe offers my flavor notes, which are listed in order of boldness on your palate. Good curry finishes big and loud because it will be eaten with lots of plain rice.

Curing the curry for even 15 minutes settles and mellows flavors. Unsure about your curry's outcome? Let it sit, then retaste and tweak.

Storing curry in the fridge is fabulous for meal prep. It will generally be good for up to 3 days. Freeze it for up to 3 months. Proteins freeze well with the sauce but remove any vegetables, as they will turn soggy.

Reheating curry should happen over gentle heat with a splash of water to avoid scorching.

1

2

3

6

4

5

พริกแกงเผ็ด | Prik Gaeng Ped

Red Curry Paste

Keep this super-versatile curry paste on hand and you'll not only be able to cook up stellar red curries but also panang curries (pages 150 and 153), steamed hor mok (pages 225 and 227), fish cakes (page 72), and a magical crispy fish cereal for topping rice (page 239). In a pinch, it can even be turned into Southern Thai curry paste (page 168). Given all that, prik gaeng ped is a "mother" curry, so I always double this recipe. The chilies define this paste's fruity heat and color, so expect lots of little chili bits. The Note offers tips to dial down the heat. New to seeding lots of chilies? See pages 20 and 142 for pointers.

INGREDIENT	X1 FOR SMALL TO MEDIUM PROCESSORS	X2 FOR BLENDER AND ALL PROCESSOR SIZES
Seeded dried prik chee fa or puya chilies	40g | 1.3 oz	80g | 2.6 oz
Seeded dried prik jinda or árbol chilies (see Note)	10g | 0.3 oz	20g | 0.6 oz
Coriander seeds	2g | 1¼ tsp	4g | 2½ tsp
Cumin seeds	1g | ½ tsp	2g | 1 tsp
White peppercorns	1g | ¼ tsp	2g | ½ tsp
Garlic cloves, coarsely chopped	50g | 1.7 oz	100g | 3.3 oz
Shallots, coarsely chopped	50g | 1.7 oz	100g | 3.3 oz
Finely chopped lemongrass (from 1 or 2 thick stalks)	25g | ¼ cup	50g | ½ cup
Peeled galangal, chopped no bigger than ¼ inch (6mm)	10g | 1 Tbsp	20g | 2 Tbsp
Cilantro root or cilantro stems, chopped	5g | 2 tsp root, or 10g | 1½ Tbsp stems	10g | 4 tsp root, or 20g | 3 Tbsp stems
Gapi (Thai shrimp paste; omit for vegan version)	20g | 1 Tbsp	40g | 2 Tbsp
Rind of 1 makrut or regular lime, finely chopped	5g | 1½ tsp	10g | 1 Tbsp
Kee Lo (Cracked Coconut Milk, page 53) or virgin coconut oil, if needed to ease grinding		
Approximate yield	1 cup (225g)	2 cups (450g)

When scaling up, toasting time for spices may be slightly longer.

The yield will be larger if kee lo or coconut oil is added.

Soak the chilies: Snip the chilies into pieces no bigger than 1 inch (2.5cm), dropping them into a medium bowl. Add warm water to cover and let soak until softened and pliable, 3 to 5 minutes. Drain in a fine-mesh strainer, then firmly squeeze or use a silicone spatula to firmly press out as much water as possible (some lingering water is inevitable). Transfer to a food processor or blender.

Toast and pound spices: In a small saucepan over medium-low heat, toast the coriander, cumin, and white peppercorns until fragrant, 2 to 3 minutes. Remove from the heat, let cool briefly, and then use a mortar and pestle (or an electric grinder) to render the spices to a powder. Add to the chilies.

Grind the paste: Add the garlic, shallots, lemongrass, galangal, cilantro root, gapi, and lime rind to the chilies and spices in the machine. (If making a vegan version, omit the gapi and add 1 Tbsp water to facilitate grinding.) Process until a finely textured, spreadable paste forms, pausing to scrape down the sides of the bowl or jar as needed. Be patient, as this grinding step takes several minutes (it's still faster than hand pounding). If moisture is needed to get things moving in the machine, add the kee lo by the 1 Tbsp, using up to ¼ cup (60ml) total for a single batch.

Use the curry paste right away, or transfer to a jar, cap tightly, and refrigerate for up to 3 weeks or freeze in ½-cup (120ml) portions for up to 6 months.

NOTE

For less chili heat, omit the prik jinda or árbol chilies and increase the prik chee fa or puya chilies to 50g (1.7 oz) per batch. For an even milder paste, use a one-to-one combination of dried puya and guajillo (or even milder New Mexico or California) chilies.

แกงเผ็ดเป็ดย่างใส่ผลไม้ | Gaeng Ped Sai Polamai

Quickie Roast Duck Red Curry

SERVES 4

Need a Thai curry to make on the fly on a weeknight or weekend to impress yourself or company? This is it. Gaeng ped sai polamai is a beginner curry that's beloved by many Thais. Traditionally, it features bone-in pieces of roast duck, which are easily procured from a Chinese barbecue shop, where a clerk will cut the duck for you. To counter the duck's roasty richness, fresh fruit finishes the curry. Pineapple is traditional, but I adore tart-sweet stone fruit when it's in season. In summer, I often use both Thai and dark opal basil, as photographed here, to craft extra-beautiful curry.

Make this once and you'll be riffing on it. For instance, prepare this easy recipe with smoked duck. I'm partial to the version prepared at The Morris in San Francisco. Give leftover rotisserie chicken or Thanksgiving turkey a Thai makeover with this recipe. Whatever fowl you choose, make sure it's simply seasoned and cut into largish pieces, and whether bone-in or boneless, use about 2½ cups (600 ml). Scoop the thick coconut milk from the top of an unshaken can of coconut milk.

60ml | ¼ cup thick coconut milk

55 to 75g | ¼ to ⅓ cup Prik Gaeng Ped (Red Curry Paste, page 144), to taste

540ml | 2¼ cups coconut milk

½ meaty Chinese roast duck, cut into large bone-in pieces (ask the shop to do this)

1 Tbsp fish sauce, plus more to taste

1 large or 2 small firm-ripe nectarines or plums, halved, pitted, and cut lengthwise into wedges ½ inch (1.25cm) wide

3 or 4 makrut lime leaves (optional; for aroma)

1 handful fresh Thai basil leaves, plus more for garnish

Bloom the paste and cook the curry: In a medium pot over medium heat, warm the thick coconut milk. When it is bubbly hot, add the curry paste and cook, stirring actively, until it no longer smells raw, 1 to 2 minutes.

Add the coconut milk in three batches, stirring and letting things simmer briskly for 3 to 5 minutes to develop flavor and thicken slightly before adding the next batch. Remember to stir and scrape the pan bottom frequently to prevent scorching. Adjust the heat to maintain the bubbly cooking action and/or to prevent the sauce from spitting. As the coconut milk breaks and separates (cracks), look for traces of orange-red oil bubbling at the edge or a slightly dark red oily film on top. If the coconut milk didn't crack, don't worry.

If after adding all of the coconut milk you want to force further cracking for deeper flavor, splash in some water and cook at a hard boil, stirring occasionally. If oil appears in 2 to 3 minutes, success! If cracked coconut milk eludes you today, move on.

Add the duck and fish sauce. Adjust the heat to simmer the curry and continue cooking to heat the duck and release its savory richness into the sauce, 5 to 10 minutes. The finished sauce should be medium thick and velvety. To test, coat the back of a spoon with the sauce and run a finger through it. If the line holds firmly for a few seconds, the sauce is ready. Skim off as much fat from the surface of the sauce as you like.

Finesse, assemble, and serve: Gently fold most of the fruit (save some for garnish) into the sauce to add sweetness and simmer until just warmed through, about 1 minute (avoid overcooking and softening the fruit). Turn off the heat.

Taste the sauce. It should be spicy and salty, with a slight sweetness and acidity from the fruit. For more savoriness, add a dash of fish sauce or any residual juices that came with the duck, then add any fruit juices, if available, for tang.

Crumple the lime leaves to release their aroma, then drop them into the pot. Stir in the basil, submerging the leaves to prevent browning. Transfer the curry to a shallow serving bowl, garnish with extra basil, and serve.

NOTE

When stone fruits are out of season, substitute 1 cup (150g) fresh pineapple chunks. Because pineapple is heartier than stone fruit, simmer it until tender firm, 2 to 3 minutes.

แกงเผ็ดมังสวิรัติ | Gaeng Ped Jae

Red Curry with Bamboo Shoots and Thai Eggplant

SERVES 4

I feel a special kind of achievement when I make a vegetarian dish that tastes just as delicious, if not better, than its meat or seafood counterpart. The trick is to build the umami unctuousness that you'd otherwise get from meat. For this vegetarian curry and others, kee lo is key for coaxing out the oil from the coconut milk, thereby enabling the aromatic, oil-soluble components in the curry paste to bloom and fully express themselves. Learn how to achieve vegetarian nirvana with kee lo and then apply the skill to craft meatless curries that will impress everyone at your table.

300g | 10 oz mild bamboo shoots (see Notes)

150g | 5 oz medium-small Thai eggplants (see Notes)

2 Tbsp Kee Lo (Cracked Coconut Milk, page 53)

½ batch (about 110g | ½ cup) Prik Gaeng Ped (Red Curry Paste, page 144)

One 400ml | 13.5-oz can coconut milk

240ml | 1 cup water, plus more to taste

3 Tbsp Thai thin soy sauce, plus more to taste

Thai palm sugar, for finishing

5 makrut lime leaves

5 fresh red Thai chilies, lightly smashed or kept whole (optional)

1 handful fresh Thai or lemon basil leaves, plus a few tips for garnish

Prep the vegetables: Quarter the bamboo shoots lengthwise, then rinse and pat dry with paper towels. Thinly slice each quarter lengthwise into fringy, elongated triangles each a good ⅛ inch (3mm) thick. They will expand slightly in the curry. Trim the stems and remove the flaps from the eggplants. Halve each eggplant lengthwise.

Bloom the paste and cook the curry: In a medium pot over medium heat, melt the kee lo. Add the curry paste and cook, stirring actively, until it no longer smells raw, about 2 minutes.

Add the coconut milk in two or three batches, stirring and letting things simmer briskly for 3 to 5 minutes to develop flavor and thicken slightly before adding the next batch. Remember to stir and scrape the pan bottom frequently to prevent scorching. Adjust the heat to maintain the bubbly cooking action and/or to prevent the sauce from spitting. As the coconut milk breaks and separates (cracks), look for traces of orange-red oil bubbling at the edge or a slightly dark red oily film on top. If the coconut milk didn't crack, don't worry.

Add the water and bring to a hard boil to force further cracking and to develop deeper flavor, 3 to 5 minutes. This is not a thick curry, so aim for a medium tomato sauce consistency at this point. Add the soy sauce, bamboo shoots, and eggplants and bring to a gentle boil. Cook uncovered, stirring now and then, until the eggplants are just tender and the curry reduces slightly, about 5 minutes. If the sauce is too heavy, splash in water to loosen.

Finesse and serve: Taste the sauce. It should be spicy, salty, and a touch sweet at the end. If needed, gradually add soy sauce by the 1 tsp to deepen savoriness and sugar by the 1 tsp to soften edgy heat (the curry should not lead with sweetness).

Turn off the heat. Crumple the lime leaves to release their aroma, then drop them into the pot. Stir in most of the chilies (if using) and basil, submerging the leaves to prevent browning. Transfer to a shallow serving bowl and top with the remaining chilies (if using) and basil. Serve immediately, reminding guests that they can avoid the chilies or eat them at their own peril.

NOTES

Bamboo shoots sold in refrigerated vacuum-sealed packages (usually imported from Japan) have a tender texture and mild sweetness that are perfect for this curry. I prefer small or medium vacuum-sealed bamboo shoots over the canned ones, which often taste tinny.

Select Thai eggplants no bigger than 1¼ inches (3.1cm) wide for this recipe; if yours are bigger, quarter them. Or roll cut (see page 166 for details) slender Chinese or Japanese eggplant into triangles 1½ inches (3.75cm) wide. The cooking time will be roughly the same.

แพนงผักวสันต์ | Panang Pak

Panang Curry of Spring Vegetables

SERVES 4

Spring's bounty—young slender carrots, verdant asparagus, and sweet snap peas—get the spotlight here. To showcase their vibrant color and flavors, they're steam-seared and then enrobed in spicy and slightly peanutty panang curry sauce; feel free to vary the vegetables as you like. Served on a platter to allow the beautiful vegetables to shine, this stunning curry will please omnivores and vegans alike. Enjoy with lots of rice for a splendid springtime Thai celebration.

CURRY SAUCE

15g | 1½ Tbsp roasted peanuts

½ batch (about 110g | ½ cup) Prik Gaeng Ped (Red Curry Paste, page 144)

3 Tbsp Kee Lo (Cracked Coconut Milk, page 53)

One 400ml | 13.5-oz can coconut milk

120ml | ½ cup water, plus more if needed

2 Tbsp Thai thin soy sauce, plus more to taste

20g | 1 Tbsp firmly packed Thai palm sugar, plus more to taste

Make panang paste: Using a mortar and pestle, pound the peanuts to a fine, paste-like consistency. Add the curry paste and pound gently to mix well.

Bloom the paste and cook the sauce: In a large wok (or medium braiser) over medium heat, melt the kee lo. Add the peanut-curry paste mixture and cook, stirring actively, until the curry paste no longer smells raw, 2 to 3 minutes.

Add the coconut milk in two or three batches, stirring and letting things simmer briskly for 3 to 5 minutes to develop flavor and thicken slightly before adding the next batch. Remember to stir and scrape the pan bottom frequently to prevent scorching. Adjust the heat to maintain the bubbly cooking action and/or to prevent the sauce from spitting. As the coconut milk breaks and separates (cracks), look for traces of orange-red oil bubbling at the edge or a slightly dark red oily film on top.

Add the water, bring to a hard boil, and cook, stirring occasionally, to force further cracking for deeper flavor, 2 to 3 minutes. The finished sauce should be thick and velvety. To test, coat the back of a spoon with the sauce and run a finger through it. If the line holds firmly, the sauce is ready.

Turn down the heat to low, add the soy sauce and palm sugar, stir to mix, and then taste the sauce. If needed, add soy sauce by the 1 tsp for savory depth or sugar by the ½ tsp to balance the fire. Turn off the heat and cover.

FOR THE VEGETABLES AND SERVING

Generous 1 Tbsp Kee Lo (Cracked Coconut Milk, page 53) or virgin coconut oil, plus more if needed

450g | 1 lb young carrots, scrubbed or peeled and halved lengthwise if large

Fine sea salt

1 pinch of granulated sugar (optional; for caramelization)

60ml | 4 Tbsp water, divided

340g | 12 oz large asparagus spears (16 total), trimmed of woody ends

120g | 4 oz sugar snap peas, strings removed and cut lengthwise on the diagonal

5 fresh red Thai chilies, lightly smashed or kept whole (optional)

12 large fresh Thai basil leaves (optional)

4 makrut lime leaves, finely slivered (see page 31; optional)

2 to 3 Tbsp roasted peanuts, chopped

Steam-sear the vegetables: In a large skillet over medium-high heat, warm the kee lo and when it is hot, add the carrots and season with 3 big pinches of salt and the granulated sugar (if using). Let sear and sizzle, shaking the pan occasionally, until light brown patches develop, about 3 minutes. Add 2 Tbsp of the water, cover, and lower the heat to medium. Let cook, shaking the pan often, until you are just able to pierce a carrot with a knife tip, 10 to 15 minutes. In the final minutes, when there's little moisture left, uncover and cook to gain extra caramelization. Transfer to a sheet pan or plate.

Reheat the pan over high heat, add the asparagus spears and season with 2 big pinches of salt. Sear, shaking the pan occasionally, until bright green, 1 to 2 minutes. Add the remaining 2 Tbsp water, cover, lower the heat to medium-high, and cook, shaking the pan occasionally, until nearly tender when pierced with a knife tip, 3 to 4 minutes. Uncover and sear briefly for extra caramelization. Transfer to the pan or plate with the carrots.

Reheat the pan over high heat and add a nubbin of kee lo if the pan looks dry. Add the snap peas and 1 pinch of salt. Sear, shaking the pan occasionally, until bright green and still very snappy, about 1 minute. Remove the pan from the heat.

Assemble and serve: Add a small splash of water to the curry sauce, warm over medium heat, and recheck the flavors to verify a salty, spicy flavor that's a touch sweet. If needed, add soy sauce by the 1 tsp and palm sugar by the ½ tsp. Add the Thai chilies (if using), turn off the heat, and stir in the basil, submerging the leaves to prevent browning.

Spoon about half of the sauce onto a serving platter, covering the bottom. Arrange the asparagus on top. Add the carrots, followed by most of the remaining sauce (avoid completely smothering the vegetables; we want to show off their beauty!). Finish with the snap peas and the remaining sauce. Top with the lime leaves (if using) and peanuts before carrying to the table.

พะแนงซี่โครงเนื้อ | Panang Neua

Panang Beef Short Ribs

SERVES 6

Easy and over-the-top impressive, these short ribs require few ingredients. The key is homemade red curry paste, which you should keep on hand because it's so darn useful. For the panang curry paste here, you'll simply add freshly pounded peanuts to red curry paste. As the short ribs braise in the oven, they release their beefiness into the sauce, which is complex and intensely spiced but cushioned by a tinge of caramelized coconut sweetness.

2.3kg | 5 lb bone-in beef short ribs (6 chunky ones)

Salt (any kind)

30g | ¼ cup roasted peanuts

1 batch (225g | 1 cup) Prik Gaeng Ped (Red Curry Paste, page 144)

640ml | 2⅔ cups coconut milk

480ml | 2 cups water

55ml | 3½ Tbsp fish sauce, plus more to taste

2 tsp firmly packed Thai palm sugar, plus more to taste

3 makrut lime leaves, finely slivered (see page 31), 1 handful fresh Thai basil leaves, or both

Brown and braise: Position a rack in the middle of the oven and preheat the oven to 350°F (175°C). Blot moisture from the beef, then season very lightly on all sides with salt.

Using a mortar and pestle, pound the peanuts to a fine, paste-like consistency. Add the red curry paste and pound gently to mix well.

Select a wide, large braiser or casserole pan that will hold the short ribs in a single layer and set over high heat. When the pan is very hot (to test, flick in a couple of drops of water; they should sizzle and evaporate within a second or two), add the short ribs, fat-side down. Sear, turning once, until richly browned on both sides, about 2 minutes on each side. Transfer to a plate or sheet pan. Pour off the fat in the pan and wipe away any burnt bits to prevent bitterness.

Return the pot to the hot burner and pour in 2 cups (480ml) of the coconut milk, which will sizzle on contact. Stir in the peanutty curry paste, bring to a bubbling boil, and cook, stirring continuously with a silicone spatula to prevent scorching, until fragrant and the raw smell is gone, about 5 minutes. Tiny puddles of coconut oil may appear toward the end.

Add the remaining ⅔ cup (160ml) coconut milk and cook, stirring, until the sauce breaks and oil appears on the surface, about 1 minute. (The coconut milk, beef, and high-heat cooking guarantee breaking.) Stir in the water, fish sauce, and sugar.

Return the short ribs to the pot, coating them in the sauce and arranging them meatier-side down. Loosely cover the pan with aluminum foil to allow a little venting. Transfer to the oven and braise, flipping midway and replacing the foil, until tender, 2½ to 3 hours. To test, poke the beef with a fork; there should be only slight resistance in the center.

Finesse and serve: Remove from the oven, let cool briefly in the pot, and then transfer the beef to a sheet pan and cover loosely to keep warm. If you like, skim off the fat from the surface of the sauce. The sauce should thickly coat the back of a spoon and taste luxurious, with spicy, salty notes that finish just a tad sweet. (You should have about 3 cups | 720ml sauce; add water if you're short or boil down if you have too much.) If needed, stir in sugar by the ½ tsp or fish sauce by the 1 tsp. To serve, transfer the short ribs to a platter or onto individual plates, spoon on the sauce, and then top with lime leaf and/or Thai basil.

NOTE

Because there is relatively little sauce, be extra careful when reheating this dish. Add a generous splash of water and heat over medium-low heat, minding and turning the short ribs as needed to avoid scorching. Retaste and, if needed, tweak the sauce before serving.

พริกแกงมัสมั่น | Prik Gaeng Massaman

Massaman Curry Paste

Intensely aromatic, mildly hot, and deeply layered with warm spices to reflect the confluence of Persian, Indian, and Malaysian culinary traditions in Thailand, massaman curry is a beloved Thai classic. Excellent massaman offers spice notes balanced with pungent and sweet aromatics. This paste delivers the complex depth that makes massaman intriguing and delicious.

The beef, chicken, and sweet potato massaman curries on pages 157, 159, and 160 employ half or full batches of paste. Machines cannot handle half batches (you're better off hand pounding with a mortar and pestle for that), so make at least a full batch because the prep effort is the same. That said, go for a double batch of prik gaeng massaman to try all three curries and ensure that you have extra for your favorite!

INGREDIENT	X1 FOR SMALL TO MEDIUM PROCESSORS	X2 FOR BLENDER AND ALL PROCESSOR SIZES
Cinnamon stick	5g | 5 inches	10g | 10 inches
White peppercorns	5g | 1½ tsp	10g | 1 Tbsp
Mace blades, lightly crumbled (see Notes)	2g | 3 or 4	4g | 6 to 8
Whole star anise, broken into petal-like segments	1.5g | 1	3g | 2
Green cardamom pods (see Notes)	1.5g | 5	3g | 10
Coriander seeds	5g | 1 Tbsp	10g | 2 Tbsp
Cumin seeds	4g | 1¾ tsp	8g | 1 Tbsp plus ½ tsp
Seeded dried prik chee fa or puya chilies (see Notes)	30g | 1 oz	60g | 2 oz
Virgin coconut oil	30ml | 2 Tbsp	60ml | ¼ cup
Shallots, quartered if large, halved if medium	85g | 3 oz	170g | 6 oz
Garlic cloves	75g | 2.5 oz	150g | 5 oz
Finely chopped lemongrass (from 1 or 2 thick stalks)	25g | ¼ cup	50g | ½ cup
Peeled galangal, sliced ¼ inch (6mm) thick	15g | 0.5 oz	30g | 1 oz
Gapi (Thai shrimp paste; omit for vegan version)	40g | 2 Tbsp	80g | ¼ cup
Kee Lo (Cracked Coconut Milk, page 53) or virgin coconut oil, if needed to ease grinding		
Approximate yield	1¼ cups (300g)	2½ cups (600g)

The yield will be larger if kee lo or coconut oil is added.

Make the spice blend: Using a mortar and pestle, crush the cinnamon stick into small pieces. Put the pieces into a small saucepan and add the white peppercorns, mace, star anise, and cardamom. Toast over medium heat, stirring, until fragrant, 2 to 3 minutes. Add the coriander and cumin seeds and continue toasting until the aromas are activated, 30 to 60 seconds. Remove from the heat, transfer to a small bowl to cool, and then use an electric grinder to render the spices to a powdery blend.

Rinse the chilies: Put the dried chilies into a strainer, rinse briefly with water, and drain well. Use a paper towel to pat away moisture (wet chilies won't fry well for the paste).

Fry and process the paste: Set a large wok over medium heat and add the coconut oil. After it melts, add the shallots and garlic and stir-fry until slightly softened and caramelized, 3 to 4 minutes. Add the lemongrass and galangal and continue to stir-fry until aromatic, about 1 minute. Then toss in the chilies and keep stirring until they are very fragrant and have darkened a bit, 1 to 3 minutes. Remove the wok from the heat, let cool briefly, then transfer the contents to a food processor or blender. Add the shrimp paste and process until a fine paste forms. If moisture is needed to get things moving in the machine, add the kee lo by the 1 Tbsp, using up to ¼ cup (60ml) total for a single batch. Add the spice blend and process to mix well.

Use the curry paste right away, or transfer to a jar, cap tightly, and refrigerate for up to 1 month or freeze in ½-cup (120ml) portions for up to 3 months.

NOTES

Instead of cardamom pods, use 1g (mounded ¼ tsp) cardamom seeds per batch of paste. Instead of mace blades, use an equal weight amount of ground mace, adding it when grinding the spices. If mace is totally unavailable, skip it!

For less chili heat, use a three-to-one combination of dried puya and guajillo (or even milder New Mexico or California) chilies. See pages 20 and 142 for tips on seeding chilies.

มัสมั่นเนื้อแก้มวัว | Massaman Gam Wua

Massaman Curry with Beef Cheeks, Potatoes, and Burnt Shallots

SERVES 6 TO 8

Beef massaman curry has been on the Kin Khao menu since opening day. Our signature recipe is based on my grandmother's recipe—a rich, long braise of beef, potato, and charred shallots that's finished with a shower of fried shallots. Some cooks add peanuts to lend fatty sweetness, but that's not what my aunties taught me, so I don't do it. There's plenty of depth and nuttiness from the alliums and spices.

For the best flavor, select beef cuts suitable for low and slow cooking and prep them as biggish chunks. I adore beef cheeks not only because it's a cut that could use more love but also because it's so perfect for this long braising preparation. Its plentiful connective tissues and collagen ensure that during the extended cook time the meat remains toothsome yet tender enough to cut with a spoon, yielding a finished dish that soaks up all the flavors of the curry. Beef cheeks can be hard to source, so check good butcher shops. When beef cheeks are unavailable, try chuck or tri-tip and see page 158 for a short rib variation.

800ml to 1L | 3½ to 4¼ cups coconut milk (1 big box or 2 to 2½ cans), unshaken

1 batch (300g | 1¼ cups) Prik Gaeng Massaman (Massaman Curry Paste, page 154)

2kg | 4.4 lb trimmed beef cheeks, boneless chuck, or tri-tip, cut into 2- to 3-inch (5 to 7.5cm) pieces

60ml | ¼ cup fish sauce, plus more to taste

500g | 4 medium waxy potatoes (such as red or Yukon Gold), peeled and quartered

150g | 5 small shallots, unpeeled

60ml | ¼ cup Nam Makam (Tamarind Liquid, page 52), plus more to taste

60g | 3 Tbsp firmly packed Thai palm sugar, plus more to taste

120ml | ½ cup fried shallots

2 dried prik chee fa or puya chilies, toasted, for garnish (optional)

Bloom the paste and build the sauce: Collect ¾ cup (180ml) thick coconut milk from the top of the box or cans and add to a large pot. Set over high heat and bring to a boil. Add the curry paste and stir vigorously to mix. Turn down the heat a bit if the mixture spatters and sputters too enthusiastically. Continue stirring and scraping the pan bottom until bubbles of reddish oil emerge from the gently sizzling paste, about 2 minutes.

Add the remaining coconut milk in four or five batches, stirring and letting things bubble vigorously for 3 to 8 minutes to reduce and thicken slightly before adding the next batch. Remember to stir and scrape the pan bottom frequently to prevent scorching. Adjust the heat to maintain the bubbly cooking action and/or to prevent the sauce from spitting. As the coconut milk breaks and separates (cracks), look for traces of reddish oil bubbling at the edge or a slightly dark red oily film on top. Because the paste contains a bit of oil, cracking the coconut milk for this curry should happen easily.

Braise the beef: Gently place the beef in the simmering curry, then add the fish sauce and water just to cover the meat. Adjust the heat to maintain a gentle simmer, cover partially, and braise the beef until tender, 3 to 4 hours, adding the potatoes 2½ hours into the braising. The beef is ready when a fork or small knife pierces it with barely any resistance.

Before the potatoes go into the pot, set a perforated skillet or vegetable grill pan over a medium-high flame on a gas stovetop. When the pan is hot, add the whole shallots and char, turning often, until the skin blackens here and there, about 3 minutes. (Or place under the broiler close to the heat source for about 5 minutes, grill outdoors, or use a ripping-hot cast-iron skillet on the stovetop.)

CONTINUED

Let cool briefly, then peel and trim (it's OK if some burnt bits remain or the shallot clusters separate). Add the shallots to the curry about 30 minutes after adding the potatoes. The vegetables will cook along with the curry to absorb flavors without overcooking.

Fine-tune and serve: Turn off the heat and skim off as much fat from the surface of the sauce as you like. Add the tamarind and sugar and mix well. Taste the sauce. It should be well spiced (not spicy hot), salty, and with a good balance of tamarind acidity and sweetness from the sugar. If needed, soften the spicy heat by stirring in tamarind by the 1 Tbsp and sugar by the 1½ tsp. For extra savory oomph, stir in fish sauce by the 1½ tsp. To mellow the flavor, stir in a splash of water. The finished sauce should be medium thick and velvety. To test, coat the back of a spoon with the sauce and run a finger through it. If the line holds firmly for a few seconds, the sauce is ready. Transfer the curry to a shallow serving bowl, garnish with the fried shallots and toasted chilies (if using), and serve.

VARIATION

มัสมั่นซี่โครงวัว | Massaman Sikrong Wua
Beef Short Rib Massaman Curry

Use 4.4 lb (2kg) bone-in beef short ribs (6 to 8 meaty English-cut pieces) for the boneless beef. For a little extra flavor and character, sear the short ribs in the pot with a splash of neutral oil (such as rice bran) over high heat, then hold them on a plate. Bloom the paste and build the sauce as usual, then return the short ribs to the pot. The rest of the recipe is the same, though for even cooking, turn the short ribs twice during the first 2 hours of cooking.

มัสมั่นไก่ | Massaman Gai

Massaman Curry with Chicken, Potatoes, and Burnt Shallots

SERVES 6 TO 8

Massaman curry works with many proteins, including chicken, which cooks up quickly for weeknight curry. Life is too short for lean chicken-breast curry, so braise bone-in thighs for fabulous flavor and texture. Prepare a half batch in a medium-large pot if you like. The cook time is the same.

800ml to 1L | 3½ to 4¼ cups coconut milk (1 big box or 2 to 2½ cans), unshaken

1 batch (300g | 1¼ cups) Prik Gaeng Massaman (Massaman Curry Paste, page 154)

2kg | 4.4 lb bone-in, skin-on chicken thighs

60ml | ¼ cup fish sauce, plus more to taste

500g | 4 medium waxy potatoes (such as red or Yukon Gold), peeled and quartered

150g | 5 small shallots, unpeeled

60ml | ¼ cup Nam Makam (Tamarind Liquid, page 52), plus more to taste

60g | 3 Tbsp firmly packed Thai palm sugar, plus more to taste

120ml | ½ cup fried shallots

2 dried prik chee fa or puya chilies, toasted, for garnish (optional)

Bloom the paste and build the sauce: Collect ¾ cup (180ml) thick coconut milk from the top of the box or cans and add to a large pot. Set over high heat and bring to a boil. Add the curry paste and stir vigorously to mix. Turn down the heat a bit if the mixture spatters and sputters too enthusiastically. Continue stirring and scraping the pan bottom until you see bubbles of reddish oil emerge from the gently sizzling paste, about 2 minutes.

Add the remaining coconut milk in four or five batches, stirring and letting things bubble vigorously for 3 to 8 minutes to reduce and thicken slightly before adding the next batch. Remember to stir and scrape the pan bottom frequently to prevent scorching. Adjust the heat to maintain the bubbly cooking action and/or to prevent the sauce from spitting. As the coconut milk breaks and separates (cracks), look for traces of reddish oil bubbling at the edge or a slightly dark red oily film on top.

If after adding all the coconut milk you want to force further cracking for deeper flavor, splash in some water and cook at a hard boil, stirring occasionally. If oil appears in 2 to 3 minutes, success! If cracked coconut milk eludes you today, move on.

Braise the chicken: Place the chicken thighs in the simmering curry. Add the fish sauce and water to cover the chicken. Adjust the heat to maintain a gentle simmer, cover partially, and braise the chicken until tender, 1 to 1½ hours, adding the potatoes about 20 minutes into the braising. The chicken is ready when a fork or small knife pierces a thigh with only slight resistance.

Before the potatoes go into the pot, set a perforated skillet or vegetable grill pan over a medium-high flame on a gas stovetop. When the pan is hot, add the whole shallots and char, turning often, until the skin blackens here and there, about 3 minutes. (Or place under the broiler close to the heat source for about 5 minutes, grill outdoors, or use a ripping-hot cast-iron skillet on the stovetop.) Let cool briefly, then peel and trim (it's OK if some burnt bits remain or the shallot clusters separate). Add the shallots to the curry about 20 minutes after adding the potatoes. The vegetables will cook along with the curry to absorb flavors without overcooking.

Fine-tune and serve: Turn off the heat and skim off as much fat from the surface of the sauce as you like. Add the tamarind and sugar and mix well. Taste the sauce. It should be well spiced (not spicy hot), salty, and with a good balance of tamarind acidity and sweetness from the sugar. If needed, soften the spicy heat by stirring in tamarind by the 1 Tbsp and sugar by the 1½ tsp. For savory oomph, stir in fish sauce by the 1½ tsp. To mellow the flavor, stir in a splash of water. The finished sauce should be medium thick and velvety. To test, coat the back of a spoon with the sauce and run a finger through it. If the line holds firmly for a few seconds, the sauce is ready. Transfer the curry to a shallow serving bowl, garnish with the fried shallots and toasted chilies (if using), and serve.

มัสมั่นมันเผา | Massaman Mun Pao

Massaman Curry with Roasted Sweet Potatoes

SERVES 4 TO 6

Here's a meal-prep game plan: Make a vegan massaman curry sauce days in advance, then roast off some sweet potatoes and unite the two for an easy, satisfying main course or side dish. The sweet, warm spice notes and tangy heat of massaman are terrific with the potato chunks, which take on a chewy exterior during roasting. Enjoyed with jasmine rice, this spicy-sweet curry is perfect for a meatless meal or alongside grilled or roast chicken. If you serve this curry at Thanksgiving to Thai-up your menu, that turkey won't know what hit it, and your vegetarian guests will be so delighted.

Kee lo lends a natural sweetness and builds umami richness. Do not substitute coconut oil, even though it's used for roasting the potatoes. Firm-fleshed sweet potatoes, such as Japanese or purple ones, hold up well in the sauce.

800g | 1¾ lb sweet potatoes

1 Tbsp virgin coconut oil, melted or softened

2 big pinches of fine sea salt

2 Tbsp Kee Lo (Cracked Coconut Milk, page 53)

½ batch (150g | about ⅔ cup) Prik Gaeng Massaman (Massaman Curry Paste, page 154)

One 400ml | 13.5-oz can coconut milk

240ml | 1 cup water

60ml | ¼ cup Thai thin soy sauce, plus more to taste

Scant 1½ Tbsp Nam Makam (Tamarind Liquid, page 52), plus more to taste

20g | 1 Tbsp firmly packed Thai palm sugar, plus more to taste

60ml | ¼ cup fried shallots

Roast the sweet potatoes: Position a rack in the middle of the oven and preheat the oven to 425°F (220°C). Line a sheet pan with parchment paper. Peel the potatoes, then cut into husky but manageable 1½- to 2-inch (3.75 to 5cm) chunks. Or for even roasting and an arty curry, roll cut (see page 166) the potatoes into pieces measuring 1½ to 2 inches (3.75 to 5cm) wide.

In a medium bowl, toss the sweet potatoes with the coconut oil and salt. Transfer to the prepared sheet pan, spreading the chunks, with a cut-side down, into a single layer. Roast the sweet potatoes, turning once or twice with a metal spatula, until tender and browned here and there, 25 to 40 minutes, depending on the potato type and size.

Bloom the paste and cook the sauce: While the potatoes are roasting, set a large wok (or a medium braiser) over medium heat and melt the kee lo. Add the curry paste and cook, stirring actively, until it no longer smells raw, 2 to 3 minutes.

Add the coconut milk in two or three batches, stirring and letting things bubble vigorously for 3 to 5 minutes to reduce and thicken slightly before adding the next batch. Remember to stir and scrape the pan bottom frequently to prevent scorching. Adjust the heat to maintain the bubbly cooking action and/or to prevent the sauce from spitting. As the coconut milk breaks and separates (cracks), look for traces of dark red oil bubbling at the edge or a slightly dark red oily film on top.

Add the water, bring to a hard boil, and cook, stirring occasionally, until slightly thickened and the sauce cracks, about 5 minutes. At this point, the sauce should be velvety and lightly thickened. To test, coat the back of a spoon with the sauce and run a finger through it. If the line gently holds, the sauce is ready. The sauce will thicken slightly as it sits, which is normal.

Turn down the heat to low, add the soy sauce, tamarind, and sugar, and stir well. Taste the sauce. It should have a salty, spicy tang followed by a bit of heat. As needed, add soy sauce, tamarind, and sugar by the ½ to 1 tsp. Err on the tangy side because the sweet potato will add sweetness. Turn off the heat and cover (or let cool, transfer to an airtight container, and refrigerate for up to 3 days).

Unite and serve: When the potatoes are done, reheat the curry sauce over medium heat with 1 to 2 Tbsp water to prevent scorching. After a gentle boil begins, add the warm potatoes, stir gently, and let cook to meld the flavors and thicken slightly, 3 to 5 minutes. Taste in case some last-minute flavor finessing is needed. Transfer the curry to a shallow serving bowl, shower with the fried shallots, and serve.

พริกแกงเขียวหวาน | Prik Gaeng Kiew Wan

Green Curry Paste

Compared to curry pastes made with dried chilies, jade-green prik gaeng kiew wan shines because of its fresh, vegetal flavor bursts. Fresh green chilies star in this paste, which also includes a warm spice blend, lime rind, lemongrass, and lots of garlic. Cilantro root or stems add earthy coriander notes (we never include cilantro leaves). For the chilies, start with 3 oz (90g) of each kind to yield the prepped amount needed (see seeding tips on page 20).

Use the paste soon after making it, or freeze it to preserve its layered nuances. Feature this paste in the beef and eggplant curry on page 165, or easily tweak it to make gaeng rawang curry paste (check out the Variation on page 163) for preparing the lemongrass-laced chicken curry on page 167. Versatility is a virtue of good Thai curry pastes.

INGREDIENT	X1 FOR SMALL TO MEDIUM PROCESSORS	X2 FOR BLENDER AND ALL PROCESSOR SIZES
Coriander seeds	2g | 1¼ tsp	4g | 2½ tsp
Cumin seeds	1g | ½ tsp	2g | 1 tsp
Whole star anise	1g | 1 small	2g | 2 small
Mace blade or ground mace (omit if unavailable)	0.25g | blade ¼ inch (6mm) wide, or 1 pinch of ground	0.5g | blade ½ inch (1.25cm) wide, or 2 pinches of ground
Shallots, coarsely chopped	75g | 2.5 oz	150g | 5 oz
Seeded fresh green Thai chilies	60g | 2 oz	120g | 4 oz
Seeded fresh green jalapeño or serrano chilies, chopped (see Notes)	60g | 2 oz	120g | 4 oz
Garlic cloves, coarsely chopped	50g | 1.7 oz	100g | 3.3 oz
Lemongrass, finely chopped (from 1 or 2 thick stalks)	30g | ⅓ cup	60g | ⅔ cup
Makrut or regular lime rind, chopped	5g | 1½ tsp	10g | 1 Tbsp
Peeled galangal, chopped	10g | 1 Tbsp	20g | 2 Tbsp
Chopped, unpeeled grachai (fingerroot; optional)	5g | 1½ tsp	10g | 1 Tbsp
Finely chopped cilantro root or cilantro stems	1 tsp packed root, or 2 tsp stems	2 tsp packed root, or 4 tsp stems
Gapi (Thai shrimp paste; omit for vegan version)	10g | 1½ tsp packed	20g | 1 Tbsp packed
Kee Lo (Cracked Coconut Milk, page 53) or virgin coconut oil, if needed to ease grinding		
Approximate yield	1¼ cups (300g)	2½ cups (600g)

The yield will be larger if kee lo or coconut oil is added.

Toast and grind the spices: In a small saucepan, combine the coriander, cumin, and star anise, breaking the star anise into individual petals. Toast over medium-low heat, stirring, until fragrant, 2 to 3 minutes. Add the mace blades, crumbling them (or the ground mace). Stir to combine and activate the aroma. Remove from the heat, let cool briefly, and then use a mortar and pestle (or an electric grinder) to render the spices to a powder.

Make the paste: In a food processor or blender, combine the shallots, all of the chilies, garlic, lemongrass, lime rind, galangal, grachai (if using), cilantro root, gapi, and spice blend and process to a fine texture, pausing to scrape down the sides of the bowl or jar as needed. If moisture is needed to get things moving in the machine, add the kee lo by the 1 Tbsp, using up to ¼ cup (60ml) total for a single batch.

Use the curry paste right away, or transfer to a jar, cap tightly, and refrigerate for up to 1 week. To freeze, see Notes.

NOTES

For moderate heat, select biggish green Thai chilies roughly 2 to 2½ inches (5 to 6.25cm) long and employ jalapeños. Choose smaller Thai chilies and serranos for extra palate excitement—if you dare.

To preserve this curry paste's fresh flavor and verdant color well for 1 month, add ¼ cup (60ml) Kee Lo (Cracked Coconut Milk, page 53) or 3 Tbsp virgin coconut oil to the processor or blender when making the paste. Freeze the paste in ½-cup (120ml) portions. When using frozen paste for the beef or chicken curry on pages 165 and 167, over medium heat, warm the paste with ¼ cup (60ml) of the total amount of coconut milk called for in the recipe. Heat until the paste melts, sizzles, and starts blooming. There's no need to add kee lo (or coconut oil) to bloom the paste. The rest of the recipe remains the same.

VARIATION

พริกแกงระแวง | Prik Gaeng Rawang
Gaeng Rawang Curry Paste

To prepare curry paste for the chicken curry on page 167, make the green curry paste as directed. For each batch, add 3 Tbsp (25g) coarsely chopped, peeled fresh turmeric (or scant 1 Tbsp ground turmeric) when processing the paste. Use the chartreuse-yellow paste right away, or refrigerate or freeze as directed in the green curry paste recipe Notes. Each batch yields about 1⅓ cups (325g).

แกงเขียวหวาน | Gaeng Kiew Wan Neua

Green Curry with Beef and Thai Eggplant

SERVES 6

Many Thai curries come together via a lengthy braise, but gaeng kiew wan neua (photographed opposite, lower left) is a quick one. That's on purpose, as the green curry paste becomes muted during a low-and-slow cook. Instead, I briefly simmer sliced beef and fast-cooking Thai eggplants in the piquant sauce. Rib eye's rich flavor and tender texture are perfect. Bavette (flap) yields great curry too.

Have the curry paste made (or thawed!) so you can enjoy this sumptuous curry in little time. Pre-cracked coconut milk (kee lo) lends a touch of elegant sweetness. Don't be alarmed by green curry's initial assertive heat, as it will mellow during cooking.

- 750g | 1⅔ lb well-marbled boneless rib eye or bavette (flap) steaks
- 55ml | 3½ Tbsp fish sauce, plus more to taste
- 300g | 10 oz medium Thai eggplants or slender Japanese or Chinese eggplants
- 60ml | ¼ cup Kee Lo (Cracked Coconut Milk, page 53), or 45ml | 3 Tbsp virgin coconut oil
- 1 batch (300g | 1¼ cups) Prik Gaeng Kiew Wan (Green Curry Paste, page 162)
- 800ml to 1 L | 3½ to 4¼ cups coconut milk (1 big box or 2 to 2½ cans)
- 80ml | ⅓ cup water
- 4 or 5 makrut lime leaves (optional)
- 1 to 3 tsp firmly packed Thai palm sugar, to taste (optional)
- 2 handfuls fresh Thai basil leaves (optional; for extra complexity)
- 5 to 10 fresh red Thai chilies, lightly smashed or kept whole (optional)

Marinate the beef: Cut the beef across the grain into strips ¼ inch (6mm) thick and 2 to 3 inches (5 to 7.5cm) long. Put into a large bowl, add the fish sauce, and massage the seasoning into the meat. The beef should absorb it all. Cover and let marinate in the refrigerator for at least 1 hour or up to 4 hours. It's fine to use the beef straight from the fridge.

Prep the eggplant: Remove the stems and flaps from the eggplants. If using Thai eggplants, halve them. If using Japanese or Chinese eggplants, roll cut (see page 166) them into triangles 1 inch (2.5cm) wide.

Bloom the paste and build the sauce: In a large pot over medium heat, melt the kee lo. Add the curry paste and cook, stirring actively, until it is pleasingly aromatic and no longer smells raw, about 3 minutes.

Add the coconut milk in four or five batches, stirring and letting things bubble vigorously for 3 to 8 minutes to reduce and thicken slightly before adding the next batch. Remember to stir and scrape the pan bottom frequently to prevent scorching. Adjust the heat to maintain the bubbly cooking action and/or to prevent the sauce from spitting. As the coconut milk breaks and separates (cracks), look for traces of greenish oil bubbling at the edge or a slightly dark green oily film on top.

If after adding all of the coconut milk you want to force further cracking for deeper flavor, splash in some water and cook at a hard boil, stirring occasionally. If oil appears in 2 to 3 minutes, success! If cracked coconut milk eludes you today, move on.

Cook the eggplant and beef: Add the water to loosen the sauce and amplify the curry's verdant, floral heat. Bring to a brisk simmer and add the eggplants. Gently crumple the lime leaves (if using) and drop them into the pot. Cook until the eggplants are tender firm and nearly done, 3 to 5 minutes.

Lower the heat to a very gentle simmer and add the beef, stirring to separate the slices and distribute evenly. Cook until the beef is *just* done and no longer red, about 3 minutes. The eggplants should be tender now too.

Finesse the flavor: Turn off the heat, then taste the sauce. It should be spicy and salty, with some brightness from the lime leaf (if using) and aromatics, followed by barely a hint of sweetness at the end. For extra savory oomph, stir in fish sauce by the 1 tsp. The coconut milk should already set a sweet flavor finish, but if there is a rough edge, cautiously stir in the sugar by the ½ to 1 tsp.

CONTINUED

Don't use too much sugar, as the curry can quickly turn cloying. To mellow the flavor, stir in a splash of water. The finished sauce should be medium thick and velvety. To test, coat the back of a spoon with the sauce and run a finger through it. If the line holds firmly for a few seconds, the sauce is ready.

Finish and serve: Stir in the basil, if using, submerging the leaves to prevent browning. For extra heat, drop in the red chilies. Transfer to a shallow serving bowl and serve. Remind guests that they can avoid the chilies or eat them at their own peril.

NOTE

At Asian markets, select golf-ball-size Thai eggplants (no more than 1¾ inches | 4.4cm wide), or look for slender Japanese or Chinese eggplants, each about 1½ inches (3.75cm) thick.

HOW TO ROLL CUT VEGETABLES

To get long vegetables like Japanese and Chinese eggplant or sweet potato to cook evenly and look interesting, use a roll cut (also called oblique cut) to cut them. Wield your knife at a 45-degree angle from the vegetable to make a diagonal cut. Roll (rotate) the vegetable toward you 180 degrees (a half turn) or 90 degrees (a quarter turn) and repeat the angled cut to make pieces that look like triangles or trapezoids. If the vegetable is extra large, halve it lengthwise before cutting.

แกงระแวงไก่ | Gaeng Rawang Gai

Life-Changing Chicken Curry

SERVES 6

Aromatic with lemongrass, spices, and fresh chilies, gently hot gaeng rawang is one of my go-to chicken curries. Found only in some historic Thai cookbooks, it is not well known—but ought to be. It's simply made by tweaking iconic Thai green curry paste with fresh turmeric. At Nari, we've prepared this curry with whole poussin, but easier-to-source chicken legs and thighs work well. Photographed on page 164, the rich results are great with rice, or for a supreme experience, offer the curry with flaky roti flatbread (purchased frozen paratha works too). *Food & Wine* magazine included my recipe in a feature on life-changing dishes. Add it to your repertoire.

60ml | ¼ cup Kee Lo (Cracked Coconut Milk, page 53), or 45ml | 3 Tbsp virgin coconut oil

1 batch (320g | 1⅓ cups) Prik Gaeng Rawang (Gaeng Rawaeng Curry Paste, page 163)

800ml to 1L | 3½ to 4¼ cups coconut milk (1 big box or 2 to 2½ cans)

1.8 kg | 4 lb bone-in, skin-on chicken legs, thighs, or a combo

120g | 2 large lemongrass stalks, trimmed, cut into 3-inch (7.5cm) lengths, and smashed to release scent

60ml | ¼ cup fish sauce, plus more to taste

120g | 4 to 6 mini sweet peppers, quartered lengthwise and seeded

7 to 20g | 1 to 3 tsp firmly packed Thai palm sugar

2 handfuls fresh Thai or lemon basil leaves (optional)

5 to 10 fresh red Thai chilies, lightly smashed or kept whole (optional)

Bloom the paste and build the sauce: In a large pot over medium heat, melt the kee lo. Add the curry paste and cook, stirring actively, until the paste becomes pleasingly aromatic and no longer smells raw, 2 to 3 minutes.

Add the coconut milk in four or five batches, stirring and letting things bubble vigorously for 3 to 8 minutes to reduce and thicken slightly before adding the next batch. Stir and scrape the pan bottom frequently to prevent scorching. Adjust the heat to maintain the bubbly cooking action and/or to prevent the sauce from spitting. As the coconut milk breaks and separates (cracks), look for traces of yellow-green oil bubbling at the edge or a slightly dark yellow-green oily film on top.

If after adding all of the coconut milk you want to force further cracking for deeper flavor, splash in some water and cook at a hard boil, stirring occasionally. If oil appears in 2 to 3 minutes, success! If cracked coconut milk eludes you today, move on.

Braise the chicken and lemongrass: Add the chicken, lemongrass, and fish sauce. If needed, add water just to cover the chicken. Adjust the heat to maintain a gentle simmer and cook uncovered, turning the chicken occasionally, until it is tender, 35 to 55 minutes, depending on the size of the pieces. To test, poke a chicken piece with a knife, and if the juices run clear, the chicken is ready. Add the sweet peppers and cook until just softened, about 2 minutes.

Fine-tune and serve: Turn off the heat, then taste the sauce. It should be spicy, fresh (you can detect the lemongrass and turmeric), salty, and barely sweet. For extra savory oomph, stir in fish sauce by the 1 tsp. Stir in 1 tsp of the sugar, taste, and cautiously add more by the ½ tsp if needed to round out the flavors. (Don't add more than 3 tsp of sugar total, or the curry will be candy sweet.) To mellow the sauce, splash in some water. The finished sauce should be medium thick and velvety. To test, coat the back of a spoon with the sauce and run a finger through it. If the line holds firmly for a few seconds, the sauce is ready.

Stir in the basil, if using, submerging the leaves to prevent browning, then drop in the Thai chilies (if using). Transfer to a shallow serving bowl and serve. Remind guests that the lemongrass is inedible. Remind them, too, that that they can avoid the chilies or eat them at their own peril.

NOTES

When using frozen or mild-tasting lemongrass, add 1 or 2 extra stalks to pump up flavor.

To serve fewer people, halve the recipe (and use a smaller pan). The cook time should be the same.

พริกแกงใต้ | Prik Gaeng Tai

Southern Curry Paste

Bright with chili heat, this orange-yellow paste lays the foundation for Southern Thai preparations such as the sensational grilled beef and crab curries on pages 171 and 172 and the stir-fried pork on page 175. Earthy turmeric and pungent black pepper are two ingredients that set fiery Southern curry paste apart from those of other regions. They also are anti-inflammatory and aid in digestion, so don't be alarmed by the amount used.

To help the paste ingredients process to a fine texture in a machine, soak and finely chop the small dried chilies. A long soak also helps to reduce some of the heat. That said, prik gaeng tai is characteristically very hot, so use as much chili as you can stand. You'll find additional tips in Notes on how to step down the heat, but don't take it down too far. Like my father loves to say, "Southern curries shouldn't be polite."

INGREDIENT	X1 FOR SMALL AND MEDIUM PROCESSORS	X2 FOR BLENDER AND ALL PROCESSORS
Seeded dried prik jinda or árbol chilies (see Notes)	24 to 30g | 0.8 to 1 oz	48 to 60g | 1.6 to 2 oz
Garlic cloves, coarsely chopped	90g | 3 oz	180g | 6 oz
Shallots, coarsely chopped	60g | 2 oz	120g | 4 oz
Lemongrass, finely chopped (from 2 or 4 thick stalks)	45g | 1.5 oz	90g | 3 oz
Peeled fresh turmeric, chopped (from 2 big knobs)	30g | 1 oz	60g | 2 oz
Gapi (Thai shrimp paste)	20g | 1 Tbsp packed	40g | 2 Tbsp packed
Chopped makrut or regular lime rind	1 Tbsp packed	2 Tbsp packed
Freshly ground black pepper	3.6g | 1½ tsp	7.2g | 1 Tbsp
Kee Lo (Cracked Coconut Milk, page 53) or virgin coconut oil, if needed to ease grinding		
Approximate yield	1 cup (275g)	2 cups (550g)

The yield will be larger if kee lo or coconut oil is added.

Soak and chop the chilies: Put the seeded chilies into a medium bowl, add warm water to cover, and let soak until softened and pliable, about 10 minutes. Drain in a fine-mesh strainer, then firmly squeeze or use a silicone spatula to firmly press out as much water as possible (some lingering water is inevitable). Transfer to a food processor or blender.

Assemble and make the paste: Add the garlic, shallots, lemongrass, turmeric, gapi, lime rind, and black pepper and process until a finely textured paste forms, pausing to scrape down the sides of the bowl or jar as needed. If moisture is needed to get things moving in the machine, add the kee lo by the 1 Tbsp, using up to ¼ cup (60ml) total for a single batch.

Use the curry paste right away, or transfer to a jar, cap tightly, and refrigerate for up to 2 weeks or freeze in ½-cup (120ml) portions for up to 3 months.

NOTES

For less chili heat, use a one-to-one combination of 12 to 15g seeded dried prik chee fa or puya chilies and 12 to 15g seeded dried prik jinda or árbol chilies per batch.

When fresh turmeric is unavailable, use 1 Tbsp high-quality ground turmeric per batch, adding it toward the end of processing.

If you already have Prik Gaeng Ped (Red Curry Paste, page 144) made, use it for a quick Southern curry paste hack. Mix ½ cup (110g) prik gaeng ped with 2 tsp ground turmeric and 1 tsp freshly ground black pepper. You'll have about ½ cup (130g) to play with.

แกงเนื้อย่างใบชะพลู | Gaeng Neua Yang Bai Chaplu

Southern Curry with Grilled Beefsteak and Bai Chaplu

SERVES 4

When beef is used in Thai curries, it's often simmered for a long time, until tender and falling apart, like the massaman beef cheeks and panang short ribs on pages 157 and 153. This outstanding Southern Thai curry takes a different route. Sliced grilled rare steak is added to the spicy, herbaceous curry right at the end so it never gets tough. The beef, which has acquired a layer of caramelized, fatty flavor from being seared over high heat, takes up the curry's boldness but still retains its original beefiness. The curry is finished with wild betel leaf (bai chaplu; see page 28), which imparts unique piquant notes. If you cannot find wild betel leaves, use a big handful of fresh Thai or holy basil leaves (and tweak the curry's name!). Use the best steak you can afford, and your curry will taste ไฮโซ—"hi(gh) so(ciety)" Thai.

---

450 to 680g | 1¼ to 1½ lb boneless rib eye or sirloin steak, about 1¼ inches (3.1cm) thick

60ml | 4 Tbsp fish sauce, divided, plus more to taste

Two 400ml | 13.5-oz cans coconut milk

130g | ½ cup Prik Gaeng Tai (Southern Curry Paste, page 168)

1 tsp firmly packed Thai palm sugar

Crushed dried Thai chili or Prik Pon (Toasted Chili Flakes page 46), optional

8 large wild betel leaves, fresh or thawed

1 small lime, halved

Marinate and sear the beef: Use a paper towel to pat excess moisture from the beef, then rub 2 Tbsp of the fish sauce all over the beef. Refrigerate, uncovered, for about 2 hours.

Prepare a charcoal or gas grill for direct-heat cooking over a very hot fire. Sear the cold, wet beef over the fire, turning once, until light brown on both sides, 30 to 60 seconds on each side. Alternatively, use a cast-iron or carbon-steel pan over high heat, adding a light film of oil if needed. Set the rare beef aside to cool.

Bloom the paste and build the sauce: Set a large wok or medium-large pot over medium heat until warm, about 2 minutes, then add a good ¼ cup (60ml) of the coconut milk. When the coconut milk comes to a boil, add the curry paste and cook, stirring actively, until the paste is fragrant and no longer smells raw, about 2 minutes.

Add the remaining coconut milk in four or five batches, stirring and letting things bubble vigorously for 3 to 8 minutes to reduce and thicken slightly before adding the next batch. Remember to stir and scrape the pan bottom frequently to prevent scorching. Adjust the heat to maintain the bubbly cooking action and/or to prevent the sauce from spitting. As the coconut milk breaks and separates (cracks), look for traces of bright orange-red oil bubbling at the edge or a slightly dark red oily film on top.

If after adding all of the coconut milk you want to force further cracking for deeper flavor, splash in some water and cook at a hard boil, stirring occasionally. If oil appears in 2 to 3 minutes, success! If cracked coconut milk eludes you today, move on.

Stir in the remaining 2 Tbsp fish sauce and the sugar, then taste the sauce. It should be hot and salty with no pronounced sweetness. As needed, stir in fish sauce by the 1 tsp for a saltier finish or crushed chili by the pinch for extra fire. Let the sauce finish loud. The finished sauce should be medium thick and velvety. To test, coat the back of a spoon with the sauce and run a finger through it. If the line holds firmly for a few seconds, the sauce is ready. Turn down the heat to low and cover partially to keep warm.

Add the beef and wild betel leaves and serve: Cut the beef across the grain into slices about ⅓ inch (8mm) thick. Return the sauce to a swift simmer, add the beef, give the pot a stir, and then turn off the heat. Tear the wild betel leaves into large pieces, drop them into the pot, and gently stir them into the curry. Squeeze in lime juice to brighten, then transfer to a shallow serving bowl and serve.

NOTE

Instead of beef, feature an equal amount of big shrimp or scallops and skip the fish sauce marination before grilling.

แกงกะทิปู | Gaeng Gati Pu

Southern Thai Crab Curry

SERVES 4

Delicate crabmeat can withstand a bath in feisty prik gaeng tai with no problem: The curry sauce has the fatty, briny, sweet, salty, spicy notes to match and amplify the crab without overwhelming it. Crab goes well with black pepper, and the prik gaeng tai contains a healthy amount. Use the best quality crabmeat possible. I prefer to pick my own, but you can buy lump crabmeat, if you like. Add fragrant wild betel leaves (bai chaplu; see page 28) for a home run. Enjoy gaeng gati pu with lots of rice to absorb and distribute the intense flavors. Or serve the curry Phuket-style with noodles, as photographed (see Note).

Two 400ml | 13.5-oz cans coconut milk, unshaken

130g | ½ cup Prik Gaeng Tai (Southern Curry Paste, page 168)

2 Tbsp fish sauce, plus more to taste

10g | 1½ tsp firmly packed Thai palm sugar, plus more to taste

300g | 10 oz cooked crabmeat

12g | 10 medium wild betel leaves, fresh or thawed, cut into chiffonade

Prep the coconut milk: Collect ½ cup (120ml) thick coconut milk from the top of one of the cans and reserve for garnish. Whisk the remaining coconut milk to blend.

Bloom the paste and cook the curry: Set a medium pot or wok over medium heat until warm, about 2 minutes, then add a good ¼ cup (60ml) of the coconut milk. When the coconut milk comes to a boil, add the curry paste and cook, stirring actively, until the paste is fragrant and no longer smells raw, about 2 minutes.

Add the remaining coconut milk in three or four batches, stirring and letting things bubble vigorously for 3 to 8 minutes to reduce and thicken slightly before adding the next batch. Remember to stir and scrape the pan bottom frequently to prevent scorching. Adjust the heat to maintain the bubbly cooking action and/or to prevent the sauce from spitting. As the coconut milk breaks and separates (cracks), look for traces of orange-red oil bubbling at the edge or a slightly dark red oily film on top.

If after adding all of the coconut milk you want to force further cracking for deeper flavor, splash in some water and cook at a hard boil, stirring occasionally. If oil appears in 2 to 3 minutes, success! If cracked coconut milk eludes you today, move on.

Stir in the fish sauce and sugar. After the sugar melts, turn down the heat to low and stir in the crab, saving a little for garnish. When the crab has warmed through, after 2 to 3 minutes, turn off the heat. The finished sauce should be medium thick and velvety. To test, coat the back of a spoon with the sauce and run a finger through it. If the line holds firmly for a few seconds, the sauce is ready.

Taste the sauce. It should be hot and salty with a slight sweetness at the end. As needed, stir in fish sauce by the 1 tsp for a saltier finish or sugar by the ½ tsp to temper the heat. You should taste the crab's sweet brininess along with the rich, hot curry.

Finish and serve: Gently stir most of the wild betel leaves into the curry (save some for garnish) and transfer the curry to a shallow serving bowl. Spoon as much of the reserved thick coconut milk in the center as you like, then crown with the reserved crabmeat and wild betel leaves and serve.

NOTE

For Phuket-style eating, serve the curry with sen mee (fine or small round rice noodles such as Wai Wai brand). Top the noodles with crumbled Gratiem Grob (Garlic Chips, page 56) plus a drizzle of the tasty oil left over from frying the garlic. You'll get bonus Phuket street cred for enjoying gaeng gati pu this way.

คั่วกลิ้งหมู | Kua Kling Moo

Hunter's Dry Curry

SERVES 4

Kua kling originated as a dry curry made from game meat. In the jungles of Southern Thailand, hunters would cook their kill twice, initially grilling or smoking the meat after butchering to preserve it for transport home. Before being eaten, the smoked meat was cooked again with a very spicy, pungent curry paste full of chili (which is antiseptic) and plenty of soothing turmeric to tame the wildness.

Nowadays, kua kling is very popular in Thailand, where it's commonly prepared with ground pork. The key is prik gaeng tai, so make the curry paste ahead and keep it in the fridge (or freezer) to put together this spicy, savory Southern classic in a snap. Instead of pork, you can use ground lamb or beef. If you want to walk on the wild side and honor the dish's origins, make kua kling with game meat, like venison or boar. Serve this crowd-pleaser with lots of rice to absorb the flavors. To cool the heat, enjoy the stir-fry with thickly sliced cucumber.

1½ Tbsp neutral oil, such as rice bran, or virgin coconut oil

90 to 130g | ⅓ to ½ cup Prik Gaeng Tai (Southern Curry Paste, page 168), to taste

450g | 1 lb ground pork, about 80 percent lean, broken into big chunks

1 to 2 Tbsp fish sauce

20g | 1 Tbsp firmly packed Thai palm sugar, plus more to taste

1 fresh Fresno or other medium-hot chili, seeded and thinly sliced

3 to 4g | 3 to 4 Tbsp finely slivered makrut lime leaf (see Note)

Bloom the paste: In a large wok over medium heat, warm the oil. Add the curry paste and stir-fry until it is slightly darkened and no longer smells raw, 2 to 3 minutes.

Stir-fry the meat: Increase the heat to medium-high and add the pork. Stir, mash, and separate the meat into nubbins coated with curry paste, then stir-fry the pork until it is no longer a raw pink, 2 to 3 minutes. Season with 1 Tbsp of the fish sauce and the sugar, then keep stir-frying to incorporate the seasonings, fully cook the pork, and concentrate flavor, 3 to 5 minutes. Taste the curry. It should have a spicy, salty finish. Gradually add as much of the remaining 1 Tbsp fish sauce as needed. When done, the pork nubbins should be a rich brown with a yellow tinge. You can overcook the pork a little and it will still be OK.

Finish and serve: Turn off the heat and stir in most of the chili slices and lime leaf slivers. Transfer the curry to a serving plate, leaving any excess fat behind in the pan if you wish. Top with the remaining lime leaf and chili for flavor and flair and serve.

NOTE

Makrut lime leaves finish this stir-fry with the perfect perfume and flavor. Although it is fine to skip them if you don't have them, they do make kua kling extra special. You'll find tips on slivering the leaves on page 31 to encourage you.

แกงหมูชะมวง | Gaeng Moo Chamuang

Pork and Sour Leaf Curry

SERVES 6 TO 8

The eastern coast of Thailand is famous for this rich and slightly tart curry, which is typically made with bai chamuang, the sour leaves of the *Garcinia cowa* (cowa mangosteen) tree. When I'm in Thailand, I always use the slender leaves (as photographed on the opposite page). But when I'm in my kitchen elsewhere and chamuang is nowhere to be found, I make this curry with bright green, tart sorrel. If you're lucky to have chamuang within reach, see the Notes.

Devoid of coconut milk, gaeng moo chamuang has an unusual savory richness from the long-cooked pork plus a healthy amount of shrimp paste and aromatics. It's all balanced out by a tangy brightness from the sour leaf, a light sweetness from the palm sugar, and a hint of smoky chili. This recipe, a specialty of my aunt Pah Tum (Dr. Pathum Snitwongse), beguiles with its friendly yet intense, distinctive character. Few people appreciate and know "how to eat it," let alone make it well. Prepare this curry once and you'll fall in love with it as I have.

CHAMUANG PASTE

40g | 1.3 oz seeded dried prik chee fa or puya chilies

1 Tbsp neutral oil, such as rice bran

80g | 2.6 oz shallots, quartered (2 medium-large)

50g | 1.7 oz garlic cloves (⅓ cup)

20g | 2 Tbsp coarsely chopped, peeled galangal

60g | 3 Tbsp packed gapi (Thai shrimp paste)

Make the curry paste: Put the dried chilies into a strainer, rinse briefly with water, and drain well. Use a paper towel to pat away moisture (wet chilies won't fry well for the paste).

Set a large wok over medium heat. When the pan is hot, add the oil and swirl the pan to coat with the oil. Add the shallots, garlic, and galangal and stir-fry until fragrant and beginning to turn a little golden brown, a good 2 minutes. Add the chilies and stir-fry until fragrant, glistening, and lightly toasted, about 1 minute.

Remove the pan from the heat and transfer the contents to a small to medium food processor (this smallish batch of paste won't come together in a blender). Add the gapi and process, pausing often to scrape down the sides of the bowl (be patient!), until a fine paste forms, 3 to 5 minutes. If moisture is needed to ease processing, add water by the 1 Tbsp but no more than ¼ cup (60ml). Use immediately, or scrape into an airtight container and refrigerate for up to 2 weeks or freeze for up to 3 months. You should have about 1 cup (250g) of paste.

CURRY

2½ Tbsp neutral oil, such as rice bran

750g | 1⅔ lb boneless pork shoulder, cut into 2- to 3-inch (5 to 7.5cm) cubes

750g | 1⅔ lb boneless pork belly, cut into 2- to 3-inch (5 to 7.5cm) cubes (see Notes)

120g | 6 Tbsp firmly packed Thai palm sugar, plus more to taste

160ml | ⅔ cup Nam Makam (Tamarind Liquid, page 52)

90ml | brimming ⅓ cup fish sauce, plus more to taste

1.1L | 5 cups water

250g | generous 8 oz sorrel leaves, roughly torn, plus some small leaves for garnish (see Notes for using chamuang)

Unseasoned rice vinegar, for finishing

Bloom the paste and cook the curry: Set a large pot over medium heat and add the oil. When the oil is barely shimmering, add all of the paste and cook, stirring vigorously, until the paste stains the pot orange-red, is fragrant, and has darkened slightly, 2 to 3 minutes. Add the pork shoulder and belly and stir to coat well with the paste. If things look too dry, add a bit of water to moisten. Continue cooking, stirring continuously, until the pork is lightly browned, 3 to 4 minutes. Stir in the sugar, tamarind, and fish sauce, then continue to cook to further caramelize the pork, about 2 minutes. Pour in the water to just barely cover the pork; add a bit more, if needed.

Bring the pot to a boil over medium-high heat, then immediately lower the heat to a simmer. Cover partially and cook, stirring now and then, until the pork is tender, 2 to 3 hours, adjusting the heat as needed to maintain a gentle simmer. Uncover, skim off some of the fat from the top if you like, and then stir in the sorrel leaves. They will quickly wilt and infuse the sauce.

Fine-tune and serve: Taste the sauce. It should be about equally sour and salty, with a little sweetness to finish. If needed, add a splash of vinegar or fish sauce or a bit of sugar. The sauce will also taste rich and luscious from all the collagen in the pork. Turn off the heat, transfer to a shallow serving bowl, garnish with extra sorrel leaves, and serve.

NOTES

To use chamuang leaves for this curry, you will need a generous 8 oz (250g) of roughly torn leaves. Add half of them before adding the water to the pork. Use only ⅓ cup (80ml) tamarind liquid because the leaves will add enough acidity to flavor the curry. Add the other half of the leaves when the pork is tender.

The curry paste can be split into two equal batches. Simply halve all of the curry ingredients and cook the curry in a medium-large pot. The timing will be the same. Refrigerate or freeze the second batch of paste until you have a hankering for this curry.

Select meaty pork belly, with or without skin. Chamuang curry can also be made with all pork shoulder, if you prefer a leaner curry.

แกงส้มชะอมทอด | Gaeng Som Cha-Om Tod

Sour Curry with Shrimp and Fluffy Herb Omelet

SERVES 4

If I had to choose only one curry to eat for the rest of my life, it would be this one, Central Thai-style gaeng som. It is such a comforting curry to me—tangy, salty, and just spicy enough to hurt a little, but never too much because of the tiny bit of sweetness at the end.

This version of gaeng som, with a fluffy crisp omelet stuffed full of herbaceous, slightly bitter cha-om (climbing wattle; see page 28) is a favorite of my mom's. Fresh cha-om is rare, so I sometimes fry up the eggs with other tender leaves, such as a mix of herbs, spring onions, or arugula. Use what's around. Feel free to make the kai jeow (fried omelet) to enjoy as a side dish for rice.

SOUR CURRY PASTE

10g | 0.3 oz seeded dried prik chee fah or puya chilies

2g | 0.07 oz seeded prik jinda or árbol chilies (see Notes)

25g | 0.8 oz coarsely chopped garlic (2½ Tbsp)

50g | 1.7 oz coarsely chopped shallots (scant ½ cup)

10g | 1 Tbsp chopped, peeled galangal

5g | 1½ tsp chopped, unpeeled grachai (fingerroot)

10g | 1½ tsp packed gapi (Thai shrimp paste)

Make the curry paste: Snip the chilies into pieces no bigger than 1 inch (2.5cm), dropping them into a small bowl. Add warm water to cover and let soak until softened and pliable, 3 to 5 minutes. Drain in a fine-mesh strainer, then firmly squeeze or use a silicone spatula to firmly press out as much water as possible (some lingering water is inevitable!). Transfer the chilies to a small to medium food processor (see Notes).

Add the garlic, shallots, galangal, grachai, and gapi to the processor and process to a fine texture. If needed, let the partially ground paste sit for 5 to 10 minutes to soften stubborn chili pieces, then restart the machine; add 1 Tbsp water if you must. Scrape the rusty-red paste into a measuring cup. You should have about ⅔ cup (150g), depending on the amount of water used.

CURRY

600g | 1⅓ lb large shell-on, head-on shrimp (see Notes)

1.1L | 5 cups water

90ml | 6 Tbsp Nam Makam (Tamarind Liquid, page 52), plus more to taste

50g | 2½ Tbsp firmly packed Thai palm sugar, plus more to taste

60ml | ¼ cup fish sauce, plus more to taste

Prep the shrimp: Peel the shrimp, dropping the shells and heads into a medium pot. Then devein the shrimp bodies, transfer the shrimp to a medium bowl, cover, and refrigerate until needed. Add the water to the pot holding the shrimp shells and bring to a boil over high heat. Turn down the heat to maintain a brisk simmer and simmer, uncovered, until the liquid has reduced by one-third, 20 to 30 minutes.

Cook the curry: Strain the shrimp broth through a fine-mesh strainer set over a large measuring cup. You should have about 3⅓ cups (800ml). If you are way off the mark, add water as needed to equal the measure, or return the broth to the heat, boil down as needed, and then return to the measuring cup. Wash the pot, return the broth to it, and bring to a boil over high heat. Stir in the curry paste, then turn down the heat to maintain a low, steady boil and cook to slightly mellow the raw acridness of the paste and to reduce the broth by about 20 percent to create a light sauce, about 5 minutes.

Lower the heat to a simmer, then stir in the tamarind, sugar, and fish sauce. Taste the curry. The flavor should be tart, salty, and a tad sweet followed by a slightly edgy heat that hurts just a little. If needed, add tamarind by the 1½ tsp, sugar by the 1 tsp, and fish sauce by the 1 tsp to adjust the balance. Remember that the curry broth should be quite robustly flavored because it's a sauce and not a soup! Turn down the heat to low and cover partially.

CONTINUED

FRIED OMELET

3 large eggs, at room temperature

2 tsp fish sauce

240ml | 1 cup fresh cha-om or coarsely chopped mixed fresh herbs (such as any kind of basil, dill, chives, or green onions), spun dry

1½ tsp cornstarch (optional)

Neutral oil, such as rice bran, for deep-frying

Fry the omelet: In a small bowl, combine the eggs and fish sauce. Use a fork to beat vigorously until free-flowing and foamy, 30 to 45 seconds. Coat the leafy bits in the cornstarch (if using) and then stir into the eggs.

For frying, select a tall pan about 6 inches (15cm) wide at the bottom, such as a 2.5-qt (2.5L) saucier or Windsor pan (see Notes for an equipment tip). Warm the pan over medium heat, add oil to a depth of 1 inch (2.5cm), and swirl the pan to coat the sides. Raise the heat to medium-high and heat the oil to 375°F (190°C). The oil is ready if, when you flick a bit of egg into it, the egg floats on top in small puffs.

From about 6 inches (15cm) above the surface of the oil, pour in all of the egg mixture. The oil will dramatically bubble up and then mellow. Using the fork, gently stir to fluff the mixture and, if needed, distribute the greenery. Fry until the edges are golden and lightly crisp, 3 to 4 minutes. The underside should be golden brown (use a spider or a spatula to lift an edge and sneak a peek).

Scoot the spider under the omelet and, with the help of the spatula to hold the omelet in place, gently flip the omelet. Lower the heat to medium and fry the second side to a luscious golden brown, 2 to 3 minutes. To show the prettier side, turn the omelet over as you remove it from the oil. Remove from the heat. Rest the spider with the omelet on top of the pot to drain. The omelet will lose its puffiness and soften as it sits. It's fine to enjoy it at room temperature.

Assemble and serve: Return the curry to a roaring boil, add the shrimp, stir to separate, and then turn off the heat. Let sit for 3 to 5 minutes while the residual heat cooks the shrimp to perfection (trust me). Transfer to a warm shallow serving bowl, top with the omelet, and present your gaeng som immediately. Use serving spoons to portion the egg into wedges and serve with the shrimp and sauce.

NOTES

For a milder curry, omit the dried jinda (árbol) chilies and use 0.4 oz (12g) total of dried prik chee fa, puya, guajillo, New Mexico, or California chilies. If you decide to make a double batch of the curry paste, any size processor or a blender can be used.

If head-on shrimp are unavailable, buy 1 lb (450g) shell-on shrimp and use the shells for the broth.

Prep the curry sauce and shrimp hours in advance and refrigerate. Reheat the curry, fry the omelet, cook the shrimp in the curry, and assemble to serve.

A smallish saucier or Windsor pan is ideal for frying the omelet because its narrow shape constrains the omelet size, making the fluffy, thicker result easy to manage and flip. A medium wok works too.

Adding cornstarch to the beaten egg mixture yields a crispier result.

แกงฮังเล | Gaeng Hunglay

Pork Belly Hunglay Curry

SERVES 6 TO 8

The Northern provinces of Thailand, bordering Myanmar, influenced this brick-red curry, which entices you with a heady fragrance that bridges traditions from the Indian subcontinent with those of Southeast Asia. Its sweet, tart, and exquisitely rich flavor comes from a long simmer of pork belly in an intricately spiced curry.

Gaeng hunglay is defined by a special masala, which you should really make yourself. Substitute regular curry powder, if you *really* must. My masala formula is organized into groups so the spices can be phased into the pan, enabling you to toast them all evenly and avoid scorching. While you're at it, make extra masala for the khao soi gai noodle soup on page 275. See the Notes for additional tips on the spices and other ingredients.

HUNGLAY MASALA

Group 1

3g | 1 Tbsp whole star anise, broken into petal-like segments

2g | 2-inch piece cinnamon stick, crushed into small pieces in a mortar

2g | 2 or 3 long peppers, gently crushed into small pieces in a mortar

3g | 1 tsp black peppercorns

1g | ½ tsp whole cloves

Group 2

5g | 1 Tbsp coriander seeds

2g | 1 tsp green cardamom pods, hulled, or scant ½ tsp cardamom seeds

2g | scant 1 tsp fenugreek seeds

3g | 1½ tsp cumin seeds

2g | ¾ tsp fennel seeds

1g | 1 or 2 mace blades, crumbled into small pieces

Group 3

3g | 1 tsp ground turmeric

1g | 1 tsp freshly grated nutmeg

1g | ¼ plus ⅛ tsp ground sand ginger

Prepare the masala: Measure the three groups of spices into three separate small bowls. Set the bowls near the stovetop.

In a small saucepan over medium-low heat, toast the Group 1 spices (star anise, cinnamon, etc.), shaking the pan often, until sweetly fragrant, about 2 minutes. Add the Group 2 spices (coriander, cardamom, etc.) to the Group 1 spices in the pan and toast, shaking the pan often, until the mixture is perfumy, about 1 minute.

Remove the pan from the heat, pour the Group 3 ground spices into the pan, and stir to blend well. The residual heat will be enough to warm and toast the final group of spices.

Let cool briefly, then transfer the toasted spices to an electric grinder and grind to a fine powder (or pound with a mortar and pestle). You should have about ¼ cup (30g), enough for a batch of this curry. Set aside to make this curry, or transfer to a tightly capped glass jar and store in a cool cupboard for up to 3 months or freeze for up to 1 year.

HUNGLAY CURRY PASTE

25g | 0.9 oz seeded dried prik chee fa or puya chilies

100g | 3.3 oz shallots, coarsely chopped (scant 1 cup)

40g | 1.3 oz garlic cloves, coarsely chopped (¼ cup)

30g | 1 oz lemongrass, chopped (⅓ cup, from 1 thick stalk)

2 Tbsp extra-virgin coconut oil, softened or melted

5g | 1½ tsp finely chopped, peeled turmeric, or 1.5g | ½ tsp ground turmeric

30g | 1 Tbsp plus 2 tsp hatcho or red (aka) miso

Make the curry paste: Put the seeded chilies into a small bowl, add warm water to cover, and let soak until softened and pliable, 3 to 5 minutes. Drain in a fine-mesh strainer, then firmly squeeze or use a silicone spatula to firmly press out as much water as possible (some lingering water is inevitable!). Transfer to a small to medium food processor.

CONTINUED

Add the shallots, garlic, lemongrass, coconut oil, turmeric, and miso and process to a fine texture. This may take several minutes, including frequent pausing to scrape down the sides of the bowl. If moisture is needed to get the ingredients moving, add water by 1 Tbsp but no more than ¼ cup (60ml). You should have about 1 cup (250g) of brick-red paste. Use immediately, or transfer to an airtight container and store in the refrigerator for up to 2 weeks or freeze for up to 3 months.

CURRY

2 Tbsp extra-virgin coconut oil

1 batch Hunglay Curry Paste

1 batch Hunglay Masala

1.8 kg | 4 lb boneless meaty pork belly, cut into 2- to 3-inch (5 to 7.5cm) cubes (see Notes)

75g | ½ cup chopped pineapple, preferably fresh or thawed frozen

80ml | ⅓ cup fish sauce, plus more to taste

45ml | 3 Tbsp Thai black soy sauce

60g | 3 Tbsp firmly packed Thai palm sugar, plus more to taste

80ml | ⅓ cup Nam Makam (Tamarind Liquid, page 52), plus more to taste

50g | ½ cup matchstick-cut ginger

50g | ⅓ cup salted or unsalted roasted peanuts

50g | ⅓ cup pickled garlic cloves, homemade (page 55) or purchased

Homemade pickled garlic brine (if available)

Bloom the paste for the curry: In a large pot or Dutch oven over medium heat, melt the coconut oil. Add the curry paste and cook, stirring actively, until fragrant and slightly darkened, 2 to 3 minutes. Stir in the masala and cook, stirring, until fragrant, 15 to 30 seconds.

Simmer until tender: Add the pork and pineapple and stir vigorously and continuously to coat the pork with the seasonings, lightly sear it, render a little fat, and slightly soften the pineapple, 3 to 5 minutes. Lower the heat if needed to avoid scorching. Add the fish sauce, soy sauce, sugar, and tamarind, then stir again to mix and scrape bits sticking to the pot bottom. Add water just to cover the meat, bring the pot to a boil, and immediately turn down the heat to a gentle simmer. Continue to cook, uncovered and barely simmering, for 2 hours. Then stir in the ginger, peanuts, and pickled garlic, reserving a little of each to use for garnishing the finished dish.

Continue simmering until the pork is completely tender, about 3 hours total. Skim off as much fat from the top as you like.

Finesse and serve: Taste the sauce. It should be salty and sweet yet finish with a tart brightness. If needed, fine-tune the flavor with a bit of fish sauce, sugar, tamarind, and/or homemade pickled garlic brine (the commercial brine can have a chemical taste, so I don't suggest it). The sauce should taste rich and luscious from all the collagen in the pork.

Transfer to a shallow serving bowl, garnish with the reserved ginger, peanuts, and pickled garlic, and serve.

NOTES

For the masala, shop for the ingredients at a spice shop or Asian market (look near the Chinese five-spice powder). Long pepper may be labeled *Piper longum*. Sand ginger may be called sha ginger powder or sha jiang fen (Mandarin Chinese).

Can't find whole spices like mace blades? Weigh out ground spices and add them with the Group 3 to avoid burning.

To use the curry paste as two smaller batches, simply halve the curry ingredients (use a scant ½ cup | 125g paste and half of the masala) and cook in a medium-large pot. The timing remains the same.

Use skin-on pork belly if available for a bit of wonderful chew and richness, but skinless pork belly works fine too. Select pork belly with a fair amount of lean meat, like what may be used for Chinese roast pork or Italian porchetta. If you can't find meaty pork belly, combine pork shoulder and fatty belly in a one-to-one ratio.

พริกแกงเมือง | Prik Gaeng Mueng

Northern Curry Paste

Mildly hot and deeply umami, this curry paste serves as the mother flavor base for the summery curry on page 186, pork-and-tomato namprik ong relish on page 123, and the fried rice variation on page 258. The key is tua nao, a fermented soybean paste that is used wet like miso or dried between leaves. Tua nao is hard to source outside of Thailand, so at my restaurants in San Francisco, we dehydrate hatcho miso as thin disks (think DVD size) and keep them in our larder. The microwave method in the main recipe is a quick hack for a small quantity; check the Note for an oven method, which you can use for multiple disks and be totally set for future recipes!

INGREDIENT	X1 FOR SMALL TO MEDIUM PROCESSORS	X2 FOR BLENDER AND ALL PROCESSORS
Hatcho miso (see page 22) or tua nao (dried fermented soybean)	30g | 1½ Tbsp miso, or 20g | 0.7 oz tua nao	60g | 3 Tbsp miso, or 40g | 1.4 oz tua nao
Seeded dried prik chee fa or puya chilies, snipped into 1-inch (2.5cm pieces)	35g | 1.2 oz	70g | 2.4 oz
Shallots, coarsely chopped	100g | 3.3 oz	200g | 6.6 oz
Garlic cloves, coarsely chopped	75g | 2.5 oz	150g | 5 oz
Peeled galangal, finely chopped	25g | 3 Tbsp	50g | 6 Tbsp
Approximate yield	1 cup (250g)	2 cups (500g)

The yield will be larger if water is added.

Make shortcut tua nao: If using premade tua nao, skip to the next step. For each batch, when starting from miso, roll it into a ball, then flatten the ball into a patty ¼ inch (6mm) thick. Place the patty between two pieces of parchment paper roughly the size of a greeting card. Use a rolling pin to roll the miso into a very thin disk about 4½ inches (11cm) wide. Remove the top piece of parchment paper. Using a sharp knife, quarter the miso disk to make it easier to flip later.

To dehydrate the miso (still on the parchment), microwave it on medium-low power until a thick rim of bubbles appears, about 1½ minutes. Let cool for a few seconds, carefully flip the miso over on the parchment, then microwave again for 1½ minutes, pausing to flip every 30 to 45 seconds. You'll eventually be able to separate the miso into wedges. Expect steam to rise as the miso transforms into tua nao. There should be slight dampness at the end. If there are soft patches, lower the power a notch and microwave in 30-second bursts until dryish. (No microwave? See the recipe Note.) Let cool and dry completely. Your tua nao should weigh almost 0.7 oz (20g).

Toast the tua nao: In a vegetable grill pan or perforated skillet (or a cast-iron or carbon-steel skillet), toast the tua nao over medium heat, turning it often, until fragrant and blisters have formed here and there, 30 to 45 seconds if using a grill pan or perforated skillet (or up to 10 minutes if using a cast-iron or carbon-steel skillet). Watch the tua noa closely to avoid burning. Some smoking is OK. If needed, turn the heat down or off to coax out flavor and aroma.

Make the paste: Put the toasted tua nao into a food processor or blender, add the chilies, shallots, garlic, and galangal, and process until a dark red paste forms. If moisture is needed to get the ingredients moving, add water by the 1 Tbsp but no more than ¼ cup (60ml). Use immediately, or transfer to an airtight container and refrigerate for up to 1 month or freeze for up to 6 months.

NOTE

To dehydrate miso for tua nao in the oven, set a rack in the middle position and preheat the oven to 200°F (95°C); use convection mode for good air circulation. Place a large wire cooling rack on a sheet pan. As directed in "Make shortcut tua nao," roll out 1½ Tbsp (30g) of miso between two parchment paper sheets into a thin disk, then quarter it. Set the miso (still on the parchment) on the cooling rack. Slide the sheet pan into the oven and bake until dry, 1½ to 2 hours, flipping the miso disk around the 45-minute mark. To save time and energy, dehydrate multiple disks of miso at the same time on the rack. When cooled, store in a ziplock bag or airtight container for up to 6 months. For accuracy, weigh the tua nao for recipes.

แกงแคมังสวิรัติ | Gaeng Khae Jae

Northern Curry of Summer Vegetables and Aromatic Herbs

SERVES 4

An earthy chameleon, this brothy curry can be served over rice on a plate or in a bowl as a soup. You can prepare it to celebrate vegetables as I have here, or you can feature chicken or pork. It is light because Northern Thai curries often omit coconut milk. This version captures summer's brightness with colorful squash, crunchy corn, bright tomato, and perfumy herbs.

Shop for a mélange of interesting firm squashes because they are not watery and will look great in this curry. I favor UFO-shaped pattypans no wider than 3 inches (7.5cm), slender Costata Romanesco, and other young, crisp summer squashes. In fall, use kabocha or kuri (chestnut) squash. Aromatic wild betel leaves (bai chaplu) are added for a final slightly bitter herbal burst. In addition, climbing wattle (cha-om) is often used in this curry, but because it is rare in the United States, an alternative is included below.

750g | 1⅔ lb assorted smallish summer squashes (such as pattypan and Costata Romanesco)

120g | scant 1 cup fresh corn kernels (from 1 medium ear)

60g | ¼ cup Prik Gaeng Mueng (Northern Curry Paste, page 184)

1 L | 4 cups water

2 Tbsp Thai thin soy sauce, plus more to taste

¼ tsp fine sea salt, plus more to taste

½ tsp firmly packed Thai palm sugar

225g | generous 1 cup firm but ripe cherry tomatoes

6 to 8 squash blossoms (optional; for extra seasonal beauty)

4 or 5 large wild betel leaves, fresh or thawed, torn into medium-large pieces

2 handfuls tender climbing wattle tops, or 1 handful fresh Thai, lemon, or holy basil leaves plus 1 handful torn dill fronds

1 or 2 lime wedges

Prep the vegetables: Trim the squashes and cut into bite-size pieces. For handsome looks and varied texture, cut longish squash like Costata Romanesco into rounds ½ inch (1.25cm) thick to show off their ridges. Round pattypans are best cut into wedges, each about 1 inch (2.5cm) wide. Cut chubby squash into 1-inch (2.5cm) chunks. Put all of the squash pieces into a medium bowl with the corn.

Cook the curry: In a medium braiser or saucepan, combine the curry paste, water, soy sauce, salt, and palm sugar. Set the pan on a big burner and bring to a boil over high heat. Lower the heat to a gentle boil and cook, stirring occasionally, until the paste no longer smells raw, 3 to 5 minutes.

Add the squashes and corn, then continue cooking until the squashes are tender firm, 3 to 4 minutes. (A knife tip inserted into a squash piece should meet light resistance.) Add the tomatoes and continue cooking at a gentle boil until about half of them burst, 2 to 3 minutes. If using squash blossoms, add them now. Turn off the heat, then stir in the wild betel leaves and climbing wattle.

Finesse and finish: Let rest uncovered for about 5 minutes, then taste and brighten the flavors with a squeeze or two of lime juice. Taste again and add salt or soy sauce to arrive at a savory, earthy finish. If you want to slurp the curry like a soup, let it be moderately salty. If you're serving it with rice, make the flavor strongly salty. Either way, enjoy your beautiful curry.

6 หม้อต้ม

Soups

ใบแมงลัก 30 THB
ใบกระเพรา 30 THB
ใบโหระพา 30 THB
ใบยี่หร่า 30 THB
ช่างทอง

Brothy Enchantments

Consider Thai brothy soups, which often unite unexpected ideas and ingredients. For instance, the main character of gaeng ranjuan (page 198)—the name of which means "beguiling soup"—is funky, pungent shrimp paste relish. Tom klong (page 194), on the other hand, gets its flavor from smoked fish and lightly charred lemongrass.

Another recipe in this chapter is tom saap (page 197), a fabulous Isaan soup that deserves to be better known outside of Thailand. My rendition happens to be vegan, but the soup is easily adapted to accommodate omnivores.

From the Thai Chinese tradition, tom gai ya jeen on page 202 is an amber chicken soup laden with Chinese apothecary herbs that manages to taste so miraculously restorative without being overtly medicinal. These are the sort of interesting, unusual soups I've chosen to include in this chapter.

You will recognize some of the recipes here. While I decided against including the perennial favorite tom kha gai, I am going to teach you how to make the *other* favorite Thai soup, tom yum goong (page 193). It's such a mainstay that produce vendors at fresh markets in Thailand often sell small bundles of lemongrass, galangal, and makrut lime leaf for cooks to conveniently whip up a pot. My take on the zippy shrimp classic owes its excellence to my grandmother's incredible namprik pao (chili jam, page 44). (You have some in your fridge by now, yes?)

In Thai cuisine, soups may be served as part of a large meal, often in individual small bowls so you can take your share from the larger communal bowl without dipping your spoon directly into it. But sometimes a soup can fly solo as a stand-alone meal. Just add rice noodles to tom yum goong or tom saap to enjoy for lunch. Or spoon cooked jasmine rice directly into the stuffed cucumber soup on page 201 to instantly make a hearty breakfast soup guaranteed to cure even the worst hangover.

ต้มยำกุ้ง | Tom Yum Goong

Sour-Spicy Prawn Soup with Chili Jam

SERVES 6

Every Thai restaurant you've been to serves tom yum goong. Every Thai cookbook you own has a tom yum goong recipe. But none of those renditions are seasoned with my grandmother's superior chili jam. If you must use store-bought chili jam, the soup won't be as good. This will be the only tom yum goong for you from now on.

900g | 2 lb large shell-on, head-on shrimp or prawns (see Notes)

2.3L | 10 cups water

180g | 1 medium red onion, quartered

60g | 2 oz peeled galangal, sliced ¼ inch (6mm) thick, divided

14 large makrut lime leaves, divided

250g | 4 large lemongrass stalks, trimmed, cut into 3-inch (7.5cm) lengths, and lightly smashed to release scent, divided

120g | 6 small or 3 medium-large shallots, halved

45g | 1 fist-size cluster oyster mushrooms, torn into bite-size pieces (1 cup)

3 to 4 Tbsp Namprik Pao (Grandmother's Chili Jam, page 44), to taste

5 to 8g | 5 to 8 fresh Thai chilies, smashed or kept whole, to taste

80ml | ⅓ cup fish sauce, plus more to taste

120ml | ⅓ cup plus 3 Tbsp lime juice

Tender fresh cilantro sprigs or blossoms, for garnish

Make an aromatic broth: Twist off the shrimp heads, dropping them into a medium-large pot. Peel and devein the shrimp bodies, adding their shells to the pot and refrigerating the flesh in a covered medium bowl.

To the pot of shells and heads, add the water, onion, half of the galangal, and 8 lime leaves, crumpling them before dropping them in. Reserve 6 handsome lemongrass pieces and add the rest to the pot. Bring the pot to a boil over high heat. Turn down the heat to a simmer and continue cooking, uncovered, for 1 hour. Remove from the heat, let cool briefly, and then strain the broth through a fine-mesh strainer set over a large bowl, firmly pressing against the solids to extract all the goodness. You should have about 7 cups (1.7L). If you are way off the mark, add water as needed to equal the measure, or return the broth to the heat and boil down as needed, then return it to the bowl. Discard the solids. Clean the pot and return the broth to it.

Assemble and serve: Bring the broth to a boil over high heat, then lower the heat to a lively simmer. Add the remaining galangal, 6 lime leaves (crumple, then release into the pot), 6 lemongrass pieces, and the shallots, and then cook for 5 minutes.

Increase the heat to high and add the mushrooms, chili jam, and chilies. When the pot returns to a full boil, add the reserved shrimp meat. Stir well to break up the shrimp clumps, then immediately turn off the heat. The residual heat will cook the shrimp through. Add the fish sauce and ⅓ cup (80ml) of the lime juice. The soup should be intensely aromatic, sour, spicy, salty, and with just a touch of sweetness from the chili jam and the shrimp meat. As needed, stir in more fish sauce by the 1 tsp and the remaining 3 Tbsp lime juice.

Divide the soup among six bowls and serve. It is customary to serve tom yum with the galangal, lemongrass, and lime leaves because they continue to scent the soup at the table, but remind guests that they are not edible. Guests can also avoid the chilies or eat them at their own peril.

NOTES

Prawns and shrimp are technically different animals but similar in flavor. For this soup, select big ones suitable for grilling or shrimp cocktail. If head-on shrimp are unavailable, use 1¼ lb (565g) shell-on shrimp.

For a dinner party, prep the ingredients and the broth the day before, then spend just 15 minutes assembling and finishing the soup.

ต้มโคล้ง | Tom Klong

Smoked Fish–Tamarind Soup

SERVES 4 TO 6

Smoky, umami-laden tom klong is a lesser-known soup in the Thai repertoire, but its time in the limelight has arrived! Smoking concentrates the natural glutamates in fish, resulting in umami-rich morsels that take center stage in this soup. In Thailand, tom klong is often made with small dried fish that are briefly grilled or fried to accentuate their crispness before they are added to the soup. Outside of Thailand, I prefer using meaty, smoky chunks of fish like the smoked trout we use in this recipe. Don't skip the charring of the aromatics. It lends a strong character to this stellar soup.

- 165 to 180g | 4 medium or 8 to 10 small shallots, unpeeled
- 150g | 3 medium lemongrass stalks, trimmed and cut into 3-inch (7.5cm) lengths
- 4 to 8 dried prik chee fa or puya chilies, to taste
- 8 makrut lime leaves, divided
- 1L | 4 cups lightly salted chicken or fish broth (see Note)
- 225g | 8 oz smoked rainbow trout or smoked whitefish fillet, skin removed and reserved
- 12 cherry tomatoes
- 1 Tbsp fish sauce
- 1 tsp firmly packed Thai palm sugar
- 45 to 60ml | 3 to 4 Tbsp Nam Makam (Tamarind Liquid, page 52)
- 2 Tbsp coarsely chopped fresh sawtooth herb or cilantro (optional)

Char the aromatics: Set a perforated skillet or vegetable grill pan over medium-high heat. When the pan is hot, add the shallots and lemongrass pieces and char, turning often, until blackened here and there and very slightly softened, 3 to 4 minutes. (Alternatively, grill outdoors or use a ripping-hot cast-iron or carbon-steel skillet.) Transfer the shallots and lemongrass to a cutting board. Lower the heat to medium, add the chilies, and toast, moving them constantly, until charred in a few spots, 10 to 20 seconds. Transfer to the cutting board and let cool briefly alongside the shallots and lemongrass.

Peel and trim the shallots (it's OK if some burnt bits remain or the clusters separate), then halve any that are wider than 1 inch (2.5cm). Bruise the lemongrass with the flat side of a knife (or with a pestle). Stem the chilies, then to seed them yet keep them handsomely intact, whirl a knife or scissor blade tip inside to dislodge the seeds, shaking them out.

Cook the soup: Put the shallots, lemongrass, and chilies into a medium pot. Crumple 4 lime leaves, then drop them into the pot. Add the broth and the skin from the trout fillet, reserving the flesh. Bring to a swift simmer over medium-high heat, then lower the heat to a simmer and continue cooking for 5 minutes.

Break the trout flesh into largish pieces—about 2 inches (5cm)—and drop them into the pot. Add the tomatoes and adjust the heat to maintain a bare simmer. Let cook until a light smokiness develops and the tomatoes begin to burst, 3 to 5 minutes. Stir in the fish sauce, sugar, and 3 Tbsp of the tamarind for a tart edge. Taste and add up to 1 Tbsp more tamarind to create a pleasantly sour taste.

Finish and serve: Remove the spent lime leaves and fish skin, then crumple the remaining fresh lime leaves and drop them into the pot. Retaste to verify the flavors and adjust if needed, then ladle into a communal bowl or individual soup bowls. Top with the sawtooth herb (or cilantro) and serve.

Although the chilies are edible, the lemongrass and lime leaves are there for aroma and are not fun to eat. Pull them from the pot before serving, if you like, but you'll rob tom klong of some of its Thai-ness.

NOTE

If you are using canned or boxed chicken broth, combine it in a two-to-one ratio with water to avoid overly salty soup.

ต้มแซ่บ | Tom Saap

Delicious Isaan Mushroom Soup

SERVES 6

The word *saap* means "delicious" in Northeastern (Isaan) dialect. If you love the bright, citrusy, spicy Isaan laab on page 106, you will think this soup is extra "saap." I often joke that tom saap is basically a soup form of laab, and that's not far from the truth. It relies on some of the same seasonings used in Isaan laab, including khao kua, prik pon, sawtooth herb, and cilantro. This particular tom saap recipe is vegetarian, but you can also make it with cooked meats (see the Notes for details).

- 300g | 10 oz mushrooms (such as maitake, trumpet, shiitake, oyster, or a combo)
- About 2 Tbsp Thai thin soy sauce, divided, plus more to taste
- 1½ Tbsp neutral oil, such as rice bran, divided
- 60g | 1 large lemongrass stalk
- 1 L | 4 cups water
- ¼ tsp fine sea salt, plus more to taste
- ¼ tsp granulated sugar
- About 1 tsp Prik Pon (Toasted Chili Flakes, page 46)
- 40g | 1 medium-large shallot, thinly sliced
- 3 makrut lime leaves
- 3 Tbsp Khao Kua (Isaan Fragrant Rice Powder, page 47)
- 60ml | ¼ cup lime juice
- 4 dried árbol chilies (optional; for the brave)
- 3 Tbsp coarsely chopped or snipped fresh cilantro, sawtooth herb, or a combo

Sear the mushrooms: Trim, then cut or hand tear the mushrooms into large bite-size pieces. Put the mushrooms on a sheet pan (or large plate) and season lightly with about 1 Tbsp of the soy sauce.

Set a heavy medium skillet (cast iron or carbon steel) over high heat. When the pan is hot, add about 2 tsp of the oil and swirl the pan to coat the bottom. Working in two or three batches, add the mushrooms and sear, pressing with a spatula and turning once, until glistening and browned on both sides, 3 to 5 minutes total. Transfer the mushrooms back to the sheet pan or plate and add more oil to the pan as needed before adding the next batch.

Make the broth: Trim the lemongrass as needed, then use a sharp knife to cut superthin slices to yield 1 Tbsp and set aside. Cut the remaining stalk into 3-inch (7.5cm) lengths, smack to crush, and add to a medium pot. Add the water, the remaining 1 Tbsp soy sauce, the salt, and sugar and stir to dissolve the salt and sugar. Taste and add a bit more salt or soy sauce for a strong savory finish.

Bring the pot to a rolling boil over medium-high heat, then lower the heat to medium to maintain a gentle simmer (no need to cook much longer). Season with the prik pon for edgy heat; add extra for full-on Isaan-style burn. (The finishing agents will mellow the flavors a tad.) Add the seared mushrooms, shallot, and lemongrass slices, then crumple the lime leaves and drop them into the pot. Turn off the heat. (If not serving right away, cover the pot. Closer to serving time, reheat to a simmer, and then take off the heat to finish.)

Finish the soup: Stir the pot as you add the khao kua. Add the lime juice, chilies (if using), and herbs. Divide among six bowls, leaving the lemongrass stalk and lime leaves in the pot if you like. Remind guests they can avoid the chilies or enjoy them at their own peril.

NOTES

Instead of mushrooms, use an equal amount of boneless chicken thigh, cut as bite-size pieces; simmer the chicken in the broth with 2 Tbsp fish sauce (omit the soy sauce and salt), then add the prik pon. Or employ pork riblets and increase the water to 5 cups (1.25L); cook the riblets in the broth until tender-chewy, about 1 hour.

For mushroom curry, laab, or fried rice, use the prep and searing technique, then add the result to your recipe.

แกงรัญจวน | Gaeng Ranjuan

Beguiling Beef Soup

SERVES 4

Elegant looking but with the umami-laden punch of namprik gapi (fermented shrimp paste relish), this aromatic soup dates to the era of King Chulalongkorn (King Rama V), who reigned from 1868 to 1910. Popularly called "Beloved King," he led modernization programs and policies, including the emancipation of the enslaved, that helped Thailand avoid European colonization.

The word *ranjuan* in this soup's name means "beguiling," a descriptor bestowed by a royal guest who was enchanted by the simple soup, which relies on well-crafted namprik gapi, citrusy lemongrass, slightly smoky charred shallots, and floral basil. At the end of my rendition, boiling-hot broth kisses thinly sliced beefsteak, cooking it gently and yielding a very special soup.

50g | 1 lemongrass stalk

720ml | 3 cups lightly salted chicken broth

½ batch Namprik Gapi (Standard-but-Not-Ordinary Shrimp Paste Relish, page 119), without eggplant

Fish sauce, for seasoning

90 to 120g | 6 small shallots, unpeeled

180g | 6 oz trimmed beefsteak (see Note), semi-frozen for easier slicing

4 to 8 fresh Thai chilies, lightly smashed

2 mini sweet peppers, quartered and seeded

1 handful fresh Thai basil leaves

Season the broth: Trim the lemongrass as needed, then use a sharp knife to cut superthin slices to yield 2 Tbsp and set aside. Cut the remaining stalk into 3-inch (7.5cm) lengths, smack to crush, add to a small saucepan, and then pour in the broth.

Bring to a boil over medium heat, lower the heat to a simmer, and stir in 3 Tbsp of the namprik gapi. Taste and add more namprik gapi by the 1½ tsp until you have a strong, slightly funky umami-laden flavor. You should use about 4 Tbsp (60ml) total. Taste again and season with fish sauce for extra depth if needed. Cover, turn off the heat, and let steep while you prep the other ingredients.

Char the shallots: Set a perforated skillet or vegetable grill pan over a medium-high flame on a gas stovetop. When the pan is hot, add the shallots and char, turning often, until the skin blackens here and there, about 3 minutes. (Or place under the broiler close to the heat source for about 5 minutes, grill outdoors, or use a ripping-hot cast-iron skillet on the stovetop.) Let cool briefly, then peel and trim (it's OK if some burnt bits remain or the shallot clusters separate). Halve each shallot lengthwise, then add the shallots to the steeping broth to release flavor.

Prepare the steak: Make sure the beef is partly frozen to facilitate thin slicing. Using a sharp knife, very thinly slice the beefsteak across the grain into pieces no thicker than ⅛ inch (3mm).

Assemble and serve: Remove the lemongrass lengths from the broth, then return the broth to a simmer over medium heat. Use a slotted spoon to retrieve the shallots and divide them evenly among four shallow soup bowls. Top each portion of shallots with a low mound of beef, then crown each beef mound with 1 tsp of the sliced lemongrass (reserve the extra).

Scatter the chilies, sweet peppers, and basil around the beef. Taste the broth to verify good, strong flavor and adjust if needed, then return to a rolling boil. Ladle into the bowls (or pour into the bowls at the table to be fancy). Finish with the remaining lemongrass slices, gently rubbing to release their fragrance as you drop them into each bowl. Serve immediately, inviting diners to stir the soup to cook the beef further before eating. Remind guests to avoid the chilies or to eat them at their own peril.

NOTE

New York strip and top sirloin cap are flavorful steak cuts that are easy to trim and cut. Or use beef sliced for shabu shabu, which is sold precut in thin slices.

แกงจืดแตงกวา | Gaeng Jued Tang Kwa

Soothing Stuffed Cucumber Soup

SERVES 6

Thai soups are not all about fire, tang, or coconutty broth. For instance, cozy gaeng jued–style soups soothe the palate and balance the flavors of bold dishes. This stuffed cucumber soup is one that I regularly crave. It is garlicky and peppery with a coriander-flavor backbone, thanks to the saam kleur, which you can make on the spot or measure from the bigger-batch recipe in the Larder chapter. Removing the cucumber center is Thai fruit-carving fun! Gentle poaching yields tender but slightly crunchy cucumber. This handsome gaeng jued is everyday fare suited for dinner parties too.

SAAM KLEUR (THREE BUDDIES PASTE) OR 1¼ TSP PREMADE FROM LARDER (PAGE 57)

4g | 1 large garlic clove

2g | 1 tsp chopped cilantro roots, or ½ tsp chopped cilantro stems

0.3g | 7 white peppercorns

0.3g | 6 black peppercorns

Prep the saam kleur: If using the 1¼ tsp premade saam kleur, put them in a medium bowl and skip to the next step. To make the paste from scratch, use a mortar and pestle to aggressively pound the garlic and cilantro into a coarse paste. Make a well in the center of the paste, add the white and black peppercorns to the well, and pound the peppercorns to smithereens, gradually working the pounded aromatics into the pepper until you have a finely textured mixture, then scrape the paste into a medium bowl.

1½ tsp plus 1 Tbsp fish sauce, divided

225g | 8 oz ground pork

500g | 4 extra-big Persian cucumbers, or 600g | 2 slender English cucumbers

1.5L | 6 cups lightly salted chicken broth

Fine sea salt

Tender fresh cilantro leaves or blossoms, for garnish

Freshly ground black or white pepper, for garnish

Season the pork: Add 1½ tsp of the fish sauce to the saam kleur and mix well. Add the pork and mix in too.

Stuff the cucumbers: Peel the cucumbers completely for a jadelike effect or leave alternating stripes of unpeeled skin for an arty appearance that will darken in the soup a tad. Trim off the ends of each cucumber, then cut the cucumbers crosswise into 2-inch (5cm) sections. Use a Thai fruit carving knife, thin-blade paring knife, or basic vegetable peeler to remove and scrape out the seeds and center. Aim for a cucumber tunnel with walls ¼ inch (6mm) thick. (A chopstick is handy for busting holes through the sections.)

Stuff the pork into the cucumber sections with a small spoon or butter spreader. Stick a toothpick through the middle of each stuffed cucumber to pierce the cucumber and pork; this helps hold the stuffing in place during cooking.

Poach and serve: Pour the broth into a large Dutch oven and season with the remaining 1 Tbsp fish sauce and 2 big pinches of salt. Bring to a boil over high heat and add the stuffed cucumber sections (pour in additional stock or water to cover if needed). When they have floated to the top, lower the heat to a simmer and poach gently, uncovered, until the pork is cooked through and the cucumber is translucent and tender firm, about 10 minutes. To test, scoop out a section and cut into it!

Divide the cucumber and broth among six bowls, slipping the toothpick out of each section before adding to a bowl. Top each bowl with cilantro and a grind or two of pepper and serve.

NOTES

Got leftover seasoned ground pork? Form it into small meatballs and poach in the stock along with the stuffed cucumber.

If you like, halve the stuffed cucumber sections crosswise after removing the toothpicks.

ต้มไก่ยาจีน | Tom Gai Ya Jeen

Apothecary Chicken Soup

SERVES 6 TO 8

Growing up, I was nourished by a formidable chicken soup enriched by medicinal herbs. We had it both at home and at Chinese restaurants. Missing its flavors and benefits, I consulted a certified traditional Chinese medicine practitioner (shout out to Linda in Auckland!) to devise an herbal formula to deliver wellness plus a taste that is not too medicinal. Here is my soup, loaded with chicken in a savory-earthy-sweet broth the color of autumn leaves. It's great for when you're feeling a little down and good for balancing your overall system. Have my formula for this easy, life-giving soup filled at a Chinese herb shop. You can also find each component of the formula individually packaged for sale at Chinese markets.

WELLNESS FORMULA

15g 枸杞, **เก๋ากี้**, goji berries

15g 当归, **ตังกุย**, dong quai

15g 龙眼干, **ลำไย**, dried longans

15g 山药, **ฮวยซัว**, mountain yam

15g 黄芪, **ปักคี้**, *Astragalus mongholicus*

15g 党参, **ตังเซียม**, *Codonopsis pilosula*

10g 玉竹, **เง็กเต๊ก**, Solomon's seal

30g | 8 small dried shiitake mushrooms (optional)

1.6kg | 3½-pound whole chicken

2 tsp fine sea salt, plus more to taste

2 Tbsp fish sauce

Soak, then simmer: Fill a very large Dutch oven or 8-qt (8L) stockpot half full with water. Put the 7 wellness formula ingredients in a spice bag (or enclose in a large square of unbleached muslin and tie with kitchen twine) and drop into the pot along with the mushrooms (if using). Let soak for 30 minutes.

Add the chicken, breast-side up, to the pot, then add water just to cover and the salt. Bring to a boil over high heat, then lower the heat to a gentle simmer (tiny bubbles steadily break the surface), cover partially, and cook, skimming off any foam from the surface as it appears, for 20 minutes. Flip the bird over, then continue to simmer, skimming as needed, until the chicken is just done, 15 to 20 minutes. To test, wiggle a leg, and if it moves easily with only little resistance, the chicken is ready.

Turn off the heat and use tongs to transfer the chicken to a large sheet pan. Cover the pot to continue hydrating the mushrooms and wellness formula in the spice bag.

When the chicken is cool enough to handle, after 20 to 30 minutes, tear or cut off the chicken meat, pull off the skin, and put the meat into a very large bowl. Break up the carcass and return it and the skin to the pot. Add any cooking juices from the sheet pan. Retrieve the spice bag from the pot and add to the bowl of chicken meat.

Add 4 cups (1L) water to the pot, leaving at least 1 inch (2.5cm) of space from the rim to allow the soup to simmer well. Bring to a soft boil and adjust the heat to allow big bubbles to burst softly through the surface. Cook, partially covered, to extract flavor from the bones and skin, 30 to 45 minutes. Meanwhile, tear the chicken meat into big bite-size pieces.

Strain and simmer more: Strain the broth through a fine-mesh strainer into the chicken bowl. Discard the chicken carcass but reserve the shiitakes (if using). If you like, halve or quarter the mushrooms before adding them to the chicken.

Rinse out the pot, then return the clear, amber broth, chicken meat, spice bag, and shiitakes to the pot. Bring to a boil over high heat, lower the heat to a gentle simmer (a bit of bubbling action steadily breaks the surface), and cook, uncovered, to develop the flavor further, 15 to 20 minutes. Add the fish sauce, taste, and then, if needed, add salt by the ¼ tsp. The soup should have a savory, delicately sweet, and gently medicinal flavor. Let the soup settle off the heat, uncovered, for 5 minutes.

Finesse and serve: Retrieve the spice bag from the pot, put it into a small bowl, and let it sit for a few minutes to release any excess broth, then return this bonus broth to the pot. Taste again to check the soup's saltiness, correct if needed, and then ladle into bowls and enjoy.

7 ย่าง ปิ้ง นึ่ง

Grilled, Roasted, Simmered, Steamed

Unexpected Treasures

Inspiration can come from curious places—like many recipes in this chapter do. For instance, the idea for the ridiculously good grilled squid recipe on page 219 came from a roadside stop where my parents pulled over on the way to our family's summer holidays in Hua Hin, a seaside town southwest of Bangkok. My parents wanted the region's dessert specialty, flan-like khanom mor gaeng. But I made a beeline to a particular older vendor, with an ancient dog at his feet, who grilled fresh squid over charcoal and doused it in a tangy, spicy, garlicky sauce. It lingered in my taste memory for decades until I eventually devised my own version for diners at Kin Khao and, now, for you.

While browsing my collection of old recipe books, I stumbled upon a unique curry recipe in an early 1960s community cookbook. Attributed to the police chief of a village in Pattani, near the border with Malaysia, the recipe for gaeng gai golae (golae chicken curry) included an unusual curry paste that incorporated signature Malay (Peranakan) ingredient combinations like luk sut (ลูกซัด, fenugreek) and grated coconut, which are not typically part of a Thai curry paste. That version yielded a wonderfully nutty, well-spiced paste. Taking a cue from the chief (though I suspect his wife was the true source), I included a toasted coconut-spice mixture in my golae paste. But like many modern Thai cooks, I also use the paste as a marinade and for making a dipping sauce. Its incredible flavor works with lamb, chicken, and tofu, as you'll see in three recipes in this chapter starting on page 214.

Of course, I couldn't make a cookbook without a recipe for gai yang, Thailand's legendary grilled chicken. The inspiration for my gai yang recipe also came from an unexpected place. I'd been going to a rice porridge shop near Samyan market in central Bangkok for decades. The market is one of my two favorite fresh markets in the city, and it's where I shop weekly when I'm in town. But I had long failed to notice the unassuming grilled chicken shop across the street from the rice porridge shop. One day, wanting something easy to share to bring back to my staff at Nahm as a treat, I picked up a couple of grilled spatchcocked chickens from the shop. With some overly charred bits, it was not fancy chicken, but the lemongrass, turmeric, and

garlic paste on the bird was incredibly moreish. I had to figure out how to replicate this delectable gai yang. Find my version on page 208.

This chapter also includes recipes that use ingredients in slightly unexpected ways. Prik gaeng ped curry paste isn't just for saucy curries. It seasons the roasted fish on page 223 and hor mok, the wobbly, custardy steamed curry mousse that you can make with either fish (page 225) or seared mushrooms (page 227).

There are even more *hidden* treasures in this chapter. If you've been to my restaurants, there are a couple of recipes here that you might recognize—something squid-y and something porky that have been on the menus at Kin Khao and Nari in one form or another since the day they opened. Need I say more? Keep turning the pages and start cooking.

ไก่ย่าง | Gai Yang

Best Thai Grilled Chicken Ever

SERVES 4

The best Thai grilled chicken should be punchy to show off its Isaan roots. I load mine with garlicky, lemongrass-y, peppery, and salty notes. Cilantro root imparts hints of coriander. Serve gai yang on its own, or as photographed on pages 210 and 211, go for a full Isaan presentation by offering it with sticky rice and two sauces: herbaceous nam jim jaew and gentler nam jim gai. Add green papaya salad (page 92) for a classic menu or lettuce and herbs to fashion wraps. A refreshing green salad would let gai yang fully strut its stuff too. For a party, marinate the chicken during the day while you're working or overnight while you're sleeping. When guests arrive, grill, then sit back and wait for the compliments to flow in.

40g | ¼ cup garlic cloves

30g | ⅓ cup very thinly sliced lemongrass

5g | 1 Tbsp coarsely chopped cilantro root or packed finely chopped cilantro stems

3g | 1 tsp white peppercorns

3g | 1 tsp black peppercorns

2 tsp ground turmeric

2 Tbsp fish sauce

2 tsp Thai oyster sauce

2 tsp Golden Mountain Seasoning Sauce

1.4kg | four 12-oz (340g) chicken leg quarters

About 120ml | ½ cup Kee Lo (Cracked Coconut Milk, page 53) or coconut milk

Marinate the chicken: Use a mortar and pestle to render the garlic, lemongrass, and cilantro root to a fine texture. Make a well in the center, add all of the peppercorns, and pound to crack and pulverize. (Or put the peppercorns into a small food processor or food chopper, whirl into teeny bits, and then add the garlic, lemongrass, and cilantro root and blitz away.) Scrape the aromatics into a large bowl and mix in the turmeric and fish, oyster, and Golden Mountain sauces.

Pat excess moisture from the chicken, then rub the marinade all over the chicken, pushing some under the skin. Cover the bowl or transfer the chicken to a large ziplock bag. Refrigerate for at least 3 hours or up to overnight.

Grill or roast the chicken: Before cooking the chicken, gently scrape off the excess marinade, collecting it in a measuring cup, and set the cup aside. Let the chicken sit at room temperature, skin-side up and uncovered, for about 1½ hours to dry the skin a bit, which will help with crispiness.

Meanwhile, for a basting sauce, pour the reserved marinade into a small saucepan and add an equal amount of kee lo (you may not need the entire ½ cup | 120ml). Bring to a boil over medium heat and keep boiling for 1 to 2 minutes, until slightly reduced and aromatic. Set aside.

Prepare a charcoal or gas grill for direct-heat cooking over medium heat. Place the chicken on the grill rack and grill, turning often, until the flesh is no longer pink (cut down to the bone to check) or an instant-read thermometer inserted into a chicken quarter away from bone registers at least 165°F (75°C), 30 to 40 minutes. Brush the basting sauce on the chicken during the last 5 to 10 minutes of cooking. (Or place the chicken, skin-side up, on an aluminum foil-lined sheet pan and roast in a preheated 350°F | 175°C oven until it tests done, 30 to 40 minutes. When done, blast under the broiler close to the heat source to add color, 2 to 5 minutes.) Transfer the chicken to a large platter and let rest for 5 to 10 minutes.

SUGGESTED ACCOMPANIMENTS

1 batch Khao Niew Neung (Microwave Sticky Rice, page 257)

1 batch Som Tum (Green Papaya Salad, page 92)

Nam Jim Jaew (All-Purpose Isaan Spicy Sauce, page 209)

Nam Jim Gai (Sweet Chili "Chicken" Sauce, page 54)

Vegetables, such as lettuce leaves, radicchio leaves, fresh herbs (cilantro, mint, sawtooth herb), thickly sliced cucumber, thinly sliced radishes, and green or long beans

Ready the accompaniments and serve: Gather the accompaniments of your choosing, and then set them out on the table along with the chicken. Tear into the chicken with your hands, dip each morsel into some sauce, pop it into your mouth, and then chase it with a ball of sticky rice and nibbles of refreshing vegetables.

NOTE

One batch of marinade works for a good 3 lb (1.5kg) of chicken; try a spatchcocked (butterflied) bird or bone-in parts. Grilling time varies so use a thermometer to check doneness.

น้ำจิ้มแจ่ว | Nam Jim Jaew

All-Purpose Isaan Spicy Sauce

MAKES ABOUT ⅔ CUP (160ML)

The most basic of Northeastern dipping sauces, nam jim jaew is really an all-purpose sauce, like a Thai equivalent of Mexican pico de gallo. Serve the crimson, thickish dipping sauce with grilled meats, such as the chicken on the previous page, pan-fried pork chops, or even vegetables. You'll also detect echoes of jaew in Isaan-style salads like nam tok beans on page 112. Included in the photo on page 211, the sauce provides a veil of spicy, pungent, herby, salty tang to anything it touches.

- 60ml | ¼ cup fish sauce
- 60ml | ¼ cup lime juice
- 10 to 15g | 2 to 3 Tbsp Prik Pon (Toasted Chili Flakes, page 46)
- 20g | 2 Tbsp Khao Kua (Isaan Fragrant Rice Powder, page 47)
- 1 pinch of Thai palm sugar (optional)
- 20g | 1 small shallot, thinly sliced
- 20g | ½ cup chopped mixed fresh herbs (such as mint, cilantro, sawtooth herb, and/or green onion)

Make the base: In a bowl, stir together the fish sauce, lime juice, 2 Tbsp of the prik pon, and the khao kua. Let sit to thicken and bloom the flavors, about 5 minutes. Taste and, if needed, add extra prik pon to finish with edgy fire. Stir in the sugar if you like a sweet touch. (I don't, but lots of people do.) Develop the right flavor balance for your taste. I prefer mine spicy, sour, and salty, in that order.

Finish and serve: Stir in the shallot and most of the herb blend. Top with the remaining herbs for a handsome look and serve. Stir at the table to enjoy all the flavors.

NOTE

To make the sauce up to 2 hours in advance, combine the fish sauce, lime juice, prik pon, and sugar (if using). A short time before serving, add the khao kua and shallot, then top with the herb blend. Don't stir until you're ready to eat.

เครื่องหมักกอและ | Prik Gaeng Golae

Golae Curry Marinade

This recipe works to deliver the intriguingly spiced flavors of Southern Thailand's golae-style dishes as a marinade that also functions as a dipping sauce base. It's fabulous for grilled lamb, chicken, and tofu (pages 214, 215, and 218). Using both coconut milk and coconut flakes yields extra-nutty, caramelized bits. Prepping the ingredients requires about an hour, so make a double batch. Photographed with other favorite curry pastes on page 140, golae curry marinade freezes well. Keep it on hand for easy, impressive meals.

INGREDIENT	X1 FOR SMALL TO MEDIUM PROCESSORS	X2 FOR BLENDERS AND ALL PROCESSORS
Fenugreek seeds	4g | 1 tsp	8g | 2 tsp
Fennel seeds	3g | 1¼ tsp	6g | 2½ tsp
Coriander seeds	1.5g | ¾ tsp	3g | 1½ tsp
Unsweetened dried coconut flakes	45g | 1.5 oz	90g | 3 oz
Seeded dried prik chee fa or puya chilies, snipped into 1-inch (2.5cm) pieces	8g | 0.3 oz	16g | 0.6 oz
Shallots, coarsely chopped	60g | 2 oz	120g | 4 oz
Lemongrass, finely chopped (1 or 2 thick stalks)	30g | 1 oz	60g | 2 oz
Garlic, coarsely chopped	12g | 0.4 oz	24g | 0.8 oz
Peeled turmeric, coarsely chopped	10g | good 1 Tbsp	20g | good 2 Tbsp
Peeled galangal, chopped no bigger than ¼ inch (6mm)	8g | scant 1 Tbsp	16g | scant 2 Tbsp
Peeled ginger, coarsely chopped	6g | 2½ tsp	12g | good 1½ Tbsp
Coconut milk, plus more if needed	90ml | 6 Tbsp	180ml | ¾ cup
Fish sauce	50ml | 3½ Tbsp	100ml | 7 Tbsp
Gapi (Thai shrimp paste)	20g | 1 Tbsp	40g | 2 Tbsp
Thai palm sugar, chopped or softened	45g | 2½ Tbsp	90g | 5 Tbsp
Approximate yield	1½ cups (350g)	3 cups (700g)

When making a double batch, toasting and cooling time will increase slightly. Be patient.

Prep the spices and coconut: In a dry large wok over medium-low heat, toast the fenugreek, fennel, and coriander, stirring or shaking the pan often, until fragrant and somewhat nutty, 2 to 3 minutes. Pour into a small bowl. Add the dried coconut to the still-hot wok and toast, stirring or shaking often, until fragrant and many pieces are light brown, about 2 minutes. Add to the spices and let cool completely, 15 to 30 minutes. Using a clean spice grinder or coffee grinder, whirl together the spices and coconut until a fragrant, finely textured mixture forms (or pound with a mortar and pestle).

Make the paste: Put the chilies, shallots, lemongrass, garlic, turmeric, galangal, ginger, coconut milk, fish sauce, gapi, and sugar into a food processor or blender (see page 136 for details), then scrape in the coconut-spice mixture. Process until a finely textured, rust-orange paste forms. If moisture is needed to move the ingredients along, add extra coconut milk, 1 Tbsp at a time. Use immediately, or transfer to an airtight container and refrigerate for up to 1 week or freeze for up to 3 months.

VARIATION

เครื่องแกงกอและเจ | Prik Gaeng Golae Jae
Vegan Golae Curry Marinade

For a single batch, use 3½ Tbsp Thai thin soy sauce and ½ tsp fine sea salt in place of the fish sauce and gapi. Makes about 1½ cups (350g).

ซี่โครงแกะย่างกอและ | Gae Yang Golae

Golae Grilled Lamb Lollipops

SERVES 4 AS A MAIN COURSE, OR 8 AS A SNACK

Thai grilling is more than chicken with sweet chili sauce. Photographed on page 217, this recipe introduces you to golae lamb chops, which are seasoned with a coconutty curry marinade that looks fiery but is mild in heat and big on spice and also doubles as the sauce. Lamb chops take up the golae flavors beautifully, are hard to overcook, and you can hold them like a lollipop! When chops or a rack aren't available or are too pricey, see the Notes for other lamb options. Or opt for golae chicken on page 215. Ajaad cucumber pickle brightens flavors and refreshes the palate, so include it whether you serve golae as a snack or add rice for a meal.

---

1 batch (350g | 1½ cups) Prik Gaeng Golae (Golae Curry Marinade, page 212), divided

1kg | 2.2 lbs frenched lamb chops (8 to 12 total; see Notes)

180ml | ¾ cup coconut milk, or 90ml | 6 Tbsp Kee Lo (Cracked Coconut Milk, page 53)

120ml | ½ cup water if using coconut milk, or 180ml | ¾ cup water if using kee lo

3 Tbsp fried shallots, plus more for garnish

1 batch Ajaad (Cucumber, Pepper, and Shallot Pickle, page 113)

Season the chops: Put 1 cup (240g) of the marinade (reserve the remaining marinade for the sauce) into a large stainless-steel, glass, or other nonreactive bowl. Add the lamb chops and mix and massage well to coat each chop all over. Cover and refrigerate for at least 3 hours or, preferably, overnight.

Make the sauce and pickle: Remove the lamb chops from the marinade, gently scraping off some of the excess marinade into a small saucepan. Set the chops aside to bring them to room temperature.

Add the reserved ½ cup (about 110g) marinade to the saucepan and stir in the coconut milk and ½ cup (120ml) water (or the kee lo and ¾ cup | 180ml water). Lightly crumble the fried shallots and stir into the sauce. Bring to a boil over medium heat, lower the heat to a gentle simmer, and cook until the mixture reduces to a medium-bodied sauce that nicely coats the back of a spoon, 3 to 5 minutes. Taste to verify a savory, coconutty, gently spiced finish. Simmer longer to intensify the flavor or dilute with water if the sauce is too punchy or salty. Cover and set aside to keep warm until serving. Ready the pickle too.

Grill and serve: Prepare a charcoal or gas grill for direct-heat cooking over a medium fire. Or set a cast-iron stovetop grill over medium heat and heat until a couple of drops of water flicked onto the surface sizzle and quickly evaporate. Place the chops on the grill rack or stovetop grill and cook, turning now and then, until caramelized on both sides and an instant-read thermometer inserted into a chop away from bone registers 130°F (54°C) for medium-rare, 6 to 8 minutes total. Transfer to a platter and garnish with fried shallots (if you like). Serve immediately with the sauce and pickle.

NOTES

If the chops are not precut, buy 1½ racks of lamb that have already been frenched (trimmed of excess meat, fat, and sinewy bits), then cut between the rib bones into chops.

Instead of lamb chops, marinate racks of lamb ribs and cut into riblets after grilling. Or cut boneless leg of lamb into 1½-inch (3.75cm) chunks and grill on skewers.

ไก่กอและ | Gai Golae

Chicken Golae Skewers with Coconut Curry Sauce (the Better Satay)

SERVES 4 HUNGRY PEOPLE

Practically every Thai cookbook has a chicken satay and peanut sauce recipe. I'll give you something better: Let the coconutty, richly spiced golae marinade transform chicken into the best grilled satay and define the splendid accompanying sauce too. It's a clever double-whammy use of one superb seasoning. I developed the gaeng golae marinade as a concentrated curry sauce and always have some frozen to make these skewers, photographed on page 217 with grilled lamb and tofu golae. Follow suit and go golae for stunningly good satay.

---

1 batch (350g | 1½ cups) Prik Gaeng Golae (Golae Curry Marinade, page 212), divided

1kg | 2.2 lb boneless, skinless chicken thighs, cut into strips 1 inch (2.5cm) wide

180ml | ¾ cup coconut milk, or 90ml | 6 Tbsp Kee Lo (Cracked Coconut Milk, page 53)

120ml | ½ cup water if using coconut milk, or 180ml | ¾ cup water if using kee lo

3 Tbsp fried shallots, plus more for garnish

1 batch Ajaad (Cucumber, Pepper, and Shallot Pickle, page 113)

2 to 3 Tbsp neutral oil, such as rice bran, for grilling

Ready the skewers: If you plan to grill the chicken over a live fire using wooden skewers, soak twelve 6-inch (15cm) skewers or eight 10-inch (25cm) skewers in hot water to cover for 20 minutes. Otherwise, grab some metal skewers.

Season and skewer: Put 1 cup (240g) of the marinade (reserve the remaining marinade for the sauce) into a large stainless-steel, glass, or other nonreactive bowl. Add the chicken and mix and massage well to coat all over. Thread the meat onto the skewers, covering about two-thirds of each skewer. Gently squeeze each loaded skewer so the meat covers the skewer well, looks good, and won't dry up during grilling. Set the loaded skewers on a sheet pan, cover, and let marinate in the fridge for at least 3 hours, or overnight.

Make the sauce and pickle: Remove the chicken from the refrigerator. Gently scrape off some of the excess marinade from the skewers into a small saucepan; set the skewers aside to come to room temperature for grilling.

To the small saucepan, add the reserved ½ cup (about 110g) marinade. Stir in the coconut milk and ½ cup (120ml) water (or the kee lo and ¾ cup | 180ml water). Lightly crumble the fried shallots and stir into the sauce. Bring to a boil over medium heat, lower the heat to a gentle simmer, and cook until the mixture reduces to a medium-bodied sauce that easily coats the back of a spoon, 3 to 5 minutes. Taste to verify a savory, coconutty, gently spiced finish. Simmer longer to intensify the flavor or dilute with water if the sauce is too punchy or salty. Cover and set aside to keep warm until serving. Ready the pickle too.

Grill and serve: Prepare a charcoal or gas grill for direct-heat cooking over a medium-hot fire. Or set a cast-iron stovetop grill over medium-high heat and heat until a couple of drops of water flicked onto the surface sizzle and quickly evaporate. Lightly brush the chicken with the oil to prevent sticking, then place the skewers on the grill rack or stovetop grill. Grill, turning often, until charred, caramelized, and cooked through, 6 to 8 minutes. (Cut into a piece to check for firmness and doneness; a thermometer is inefficient.) Pile the skewers on a platter, garnish with fried shallots (if you like), and serve immediately with the sauce and pickle.

NOTE

Don't want to skewer? Use the marinade on whole boneless, skin-on or skinless chicken thighs and grill over medium heat for about 10 minutes.

กอและเต้าหู้ | Golae Tauhu

Golae Grilled Tofu Triangles

SERVES 6

The coconutty spice notes of golae are not only good for meat. They're perfect for enrobing grilled tofu too. For vegetarian diners, make the marinade's vegan variation. When serving at a party, slide a bamboo skewer (as photographed on page 216) into the finished grilled tofu so diners can easily pick it up as a skewered food. See the Note for an easy side dish suggestion.

Two 450g | 1-lb blocks extra-firm tofu

1 batch (350g | 1½ cups) Prik Gaeng Golae (Golae Curry Marinade, page 212), divided

180ml | ¾ cup coconut milk, or 90ml | 6 Tbsp Kee Lo (Cracked Coconut Milk, page 53)

120ml | ½ cup water if using coconut milk, or 180ml | ¾ cup water if using kee lo

3 Tbsp fried shallots, plus more for garnish

1 batch Ajaad (Cucumber, Pepper, and Shallot Pickle, page 113)

60ml | ¼ cup neutral oil, such as rice bran, for grilling

Cut tofu triangles: For manageable and handsome tofu, cut it into triangles 1 inch (2.5cm) thick. To do so, stand a tofu block on its long side and cut it in half lengthwise to create two slabs. Lay a slab flat and make two diagonal cuts—like an X—to yield four small triangles. Repeat with the second slab to yield four more triangles. Halve and then cut the second tofu block the same way. You'll have a total of 16 triangles.

Drain and marinate the tofu: Arrange the tofu on a clean dish towel (or double layer of paper towels). Let drain and firm up for 10 to 30 minutes. Pat off excess moisture, then place the tofu on a large sheet pan.

Using a silicone spatula, coat the tofu triangles with ¾ cup (180g) of the marinade (reserve the remaining marinade for the sauce). Aim for a thicker coating on the triangular sides than the edge because that's where you'll get more browning on the grill. Let sit at room temperature for 1 hour, or cover and refrigerate for up to 8 hours, then return to room temperature before grilling.

Make the sauce and pickle: Meanwhile, in a small saucepan, combine the remaining ¾ cup (about 170g) marinade, the coconut milk, and the ½ cup (120ml) water (or the kee lo and ¾ cup | 180ml water). Lightly crumble the fried shallots and stir into the sauce. Bring to a boil over medium heat, lower to a gentle simmer, and cook until the mixture reduces to a medium-bodied sauce that nicely coats the back of a spoon, 3 to 5 minutes. Taste to verify a savory, coconutty, gently spiced finish. Simmer more to intensify the flavor or dilute with water if the sauce is too punchy or salty. Cover and set aside to keep warm until serving. Ready the pickle too.

Grill and serve: Prepare a charcoal or gas grill for direct-heat cooking over a medium-hot fire. Or set a cast-iron stovetop grill over medium-high heat and heat until a couple of drops of water flicked onto the surface sizzle and immediately evaporate. Generously brush the tofu with the oil to prevent sticking, then place the tofu on the grill rack or stovetop grill and grill, turning often, until caramelized on both sides, 8 to 10 minutes. Transfer to a platter, garnish with fried shallots (if you like), and serve immediately with the sauce and pickle.

NOTE

Create a simple side by grilling sliced Chinese or Japanese eggplants and/or summer squashes. Slice them on the diagonal into pieces about ½ inch (1.25cm) thick, season with salt and oil, and then add them to the grill.

ปลาหมึกย่าง | Pla Muek Yang

Charred Squid with Seafood Sauce

SERVES 8 AS A SNACK, OR 4 AS A PART OF A MEAL

Sensational tasting and easy to make, this grilled squid hails from my childhood. I first tasted it at a roadside stall on the way to Hua Hin, a popular resort town on the Gulf of Thailand. One particular vendor made it, and after a quick exchange of baht, he plucked a few squid from his hot charcoal grill, deposited them into a banana leaf cup, spooned on a generous amount of garlicky, spicy, tangy sauce, and then added a big handful of peanuts, a shower of cilantro, and bamboo skewers (for eating). I loved that pla muek yang so much that I recreated it in California using local squid from the Monterey Bay, as photographed on page 221. At my restaurants, we grill the squid over a live fire, but it is easily cooked on a cast-iron stovetop grill. Pla muek yang works for a snack, but enjoy it with rice and stir-fried greens for a sensational Thai meal.

---

1 batch Nam Jim Seafood (Seafood Sauce, page 224)

600g | 1⅓ lb cleaned small squid tubes and tentacles

2 Tbsp neutral oil, like rice bran, plus more for cooking and to taste

30g | ¼ cup roasted peanuts, chopped

60ml | ¼ cup fresh cilantro leaves and tender tops

Khao Suay (Basic Jasmine Rice, page 256) or Khao Niew Neung (Microwave Sticky Rice, page 257), for serving

Prep the sauce and squid: Make the sauce, spread on a rimmed serving platter, and set the platter near the stovetop.

Pat excess moisture from the squid with paper towels. Keep the flaps on the tubes intact if they're present. To release liquid and keep the squid tubes whole, slash each tube at ½- to ¾-inch (1.25 to 1.8cm) intervals, starting the slashing about 1½ inches (3.75cm) from the pointy tip and ending each cut near the midline (think sexy Goth stockings; don't cut all of the way across into rings). Put the slashed tubes in a medium bowl, add the tentacles, and toss with the oil.

Char, assemble, and serve: Heat a cast-iron stovetop grill pan over medium-high heat until almost smoking, then brush a little oil on the pan. Working in batches, char the squid, pressing with a grill press or a flexible metal spatula to ensure maximum contact with the cooking surface and turning now and then, until medium firm, opaque white, and cooked through, 4 to 6 minutes for the tubes and about 2 minutes for the tentacles. As each batch is ready, transfer it to the serving platter.

Use tongs to turn and coat the squid in the sauce, then rearrange all of the pieces in a handsome layer. Crown with the peanuts and cilantro and enjoy with rice. Do eat the garlic and chilies in the sauce for the full Thai effect.

NOTES

Large squid will require longer cooking time. Grilled octopus tentacles or large prawns can stand in for the squid.

Serve the grilled squid with the sweet pork on page 220. It will be similar to the squid and caramelized pork jowl in seafood sauce served at my restaurant Nari.

หมูหวาน | Moo Wan

Caramelized Pork Belly

SERVES 6 TO 8

For this homey Thai favorite, less yields more. You need only four ingredients to produce a sweet-salty pork belly to enjoy on rice plates. Use good palm sugar and fish sauce to ensure the best outcome. This pork belly is so versatile that I often paired it with the grilled squid on page 219 for a post-shift snack at Kin Khao. When we opened Nari, my chef de cuisine Meghan Clark combined the two for a dish that became a guest favorite and permanent fixture on the menu. The opposite photo shows the pork and squid together to inspire you.

A gentle stovetop simmer is traditional, but oven baking at a low temperature is an easy, fail-safe restaurant approach to moo wan perfection. Serve this pork belly with lots of jasmine rice (page 256) to mix with the sauce.

900g | 2 lb boneless pork belly (skin on or skin off; see Note)

300 to 380g | scant 1 to 1¼ cups firmly packed Thai palm sugar

300g | 1 cup less 1 Tbsp fish sauce

150g | 5 oz shallots, cut into slices ¼ inch (6mm) thick

Bind the pork: Cut the pork into chunks roughly 2 by 2½ inches (5 by 6.25cm). Using kitchen twine, tie each chunk like a gift, cinching the twine a bit to ensure the fat and lean remain together during cooking.

Simmer and bake: Position a rack in the middle of the oven and preheat the oven to 275°F (135°C).

In a medium ovenproof pot over medium heat, combine 1 cup (300g) of the sugar and the fish sauce and melt the sugar, stirring often. Taste to verify a sweet-salty flavor. If needed, add up to ¼ cup (80g) extra sugar.

Add the pork chunks, turning to coat them in the sauce, then position them skin-side down. Add water just to cover the pork (about 1 cup | 240ml), then add the shallots. (Don't worry if the pork floats. That's normal.)

Increase the heat to high and bring the liquid to a boil, then take the pot off the heat. Cover loosely with aluminum foil (make a shower cap–like lid so the pot is not tightly sealed), transfer to the oven, and bake the pork belly until the flesh, fat, and skin are tender, about 3 hours. To test, poke a metal cake tester into the fat layer. It should easily penetrate to the center.

Transfer the belly chunks to a small sheet pan or medium plate. Skim off the fat from the top of the sauce. (Or better yet, let the liquid in the pot cool, cover, and refrigerate overnight, then lift the fat off the top the next day.) You should have about 3 cups (720ml) sauce. If you want a more intense flavor, boil the sauce to thicken it.

Reheat to serve: Snip and remove the twine from the pork, then return all the pieces to the sauce. Reheat gently to serve.

NOTE

Instead of pork belly, use pork shoulder or jowl, like we do at Nari.

ปลาย่างห่อใบตอง | Pla Yang Bai Tong

Banana Leaf–Roasted Fish

SERVES 4

Don't be intimidated by the idea of cooking a whole fish. This roasted fish is easier than you think, and it also delivers a huge wow factor at the table. Keep an eye out for a big, beautiful fresh fish at your seafood counter or call a fishmonger to order one. Then give it the Thai treatment by rubbing it in Thai red curry paste and wrapping it up in banana leaf (see page 226). The leaf imparts a lovely scent to the flesh during cooking, makes the fish easier to move around, and prevents the curry paste from scorching. While the fish cooks, whip up two plucky sauces and prep vegetables and some rice for a splendid meal or an impressive part of a bigger feast.

2 pieces banana leaf, each about the size of a half sheet pan

One 1.5kg | 3½-lb whole fish (such as rockfish, sea bass, or sea trout), cleaned

Fine sea salt

3 Tbsp Prik Gaeng Ped (Red Curry Paste, page 144; optional)

4 lemongrass stalks

Prep the fish: Position a rack in the middle of the oven and preheat the oven to 450°F (230°C). Lay three lengths of kitchen twine (each about 20 in | 50cm long), evenly spaced, across a half sheet pan. Cut, rinse, and dry the banana leaf pieces. Lay one of them atop the strings so it covers the sheet pan. Lay the second leaf piece on top crosswise to the first for extra aroma and protection.

Lay the fish on the banana leaves. Use scissors to trim the fins. Then use a knife to slash the fish at three places, spacing the slashes evenly and cutting down to the bone. Flip the fish and repeat the slashes on the other side. Season the exterior and belly cavity with salt. If using the curry paste, rub it all over the skin and into the cuts.

Use a heavy knife or meat mallet to smack and soften the lemongrass stalks. Insert the stalks, bulbous portion first, into the fish's mouth, shoving them into the belly cavity. The tops of the stalks should poke from the mouth; snip the tops if there's too much showing.

Bring up the edges of the banana leaf pieces to encase the fish, using kitchen scissors as needed to trim the leaves. Using the three lengths of twine, snugly tie the fish in its green corset, making sure the leaf hugs the fish well.

Roast the fish: Slide the pan into the oven and roast the fish until cooked through, 30 to 40 minutes. To test, insert an instant-read thermometer into the thickest part. The fish is ready when it registers between 130° and 135°F (54° and 57°C). Or insert a metal cake tester into the thickest part and then touch the tester to the back of your hand or below your lip. If it's hot, the fish is done.

ACCOMPANIMENTS

1 batch Nam Jim Seafood (Seafood Sauce, page 224)

1 batch Jaew Makaam (Tamarind Jaew Sauce, page 224)

1 head lettuce, leaves separated

2 Persian cucumbers, thickly sliced

1 handful mint sprigs

1 handful cilantro sprigs

1 batch Khao Niew Meung (Microwave Sticky Rice, page 257) or Khao Suay (Basic Jasmine Rice, page 256)

Ready the accompaniments and serve: While the fish roasts, prep and set the accompaniments at the table. When the fish is done, let it cool briefly in the leaf packet, then snip the twine and unveil the fish. Serve with the two sauces, the lettuce leaves, cucumber slices, mint and cilantro sprigs, and rice. Invite diners to dip the fish into the sauces, make lettuce wraps, and nibble on sticky rice to mellow the heat.

NOTE

Instead of one big fish, roast two smaller fish (2 lb | 900g each before cleaning). Wrap each separately in banana leaf and cook at 450°F (230°C) for 18 to 25 minutes.

น้ำจิ้มซีฟู้ด | Nam Jim Seafood

Seafood Sauce

MAKES ½ CUP (120ML)

Tart, spicy, garlicky, and a touch sweet, this sauce should be kick-you-in-the-face hot. Thai people called this sauce "nam jim seafood" because it is a sauce (nam jim) for seafood. It's the go-to condiment for enjoying with seafood (such as fish, squid, or shrimp) that have been simply seasoned and grilled, roasted, or steamed.

In your kitchen, you can tame it a tad to suit your palate (which is why I've included a range for the chilies). However, remember to finish bold because dishes like the mildly seasoned roasted fish on page 223 and the grilled squid on page 219 rely on the sauce for oomph. Combining fresh and pickled garlic in just the right ratio and manner allows you to enjoy raw garlic in the company of family, friends, or a date!

---

5 to 10g | 3 to 6 fresh Thai chilies, to taste

3g | ½ tsp firmly packed Thai palm sugar, plus more to taste

20g | 6 fresh garlic cloves

10g | 1 Tbsp pickled garlic cloves, homemade (page 55) or purchased

60ml | ¼ cup lime juice, plus more to taste

3 Tbsp fish sauce, plus more to taste

Using a mortar and pestle, pound the chilies and sugar to crush and flatten the chilies into small pieces. Drop in the fresh and pickled garlic, then pound gently to break the cloves apart (avoid totally crushing the garlic or it will become too harsh). Stir in the lime juice and fish sauce. Taste the sauce. It should be pleasantly garlicky, hot, salty, and slightly tart. If needed, add sugar by the ¼ tsp, fish sauce by the 1 tsp, or lime juice by the 1 tsp. Let sit for at least 10 minutes to develop flavor before serving, or refrigerate in an airtight container for up to 5 days.

NOTE

I like nam jim seafood to be chunky—the old-school way. For a modern take, double the recipe and blend all the ingredients with about ¼ cup (60ml) of coarsely chopped cilantro (use both stems and leaves).

แจ่วมะขาม | Jaew Makaam

Tamarind Jaew Sauce

MAKES ⅔ CUP (160ML)

Brick red, thick jaew makaam is spicy hot with pungent edges from shallot, zippy herbs, and earthy tamarind. Because of differences in palates (how hot is your prik pon?) and ingredients (herbs vary in weight), volume measurements work best for this recipe. Use my guidelines to formulate your own. Serve the scintillating sauce with your favorite grilled foods.

60ml | ¼ cup fish sauce

3 Tbsp Nam Makam (Tamarind Liquid, page 52), plus more to taste

1 to 2 tsp lime juice, plus more to taste

½ tsp firmly packed Thai palm sugar

2 tsp Khao Kua (Isaan Fragrant Rice Powder, page 47)

2 to 3 tsp Prik Pon (Toasted Chili Flakes, page 46)

2 Tbsp very thinly sliced shallots

2 to 3 Tbsp chopped mixed fresh herbs (such as mint, cilantro, sawtooth herb, shiso, and/or green onion)

Make the base: In a small bowl, stir together the fish sauce and tamarind. Add the lime juice and sugar and stir to mix. Taste the base. If the tamarind tang doesn't show enough, add a squeeze of lime. If fruity tang is needed, stir in tamarind by the 1 tsp. Aim for a tart, salty, slightly sweet finish. (If not using the base within a few hours, cover and refrigerate for up to 5 days.)

Finish the sauce: Stir in the khao kua, prik pon, and shallots. Let sit for about 10 minutes to bloom the flavors. Top with the herbs, then serve. At the table, stir in the herbs before spooning onto food.

ห่อหมกปลา | Hor Mok Pla

Steamed Fish Curry Mousse

SERVES 4

Banana leaf, Thai basil, and lime leaf define the aroma of this mousse-like steamed fish curry. Just a touch of red curry paste defines its central flavor, so do use homemade prik gaeng ped for a stellar outcome. Hor mok is often presented as single portions, intricately wrapped in banana leaf. That traditional approach is great for fresh market vendors selling takeaway foods. But my approach—cooking the curry in a dish or bowl lined with banana leaf—is much easier. However, I do draw the line on how the curry mixture is made. Traditionally, collagen from fish thickens the custard, but nowadays, some cooks add flour to prevent liquid from separating during steaming. That dulls the curry's flavors. Let the fish and curry do their thing and you'll get a softly set mousse to mix into your rice. Or serve hor mok with fried rice crackers (page 50) for an indulgent snack. In addition to the suggested fish, consider flounder, halibut, and rockfish. See page 226 for banana leaf basics.

300g | 10 oz skinless fish fillet (such as petrale sole, cod, or salmon; see Notes)

2 Tbsp Prik Gaeng Ped (Red Curry Paste, page 144)

½ tsp finely chopped grachai (fingerroot; optional)

½ tsp tapioca starch

½ tsp water

One 400ml | 13.5-oz can coconut milk, unshaken

1 large egg

45ml | 3 Tbsp fish sauce

3g | 3 Tbsp finely slivered makrut lime leaves (see page 31), divided

2 banana leaf pieces, each about 5 by 10 inches (12.5 by 25cm)

120ml | ½ cup loosely packed fresh Thai basil leaves

¼ fresh red Fresno chili or mini red sweet pepper, cut into narrow matchsticks

Make the fish base: Use paper towels to pat away moisture from the fish. Cut 6 oz (180g) of the thicker parts of the fillet into 2-inch (5cm) pieces and set aside. Cut the remaining fish into ½-inch (1.25cm) chunks, then pound them with a mortar and pestle to a coarse texture. Add the curry paste and grachai, if using, and keep pounding to produce a mixture with the texture of the curry paste. The mixture eventually sucks up against the pestle without letting go easily. (Or put the ½-inch | 1.25cm fish chunks, curry paste, and grachai into a food processor and whirl, pausing occasionally to scrape down the sides of the bowl, until you have a fine texture that forms a ball.)

Prep the coconut milk: In a small bowl, dissolve the tapioca starch in the water. Collect 2½ Tbsp thick coconut milk from the top of the can, stir into the tapioca starch mixture, and set aside.

Spoon the remaining thick coconut milk from the can into a large measuring cup, then add enough of the thin coconut milk from the can to yield 1 cup (240ml). Save any remaining thin coconut milk for another curry or other dish. Whisk the egg and fish sauce into the coconut milk, then add the fish mixture and 1½ Tbsp of the lime leaves and stir well. You will have about 2¼ cups (540ml) of orangish custard.

Assemble and steam: Select a soufflé dish 6 inches (15cm) wide and 3 inches (7.5cm) deep or a heat-resistant bowl of similar size. Set up a large Chinese steamer, a tall pot with a collapsible steamer insert, or a pasta pot and strainer insert. Whichever setup you use, make sure the dish sits well in the pot with the lid on. Add water to a depth of about 1½ inches (3.75cm) to the pot. It's OK if a little water touches the dish.

Rinse the banana leaf pieces and wipe dry, then line the dish with them in a crisscross pattern to cover the interior fully. Set aside two or three dainty basil leaf tips for garnish, then put the remaining leaves in the lined dish. Pour in one-third of the custard, add the reserved fish pieces, and top with the remaining custard. Shimmy the dish to level the contents.

Bring the water in the steamer pot to a boil over high heat, then turn down the heat to release steady puffs of steam (avoid hard steam). Carefully place the curry in the steamer, re-cover, and steam, checking the water occasionally and replenishing if needed, until jiggly but set, about 35 minutes. To test for doneness, use the back of a spoon to gently press the center of the surface, which should spring back.

CONTINUED

Garnish and serve: Turn off the heat, spoon the reserved coconut milk onto the center, re-cover, and leave for 2 to 3 minutes to set. Garnish the warm hor mok with the chili and remaining lime leaf slivers to release their aromas. Add the reserved basil leaf tips, then serve. Remind diners to mix the custard juices into their rice. Yes, eat all of the garnishes too!

NOTES

Because fish quality and texture can vary, here's an extra step to ensure that your curry sets nicely. Put the fish on a plate and bury the fish in a mound of salt (any kind will do). Refrigerate, uncovered, for about 1 hour. The fish will release excess liquid. Rub off all the salt, quickly rinse, then pat very dry with a paper towel. Proceed with the recipe.

For a dinner party, follow the recipe to assemble and steam the hor mok up to 3 hours ahead of serving. Set the hor mok aside to cool. Right before serving, gently resteam to warm through (insert a metal cake tester and it should feel hot), 5 to10 minutes. Then follow the "Garnish and serve" step to finish the mousse for serving.

BANANA LEAF 101

Shop for frozen banana leaves at Chinese and Southeast Asian markets as well as at Latin grocers. The large, flat packages typically come from the Philippines and contain malleable leaves selected for wrapping food. To minimize waste, partially thaw and take what you need for a recipe, then refold and refreeze.

Before using, if the brownish edges on a leaf make it hard to bend or are unsightly, use kitchen scissors to trim them off. Then rinse the leaf in cold water and wipe dry to remove any whitish residue. If the leaf is too stiff to bend, wave it over an open flame or dunk it into a pot of hot water to soften. Overlap leaves when you can't get one big enough for a dish.

ห่อหมกเห็ด | Hor Mok Hed

Steamed Mushroom Curry Mousse

SERVES 4

Many people think of hor mok as a seafood dish, but you can certainly make it with mushrooms, and the delicious result looks like the fish version photographed on page 226. At Kin Khao, we make mushroom hor mok as a starter, steamed in small ramekins to scoop up with khao tung, the fried rice crackers on page 50. At home, steam the curry in a soufflé dish or bowl to enjoy as a main dish with rice or as a snack with the crackers. Blend different mushroom varieties for texture, appearance, and flavor. If available, use white soy sauce for brighter color. See page 226 for banana leaf basics.

225g | 8 oz mixed mushrooms (such as oyster, maitake, and shiitake)

2 tsp neutral oil, such as rice bran

Fine sea salt

½ tsp tapioca starch

½ tsp water

One 400ml | 13.5-oz can coconut milk, unshaken

½ tsp finely chopped grachai (fingerroot; optional)

2 large eggs

3 Tbsp Thai thin soy sauce or Japanese white soy sauce

2 Tbsp Prik Gaeng Ped (Red Curry Paste, page 144)

3g | 3 Tbsp finely slivered makrut lime leaves (see page 31), divided

2 banana leaf pieces, each about 5 by 10 inches (12.5 by 25cm)

120ml | ½ cup loosely packed fresh Thai basil leaves

¼ fresh red Fresno chili or mini red sweet pepper, cut into narrow matchsticks

Sear the mushrooms: Trim, then cut or hand tear the mushrooms into bite-size pieces to yield about 4 cups (1L). Set a large heavy skillet (cast iron or carbon steel) over high heat. When the pan is hot, add the oil and swirl the pan to coat the bottom. Add the mushrooms, sprinkle with ¼ tsp salt, and then sear, turning occasionally, until the mushrooms have browned here and there and shrunken to about one-third of the original volume, 7 to 10 minutes. Set aside to cool.

Prep the coconut milk: In a small bowl, dissolve the tapioca starch in the water. Collect 2½ Tbsp thick coconut milk from the top of the can, stir into the tapioca starch mixture, and set aside.

Spoon the remaining thick coconut milk from the can into a large measuring cup, then add enough of the thin coconut milk from the can to yield 1 cup (240ml). Save any remaining thin coconut milk for another curry or other dish. Pound the grachai, if using, with a mortar and pestle to a fine paste, then whisk it into the coconut milk along with the eggs, soy sauce, and curry paste. Stir in 1½ Tbsp of the lime leaves. You will have a scant 2 cups (480ml) of orangish custard.

Assemble and steam: Select a soufflé dish 6 inches (15cm) wide and 3 inches (7.5cm) deep or a heat-resistant bowl of similar size. Set up a large Chinese steamer, a tall pot with a collapsible steamer insert, or a pasta pot and strainer insert. Whichever setup you use, make sure the dish sits well in the pot with the lid on. Add water to a depth of about 1½ inches (3.75cm) to the pot. It's OK if a little water touches the dish.

Rinse the banana leaf pieces and wipe dry, then line the dish with them in a crisscross pattern to cover the interior fully. Set aside two or three dainty basil leaf tips for garnish, then put the remaining leaves in the lined dish. Pour in one-third of the custard, add the seared mushrooms, and top with the remaining custard. Shimmy the dish to level the contents.

Bring the water in the steamer pot to a boil over high heat, then turn down the heat to release steady puffs of steam (avoid hard steam). Carefully place the curry in the steamer, re-cover, and steam, checking the water occasionally and replenishing if needed, until jiggly but set, about 35 minutes. To test for doneness, use the back of a spoon to gently press the center of the surface, which should spring back.

Turn off the heat, spoon the reserved coconut milk onto the center, re-cover, and leave for 2 to 3 minutes to set. Garnish the warm hor mok with the chili and remaining lime leaf slivers to release their aromas. Add the reserved basil leaf tips, then serve. Remind diners to mix the custard juices into their rice. Yes, eat all of the garnishes too!

8

ผัดๆ ทอดๆ

Stir-Fried and Deep-Fried

NIRVANA

Sacred Wok Magic

When you ask a non-Thai person what the quintessential Thai stir-fry dish is, their answer is probably pad Thai. But if you ask a Thai person the same question, their answer would likely be pad gaprao, the spicy, herbaceous, ever-so-adaptable stir-fry dish redolent with citrusy, pungent bai gaprao (holy basil, sacred basil, or tulsi). The stir-fry is commonly enjoyed with rice and is often topped with a crispy fried egg so diners can mix the runny yolk into the rice and stir-fry.

I once read in a Thai newspaper that the average Thai person eats pad gaprao *at least* once a week. That's believable because you can find pad gaprao set out in large trays at rad khao (over-rice) canteens, ready to be spooned over rice for a quick lunch. Additionally, you can order pad gaprao at any tam-sung (as-requested) shop, the type of neighborhood corner restaurant that will basically cook you anything you want as long as the ingredients are on hand. And, yes, these spots will always have holy basil.

You can pretty much order pad gaprao with any common protein: chicken, pork, beef, and sometimes even seafood. The meat can be minced or cut into larger pieces. The heat level can be adjusted by request, sometimes by specifying the precise number of chilies you want in the wok. Your order of pad gaprao typically arrives with a little bowl of fish sauce with chopped chili (nampla prik). Sometimes the sauce also contains sliced garlic or shallot and a bit of lime juice. Diners add the sauce to pad gaprao to spike flavors as they please.

I'm sure you've seen pad gaprao at your local Thai restaurant. If you're not in Thailand, the version you've had is probably technically pad horapa, prepared with bai horapa, the leaves of anisey Thai basil, which is more readily available in the United States. It's workable enough, but if you can, make the effort to try the original version with bai gaprao, or holy basil. You won't regret it. Once you've tried true pad gaprao, you might never go back.

How to ensure a supply of holy basil? Check in with Southeast Asian vendors at farmers' markets during the summer. You can also grow your own. Look for holy basil seeds and starter plants at nurseries, hardcore Southeast Asian markets, and online. I've easily grown gaprao for my kitchens in the States and in New Zealand. A pot or two should last for a few weeks or, if you're nice to your plants and live in a warm climate, for a couple of months. My neighbors in the Wynyard Quarter on the Auckland waterfront usually know that we are back for our antipodean summer when they see my window box loaded with holy basil plants. That's how much I love the dish. And that's why you'll find four pad gaprao recipes, starting on page 233!

Worry not, this chapter is not limited to pad gaprao. You'll learn to prepare other home-cooked favorites, such as black pepper crab (page 243), a dish that always reminds me of childhood summer vacations in Phuket. You'll also make use of my grandmother's chili jam as the base for stir-frying clams, a recipe that's adaptable with other proteins. There's a quick cabbage stir-fry (page 237) that's been a perennial hit at Nari, plus fried pork meatballs (page 235) from my school days. You can even stretch your skills a bit by frying up garlicky pork riblets, luscious pork belly, and a surprisingly addictive crispy fish cereal rice topping.

All of these recipes utilize the wok, so on your mark, get set, wok away!

ผัดกะเพราเนื้อ | Pad Gaprao Neua

Bougie Pad Gaprao

SERVES 4

Watching the Netflix cult favorite *Midnight Diner: Tokyo Stories*, I fantasized about a luxe Bangkok equivalent—a shophouse café on a peaceful soi (side street) owned by a skilled auntie who's always able to fulfill your food desires. I'd request a sumptuous take on pad gaprao (holy basil stir-fry with meat), and the auntie would marinate steak cubes with a few condiments, pound a trio of bold aromatics, swiftly stir-fry it all up with a shower of mild chilies, and then finish with fistfuls of earthy herbage. "More basil!" I'd say because there's rarely enough. She'd serve the dish with rice plus a tart, salty sauce (nampla prik, see Notes) to uplift flavors. Heavenly comfort. Classic pad gaprao features ground meat, but the fantasy auntie's spectacular version is reminiscent of Vietnamese shaking beef. Here's her (my) recipe for your reality. We hope the photo here entices you to prepare this bougie version and all the tasty riffs that follow; it may even inspire you to create one of your own. When using Thai basil (bai horapa), call your dish pad horapa to be linguistically accurate. Regardless, enjoy with lots of jasmine rice.

Seasoning sauce made by mixing 2 Tbsp fish sauce, 1 Tbsp Thai oyster sauce, 1½ tsp Thai black soy sauce, and 1 Tbsp water

450g | 1 lb trimmed bavette, New York, or top sirloin steak, cut into 1-inch (2.5cm) chunks (see Notes)

¼ tsp baking soda

1 big pinch of granulated sugar (optional)

20g | 3 Tbsp thinly sliced shallots

10 to 15g | 6 to 8 fresh Thai chilies, to taste

2g | 2 tsp coarsely chopped cilantro root (optional; see Notes)

40g | ¼ cup garlic cloves

90g | 3 mini sweet peppers or other mild pepper

30g | 1½ cups fresh holy or Thai basil leaves, plus tender tips for garnish

2 Tbsp neutral oil, such as rice bran, divided

Prep the meat: Mix together the seasoning sauce ingredients in a small measuring cup. Spoon 1 Tbsp of the seasoning sauce into a medium bowl. Add the beef, baking soda, and the sugar if you want a touch of sweetness. Massage the seasonings into the beef.

Pound the aromatics: Use a mortar and pestle to pound the shallots, chilies, and cilantro root to a coarse texture (recognizable pieces of chili skin and shallot pieces are normal). Drop in the garlic, then pound to flatten. Scrape the aromatics into a small bowl.

Halve the sweet peppers lengthwise, then seed and cut on the diagonal into pieces ½ inch (1.25cm) wide. Set the aromatics, peppers, beef, remaining seasoning sauce, basil, and oil by the stovetop.

Stir-fry and serve: Set a large wok over medium-low heat on the biggest burner. When the pan is hot (to test, flick in a couple of drops of water; they should sizzle and evaporate within seconds), add 1 Tbsp of the oil, swirl the pan to coat with the oil, and add the garlic mixture. Let it gently sizzle, stirring continuously, to tease the garlic and mellow its harsh raw edge, 30 to 60 seconds. Take care to avoid burning. Return the garlic mixture to its bowl. Rinse and dry the wok.

Set the wok over high heat. When it is hot, add the remaining 1 Tbsp oil and swirl the pan to coat with the oil. Add the beef cubes, spreading them out in a single layer. Let sear until browned on the underside, 1 minute.

Drizzle about 2 Tbsp of the seasoning sauce around the perimeter of the wok, letting it sizzle and caramelize as it slides down the pan wall to flavor the meat. Flip the meat, dump in the garlic mixture, and stir-fry briefly to further cook the meat, 30 to 60 seconds.

Add the sweet peppers and the remaining seasoning sauce and cook, stirring, until the peppers begin to soften, about 45 seconds. Dump in the basil leaves and stir to incorporate and wilt, about 20 seconds.

Turn off the heat, transfer to a serving dish, garnish with the basil tips, and serve immediately.

CONTINUED

NOTES

In Thailand, pad gaprao is often enjoyed with nampla prik, made by mixing 1½ Tbsp lime juice, 1½ Tbsp fish sauce (or Thai thin soy sauce), and 1 Tbsp chopped fresh Thai chilies; if you like, stir in 1 Tbsp very thinly sliced shallot. Prepare this sauce before stir-frying so you're fully ready to serve and eat. Invite dinners to spoon on some nampla prik to add salty, tangy, pungent notes to each bite.

Select Wagyu or well-marbled steak for the most tender results. Bavette may be sold as "flap" at markets. Affordable top sirloin cap (also called picanha and coulotte) is also excellent.

Baking soda helps the meat caramelize while tenderizing it a bit too.

If you don't have cilantro root, just skip it. No need to bother with subbing cilantro stems.

To add a vegetable side, use the wok to cook it before stir-frying the pad gaprao. Heat the wok over high heat until hot, then add 1 Tbsp oil and swirl the pan to coat with the oil. Add 2 or 3 garlic cloves, smashed, to the oil and heat briefly to infuse the oil, then dump in a bunch of greens, cut into bite-size pieces, and season with 1 or 2 big pinches of fine sea salt as you swiftly stir-fry. Double the serving sauce so there's plenty for the vegetable side and main dish.

For extra protein, add a fried egg for each person to enjoy with the stir-fry and rice.

VARIATIONS

ผัดกะเพราไก่ | Pad Gaprao Gai
Holy Basil Chicken

Swap the steak for 1 lb (450g) boneless, skinless or skin-on chicken thighs. Cut the chicken into 1-inch (2.5cm) chunks and season as you do the steak. Gently cook the garlic mixture as in the main recipe. Reheat the cleaned wok over high heat, swirl in 2 Tbsp oil, and then sear the chicken all over until the chunks turn opaque, feel tender firm, and are nearly cooked, 2 to 3 minutes. Drizzle in some seasoning sauce, stir-fry briefly, return the aromatics, and finish as in the main recipe.

ผัดกะเพราเนื้อสับ | Pad Gaprao Neua Sub
Holy Basil Ground Meat

Swap the steak with 1 lb (450g) ground chicken, pork, or lamb. Season it as you do the steak, using your fingertips to incorporate the seasonings. Gently cook the garlic mixture as in the main recipe. Reheat the cleaned wok over high heat, swirl in 2 Tbsp oil, and add the ground meat, spreading it out in a layer about 1 inch (2.5cm) thick. Let sear for 30 to 45 seconds, stirring and breaking it up into small pieces. Drizzle with some seasoning sauce, stir-fry briefly, return the aromatics, and finish as in the main recipe.

ผัดกะเพราเต้าหู้ | Pad Gaprao Tofu
Holy Basil Tofu

Swap the steak for 1 lb (450g) super-firm tofu that you have crumbled into pieces no bigger than ½ inch (1.25cm). For the seasoning sauce, mix together 2½ Tbsp Thai thin soy sauce, scant 2 Tbsp vegetarian oyster sauce, 2 tsp Thai black soy sauce, ½ tsp fine sea salt, and 2½ Tbsp water. Season the tofu crumbles with 1 Tbsp of the seasoning sauce, the sugar, and 1 tsp Saam Kleur (Three Buddies Paste, page 57; optional); omit the baking soda. Gently cook the garlic mixture as in the main recipe. Reheat the cleaned wok over high heat, swirl in 3 Tbsp oil, and add the tofu, spreading it out into a layer to sear and brown here and there, about 1 minute. Flip the tofu and continue to sear and brown here and there, about 1 minute. Drizzle with some seasoning sauce, stir-fry briefly, return the aromatics, and finish as in the main recipe.

หมูก้อนทอด | Moo Gon Tod

Fried Pork Meatballs

SERVES 4

Garlicky, peppery, salty moo gon tod (it literally means "fried pork lumps") were among my favorite childhood school lunch box items. I'd fill up on the deep-fried meatballs (photographed on page 236), which I dunked in lots of ketchup, and leave the rice and vegetables untouched, much to the chagrin of my mom and our cook. As an adult, I better understand the need for a balanced meal and also delight in having refreshing bites of cucumber or cilantro along with the pork and rice. As for the dipping sauce, ketchup is nostalgic, but these days, I prefer the spicy tang of Thai sriracha sauce, spicy-sweet Thai chili sauce, or jaew sauce. If you have kids, these meatballs are for them. If you're a childlike adult, these are for you too! They're easy to make and love.

SAAM KLEUR (THREE BUDDIES PASTE) OR 2½ TBSP PREMADE FROM LARDER (PAGE 57)

25g | 5 large garlic cloves

12g | generous 1½ Tbsp chopped cilantro root, or 2½ tsp chopped cilantro stems

2g | ½ tsp white peppercorns

2g | ½ tsp black peppercorns

---

1 Tbsp Thai oyster sauce

1 Tbsp fish sauce

450g | 1 lb ground pork

Neutral oil, such as rice bran, for deep-frying

Prep the saam kleur: If using the 2½ Tbsp premade saam kleur, put them in a medium bowl and skip to the next step. To make the paste from scratch, use a mortar and pestle to aggressively pound the garlic and cilantro into a coarse paste. Make a well in the center of the paste, add the white and black peppercorns to the well, and pound the peppercorns to smithereens, gradually working the pounded aromatics into the pepper until you have a finely textured mixture, then scrape the paste into a medium bowl.

Shape mini pork UFOs: Add the oyster and fish sauces to the saam kleur and mix well. Then add the pork and mix and massage the seasonings evenly into the pork. Divide the pork into 12 equal portions. For even cooking, shape mini UFOs: Roll a portion into a ball, place it on the fingers of one hand, and press on it with your other hand, creating a dome-like shape with your fingers. You'll end up with a patty roughly 2½ inches (6.25cm) wide with a bump in the center. Set on a sheet pan or plate. Repeat with the remaining portions.

Fry and serve: Line a large plate with paper towels and set it near the stovetop. Pour oil to a depth of 1½ inches (3.75cm) into a large wok and heat over medium-high heat to between 350° and 375°F (175° and 190°C). Working in three or four batches, carefully add the pork balls to the hot oil and fry, turning often, until richly browned and crisp, 2 to 4 minutes. During frying, expect the pork to puff slightly and become rounder. As each batch is ready, transfer it to the towel-lined plate to drain, then let the oil return to temperature before adding the next batch. Serve with lots of rice and the suggested accompaniments mentioned in the recipe headnote.

กะหล่ำปลีผัดน้ำปลา | Pad Galamplee

Charred Cabbage in Caramelized Fish Sauce

SERVES 4

Stir-frying cabbage with fish sauce and garlic is an old, simple Thai dish that I first put on the Nari menu in 2019. The unique flavor and aroma of wok-cooked dishes cannot be easily achieved on a home stove, so here's my trick: Singe the cabbage to mimic the smokiness that a blazing-hot professional wok setup would provide. The singeing makes this stir-fry always taste special and lightly cooks the cabbage so it spends less time in the hot wok. Regular green cabbage works great, but so do other varieties, such as flat Dutch or cone-shaped sweetheart cabbage. An average head of cabbage weighs over 2 lb (1 kg), so use a half of a head for this recipe.

---

500 to 560g | ½ head green cabbage

1½ tsp firmly packed Thai palm sugar

1 Tbsp water

2 Tbsp fish sauce or Fast Fake Fish Sauce (page 23)

2 Tbsp neutral oil, such as rice bran

3 garlic cloves, smashed

Fake the wok hei: Cut through the core of the cabbage to yield two even wedges. Set a perforated skillet or vegetable grill pan (see Note for alternative) over medium-high heat. When the pan is hot (to test, flick in a couple of drops of water; they should sizzle and evaporate within seconds), add the cabbage wedges and singe on all cut sides, pressing and turning often, until the edges are browned and slightly smoky smelling, 3 to 5 minutes. (Avoid blackening the cabbage!) Transfer the warm cabbage to a big bowl and let sit for a few minutes until cool enough to handle.

Trim the cabbage core from each wedge and cut the leaves into uneven 2- to 3-inch (5 to 7.5cm) pieces. Cut the stiff spine pieces smaller than the rest.

Make the seasoning sauce: In a small microwave-safe bowl, combine the sugar and water and microwave on high power to melt the sugar, about 15 seconds. Stir well, then mix in the fish sauce. Set near the stovetop along with the cabbage.

Stir-fry the cabbage and serve: On your biggest burner, heat the oil and garlic in a large wok over medium-low heat. Gently fry the garlic, teasing out the flavor, until golden, 1 to 3 minutes. Transfer the garlic to a serving plate, leaving the oil behind.

Raise the heat to medium-high and add the cabbage. Stir-fry and toss, coating with the oil, until heated through and glistening, about 1 minute. Pour the seasoning sauce around the perimeter of the pan, then stir-fry and toss to distribute evenly. When the cabbage begins releasing liquid, after 45 seconds or so, turn up the heat and bring to a rapid boil to reduce the cooking juices and coat the leaves. When little liquid remains, turn off the heat. Return the garlic to the wok, give things a stir, and then transfer to a serving plate and eat up.

NOTE

You can singe the cabbage in a ripping-hot cast-iron or carbon-steel skillet over medium-high heat for 3 to 5 minutes. And if the skillet is big, you can stir-fry the cabbage in it too.

พริกขิงปลาดุกฟู | Prik King Pla Duk Foo

Crispy Curried Fish Cereal

MAKES ABOUT 2½ CUPS (600ML)

Don't put this in a bowl with milk for breakfast! These sweet, salty, spicy, citrusy crispy bits are for eating with rice, just like Japanese furikake. However, because the fish cereal is deep-fried, prik king pla duk foo is also like eating bacon bits. Yes, Thai food is crazy delicious. And you never know what will happen if you share this special treat with friends. For instance, I once was treated to a meal at the Restaurant at Meadowood in Napa Valley for bringing a jar of this curry fish cereal to chef Christopher Kostow. His lovely Thai American wife, Martina, knew the value of this special food. If your makrut leaves are young and tender, hand tear them for interesting texture, as shown in the photo.

- 2 batches Pla Duk Foo (Fish Cereal, page 75)
- 20g | brimming 3 Tbsp small dried shrimp
- 1 Tbsp oil, such as rice bran, plus more to taste
- 50 to 60g | 3 to 4 Tbsp Prik Gaeng Ped (Red Curry Paste, page 144), using the max for extra fire
- 40g | 3 Tbsp granulated sugar, preferably organic, plus more to taste
- 2½ to 3 Tbsp fish sauce
- Fine sea salt
- 3g | 3 Tbsp finely slivered makrut leaves (see page 31)

Ready the fish cereal and dried shrimp: Make the fish cereal. If already on hand, bring to room temperature. Soak the dried shrimp in hot water to cover until softened, 3 to 5 minutes. Drain and pat dry with a paper towel, and then transfer the shrimp to a mortar. Start pounding the shrimp with the pestle, aiming it slightly off center up the side of the mortar, until the shrimp are transformed into tiny, flossy shreds. (If you'd rather, use a food chopper or electric grinder.)

Cook the mixture over lowish heat: Set a large wok over medium-low heat. When the pan is hot, add the oil and swirl the pan to coat with the oil. Add the curry paste and stir with a spatula until aromatic, about 1 minute. Gradually work in the dried shrimp floss to coat well and toast the bits. Expect the mixture to appear dryish.

Stir in the sugar and let it melt, about 1 minute. Pour in 2½ Tbsp of the fish sauce, stirring swiftly to create a heady, dark red mixture. Some of the mixture will stick to the spatula, so slide the wok to a cool burner to safely scrape the mixture off the spatula and return it to the pan.

Return the wok to the hot burner, taste, and add up to 1½ tsp fish sauce to boost the umami flavor. Turn down the heat to between medium-low and low.

Dump in the fish cereal and stir to coat with the seasonings. It will naturally break into small clumps. Keep stirring, pausing to scrape off bits stuck to the spatula as needed. Use a fork to break up the dark clumps of curry paste that inevitably form. If things look like they may burn, scooch down the heat.

Once the crispy fish bits are well coated, make sure to have the heat at low. Pause to taste and add pinches of sugar to soften rough edges (let it melt before retasting) or pinches of salt for savory depth.

Add the lime leaf slivers, stirring and folding constantly while drying and slightly shrinking the slivers, 2 to 3 minutes. Turn off the heat. The fish cereal is ready to eat with rice. Or spread the mixture in a thin layer on a sheet pan, let cool completely, transfer to a tightly capped glass jar, and refrigerate for safekeeping for months. Warm in a wok or skillet over low heat to re-crisp before serving.

หอยลายน้ำผัดพริกเผา | Hoy Lai Pad Namprik Pao

Chili Jam Clams

SERVES 4

When it comes to chili jam clams, there is truth in advertising—it's simply clams and chili jam. But if you want truly impressive results, use quality ingredients, and that means my grandmother's namprik pao. It will lend umami heat with a slight touch of sweetness. Additionally, select smallish clams so there are plenty to add flavor to the sauce, which is fabulous mixed into lots of rice. Instead of clams, try shrimp or scallops.

900g | 2 lb Manila or small littleneck clams

Fine sea salt

60ml | ¼ cup Namprik Pao (Grandmother's Chili Jam, page 44)

2 to 5 fresh Thai chilies, lightly smashed, to taste

1 tsp fish sauce (optional)

½ tsp firmly packed Thai palm sugar (optional)

15g | 1 big handful fresh Thai basil leaves, plus more for garnish

½ lime, halved

Soak the clams: Rinse the clams under cold running water, then transfer to a large bowl, add water to cover plus a big pinch of salt. Let the clams sit for 30 to 60 minutes to purge them of sand. Drain the clams and set near the stovetop.

Stir-fry away: On your biggest burner, heat a large wok over high until smoking hot (no oil needed!). Add the clams and cover so they release some juices, 1 to 2 minutes. Dump in the chili jam and stir swiftly to break it up and distribute it well. Cover and cook until half of the clams open, 1 to 2 minutes. Throw in the Thai chilies, cover, and continue cooking, opening occasionally to stir and check, until all the clams have opened, 3 to 5 minutes.

Taste and serve: Turn off the heat and pick out and discard any clams that failed to open. Taste the sauce and, if needed, stir in the fish sauce to curb sweetness, or add the sugar to round the salty edges. Add the basil and stir to distribute, then squeeze in lime juice to brighten the flavors. Dish out into a shallow bowl, garnish with extra basil (if you like), and dive in. Remind guests that they can avoid the chilies or eat them at their own peril.

NOTE

For appearance, toss in a handful of sliced mini sweet peppers. Be sure to color coordinate them with the Thai chilies so you can pick them out if needed.

ปูผัดพริกไทยดำ | Pu Pad Prik Thai Dam

Phuket Black Pepper Crab

SERVES 4

When it's Dungeness crab season in the San Francisco Bay Area, there are few better pleasures than diving into this quick stir-fry. The delectable hands-on dish reminds me of family visits to Phuket Island, where intrepid cooks quickly dispatched live crabs just before cooking to ensure the freshest flavor. You don't have to do that to make this dish. But please don't shy from the black pepper. The crab and sauce need it. Scrape the creamy tomalley (the soft, yellowish curds) from the shell, but if it is unavailable or you're allergic to it, skip it. Serve with rice and a simple vegetable side, plus lots of beer and paper napkins.

- 2 cooked Dungeness crabs, cleaned with tomalley reserved, or 675 to 900g | 1½ to 2 lb Dungeness crab clusters
- 1½ Tbsp Thai black soy sauce
- 1 Tbsp Thai thin soy sauce
- 1 Tbsp fermented black bean sauce or black bean garlic sauce (see Notes)
- 2 Tbsp Thai oyster sauce
- 2 Tbsp black peppercorns, cracked and crushed
- 2 tsp granulated sugar
- 50g | 3½ Tbsp salted butter
- 15 to 20 curry leaves, to taste (see Note if unavailable)
- 100g | 2 big shallots, sliced ¼ inch (6mm) thick
- 2 garlic cloves, chopped
- 80ml | ⅓ cup water if using tomalley, or 120ml | ½ cup water if not using tomalley
- 3 fresh Thai chilies, lightly smashed
- 3 dried prik jinda or árbol chilies

Prep the crab: If working with whole crab bodies, halve them vertically with a heavy knife, then snap each half into 3 roughly even pieces. If working from clusters, break each cluster into 3 pieces. Using the spine of a heavy knife, gently crack the crab to allow flavor inside and to facilitate eating later. Discard shell bits that come loose.

Mix the sauce: In a bowl, stir together the reserved crab tomalley (if using), black and thin soy sauces, black bean sauce, oyster sauce, black pepper, and sugar. Set the sauce mixture, crab, and the remaining ingredients next to the stovetop.

Wok away: In a large wok over medium-high heat, melt the butter. Add the curry leaves and shallots and stir-fry until aromatic, about 1 minute. Add the garlic and stir-fry until fragrant, about 20 seconds. Dump in the sauce, stir, and then add the crab, stirring swiftly and flipping to coat.

Add ⅓ cup (80ml) water if using tomalley or ½ cup (120ml) if not, cover, and cook for 2 minutes. Uncover, drop in the Thai and prik jinda chilies, stir swiftly, re-cover, and cook to heat through, 2 to 3 minutes. Uncover and check the sauce. If it's too runny, crank up the heat to high and boil to reduce slightly (some sauce is good for mixing with rice). Turn off the heat, transfer to a platter or bowl, and serve. Offer seafood or nut crackers plus plenty of paper napkins. Remind guests that they can avoid the chilies or eat them at their own peril.

NOTE

Many Southern Thai Chinese dishes like this stir-fried crab use a type of soft fermented black beans. It is hard to source outside of Thailand, and I have found that fermented black bean sauce and black bean garlic sauce produced by Lee Kum Kee work well as a substitute.

No curry leaves? Use a big handful of fresh Thai basil leaves in their place. Do not cook the basil with the shallots. After turning off the heat, stir in the basil to wilt, then dish out and serve.

ซี่โครงหมูทอดกระเทียม | Sikrong Moo Tod

Crispy Garlic Fried Riblets

SERVES 4 TO 6

Attention, rib lovers! Here are the fried riblets of your crunchy, garlicky dreams. In Thailand, cooks coat and deep-fry a delicious mess of pork riblets and then dump fried garlic on top. Achieving a crunchy outside and tender-juicy meat involves a little trick. My "secret" method is two-temperature frying. Collagen melts when exposed to high temperature, so the initial frying at lowish heat retains the meat's texture while preserving the punchy garlicky flavor without burning. That's followed by higher-temperature frying to ensure a crispy exterior that makes the ribs so moreish. Because the ribs are also tasty at room temperature, they're a perfect make-ahead dish. Eat with jasmine or sticky rice (pages 256 and 257) or serve as a nosh with cold beer. Dip in sriracha sauce for extra excitement.

SAAM KLEUR (THREE BUDDIES PASTE) OR 3 TBSP PREMADE FROM LARDER (PAGE 57)

30g | 1 oz garlic cloves (9 cloves)

15g | 2 Tbsp finely chopped cilantro root, or 8g | 1 Tbsp finely chopped cilantro stems

2.5g | scant 1 tsp white peppercorns

2.5g | scant 1 tsp black peppercorns

Prep the saam kleur: If using the 3 Tbsp premade saam kleur, put them in a medium bowl and skip to the next step. To make the paste from scratch, use a mortar and pestle to aggressively pound the garlic and cilantro into a coarse paste. Make a well in the center of the paste, add the white and black peppercorns to the well, and pound the peppercorns to smithereens, gradually working the pounded aromatics into the pepper until you have a finely textured mixture, then scrape the paste into a medium bowl.

---

2 Tbsp fish sauce

2 Tbsp Thai oyster sauce

675g | 1½ lbs pork riblets, cut as 1½- to 2-inch-long (4.25 to 5cm) pieces (see Note)

20g | 2 Tbsp Thai rice flour

20g | 2 Tbsp tapioca starch

¼ tsp baking powder

1 Tbsp water

Neutral oil, such as rice bran, for deep-frying

Sriraja Panich or Shark sriracha sauce, for serving (optional)

Season the riblets: Stir the fish and oyster sauces into the saam kleur, mixing well. Add the riblets and massage in the seasonings. Cover and refrigerate for at least 6 hours or up to overnight.

Coat the riblets: Remove the chilled riblets from the fridge. While they're still cold, add the rice flour, tapioca starch, and baking powder and stir to coat well. Add the water to hydrate the dry ingredients, mixing well. The riblets will look like they're covered by a beige face mask. Let sit, uncovered, while you prepare to fry.

Deep-fry low, then go high: Using your largest burner, heat a large wok over high heat until nearly smoking. Pour in oil to fill the wok almost halfway (about 2 inches | 5cm), wait until the oil registers 300° to 350°F (150° to 175°C), and then add the pork riblets, scraping the bowl to include all the goodies. Stir gently to break up the clumps of riblets.

Turn down the heat to maintain the oil at about 250°F (120°C) to allow the riblets to fry in a confit-esque, gentle Jacuzzi bath of simmering oil for 10 minutes. Avoid stirring during the first 5 minutes to allow the coating to set on the riblets. Midway through, stir the contents of the wok, scraping the bottom to prevent the garlic from burning. Gently shaking the pan is fine, and if garlic pieces appear on top, skim them off.

Now, increase the heat to high and rhythmically shake the pan to fry the riblets evenly and deliver a crispy, rich brown finish, 5 to 7 minutes. The garlic bits on the ribs should be golden, not burnt. Using a fine-mesh skimmer, transfer the pork and all of the bits to a coarse-mesh strainer set over a large bowl to drain well and yield extra-crispy results. The riblets remain crisp and crunchy for a few hours, but eat up sooner than later, dipped in sriracha if you like.

NOTE

For the riblets, ask a butcher to saw a small rack of meaty baby back ribs or St. Louis–style pork ribs crosswise into strips about 1½ to 2 inches (3.75 to 5cm) wide. At home, cut between the bones to separate into riblets. Employ the overage for Tom Saap soup (page 197; see Notes). Or just double this recipe and invite people over.

หมูกรอบ | Moo Krob

Crispy Fried Pork Belly

SERVES 8

Why fry pork belly? Because it's damn delicious! This recipe's seasoning, coating, and frying methods yield excellent flavor and texture. Buy pork belly that has an even distribution of fat and lean. Skin-on belly is best, but you can fry skinless belly too. Cut as thin dominos, moo krob is one of the best noshes ever. Serve it with nam jim jaew (page 209) and sticky rice (page 257) for a quintessential pairing (and don't forget the beer). Put the belly in a sandwich, if you want. You'll find many ways to enjoy this incredibly good, crispy pork belly.

900g | 2 lb boneless pork belly with even distribution of fat and lean, preferably skin on

Coarse salt (any kind)

Distilled white vinegar, for soaking the pork belly

Cut and chill the belly: Cut the pork belly into strips 1½ to 1¾ inches (3.75 to 4.4cm) wide. (Use a ruler and score the skin before cutting all the way through.) Rub a three-finger pinch of salt onto the skin side of each strip, flip the strip over, and then move it on your cutting board like a scouring pad. Pour vinegar to a depth of ⅛ inch (3mm) into a nonreactive eighth sheet pan (or similar pan) and add the strips, skin-side down. Chill, uncovered, for 30 to 60 minutes.

SAAM KLEUR (THREE BUDDIES PASTE) OR 2 TSP PREMADE FROM LARDER (PAGE 57)

8g | 2 medium-large garlic cloves

4g | 2 tsp chopped cilantro root, or 2g | 1 tsp chopped cilantro stems

0.6g | 14 white peppercorns

0.6g | 11 black peppercorns

Prep the saam kleur: If using the 2 tsp premade saam kleur, put them into a large bowl and skip to the next step. To make the paste from scratch, use a mortar and pestle to aggressively pound the garlic and cilantro into a coarse paste. Make a well in the center of the paste, add the white and black peppercorns to the well, and pound the peppercorns to smithereens, gradually working the pounded aromatics into the pepper until you have a finely textured mixture, then scrape the paste into a large bowl.

20g | 2½ Tbsp Thai rice flour

20g | 2½ Tbsp tapioca starch

¼ tsp baking powder

1 Tbsp fish sauce

1 Tbsp Thai oyster sauce

1 Tbsp water

Neutral oil, such as rice bran, for deep-frying

Make the seasoned coating: Add the rice flour, tapioca starch, baking powder, fish sauce, and oyster sauce to the saam kleur and mix well, then stir in the water.

Scrape and coat the pork: Pull the cold pork from the fridge, then aggressively scrape the skin with a sharp fork and/or bread knife. Pretend you're giving a Korean-style body exfoliation or you've got a really bad itch that you need to scratch. This scuffing up helps the skin to crisp later. Go for it, so the skin ends up looking all roughed up.

Use a sharp knife to make crosswise cuts through the skin and halfway down into the fat (see photo on page 248). Make short cuts a good ¼ inch (6mm) apart. (Mistakenly cutting into the meat is OK.) When done, halve each strip crosswise for easier frying later. Add the roughened belly to the bowl of seasonings and rub vigorously all over to coat. Cover and refrigerate for at least 3 hours or up to overnight.

Ready the pork for frying: Set a large wire cooling rack on a sheet pan. Straighten the belly strips and let them dry at room temperature, uncovered, on the cooling rack for about 1½ hours. You will be frying the pork belly two or three times.

Gently fry to cook the pork: Pour oil to a depth of 1½ inches (3.75cm) into a large wok and heat over medium heat to 200° to 250°F (95° to 120°C). Bend each strip to ensure the skin fully separates at the cuts. Working in two or three batches, add the strips to the hot oil and fry, turning a few times, until tender firm, 10 to 14 minutes. To test for doneness, scoop out a strip and insert an instant-read thermometer into the center; it should register about 140°F (60°C). As each batch is ready, transfer it to the cooling rack and let the oil return to temperature before adding the next batch. Let cool, uncovered, until no longer sticky from the coating, about 1½ hours. Reserve the oil in the wok.

CONTINUED

Fry again to crisp the pork: Pat excess moisture from the pork, then check the cuts on the skin, prying or recutting through the skin to reopen any cuts that have stuck together. Line the floor by the stove with newspaper, then reheat the oil in the wok over medium heat to 325° to 350°F (160° to 175°C). Fry the pork again in two or three batches, using a splatter guard to contain hot splatters and turning the pieces often to ensure the skin's full submersion in the oil, until crisp and richly browned, 4 to 5 minutes. As each batch is ready, transfer it to the cooling rack and let the oil return to temperature before adding the next batch. Let cool for about 5 minutes.

Optional frying for extra crispness: If the skin isn't crisp enough, pry open the skin again so the oil gets into those crevices! Refry the pork belly in oil heated to 350° to 375°F (175° to 190°C) for 1 to 2 minutes. This third frying is fab for refreshing tired belly too.

Let cool briefly, then cut into thin slices along the skin score lines. Indulge away!

NOTES

The salting, vinegar soak, scouring, and scraping roughens up the skin so it later takes to the marinade well and fries up crispy.

To make the pork belly for a party, after the first fry, cool and chill the belly, uncovered, overnight. Return the pork to room temperature the next day and follow the rest of the recipe to finish as usual.

9 ข้าวๆ เส้นๆ

Rice and Noodles

Grateful for Grains

A day of eating Thai food without rice or noodles is a sad one. Grains anchor pleasurable meals and dishes in countless ways, from fluffy mounds of rice topped by sassy curries and balls of sticky rice dipped into jaew sauce to a tangle of noodles floating in broth or a snack made from rice flour.

Among my most special food memories were the Sunday lunches at my grandfather's home. The midday menu usually included an element of fun. Unlike at dinnertime when you were required to sit nicely at the table and eat politely with the adults, lunches were much more flexible. Often you could even make your *own* plate or bowl of noodles or rice. You got to choose your own adventure! What a treat for a curious troublemaker like me!

Many of those lunches were one-dish meals, but they were never monotonous or boring. Instead, such meals focused on one spectacular dish with its own constellation of condiments and add-ons. The family got to freely compose the food to each person's liking. I was gleeful if Sunday lunch featured kanom jeen, the Thai category of dishes of tender rice noodles (kanom jeen) served with rich curry sauces. My favorite was sumptuous kanom jeen nam prik, a preparation that was seldom available at restaurants back then, not even at the shops that specialized in kanom jeen. It was among my late grandmother's specialties, one that she taught to my favorite aunt, Pah Pui.

On Sunday morning, Pah Pui would oversee a cadre of cooks to prepare the savory-sweet shrimp and coconut namprik sauce. They'd begin with our family's heady seasoning paste, then enrich it with freshly squeezed coconut milk. (For my recipe, I insist on homemade paste, but I'll allow you, and myself, boxed coconut milk.) The myriad of accompaniments were organized into three categories for prep: fried things (เหมือดทอด), oil-"blanched" things (เหมือดผัด), and raw things (เหมือดดิบ). Meanwhile, someone would make a special trip to the early-morning market to purchase stellar old-fashioned fermented rice noodles from a favorite maker.

By lunchtime, an intricate setup would be displayed on the table. The centerpiece was a big tray of rice noodles carefully formed into delicate spirals and a shimmering pot of sauce. Alongside was an array of accompaniments, ranging from rafts of fried small shrimp and tempura-fried frilly Ming aralia leaves and delicate bougainvillea flowers to gently stir-fried winged beans, slightly bitter tips of very young raw acacia leaves, and the crisp inner petals of banana blossoms.

Each person grabbed a plate, added one or two noodle spirals, spooned on some of the salty-sweet-rich sauce, and then selected what they wanted from the bounty of accompaniments. I, of course, always went for the noodles and the fried things first, much to the consternation of my elder relatives.

Those kanom jeen lunches seeded my fondest memories of family and food. I want you to have them too. These heritage dishes are in need of a wider audience to appreciate them, or they risk being forgotten. To that end, I've included my family's recipes for kanom jeen nam prik on page 269 and kanom jeen nam ya on page 265. Others are dishes that I sorely miss, like kueytiew ped (page 273), a duck noodle soup from specialty shops in the town of Nahkon Chaisri, where my khun yai (maternal grandmother) was born. The khao soi spicy coconut and chicken noodle soup on page 275 honors my paternal grandmother, who was from Chiang Mai. Master any of those project dishes to vault yourself into an elite group of top-notch cooks.

If you are not in the mood for a rice noodle feast or hearty soup noodles, there are easy recipes for fried rice and stir-fried rice noodles (the crab sen chan on page 263 will beat out pad Thai any day). Add dishes from other chapters for a special meal, or just revel in serving a plate of fried rice or stir-fried noodles as a one-dish meal.

Whatever you choose, I want you to have a special Thai-style weekend lunch gathering of your own. Do all the prep—some of which can be done days in advance—and set out all the elements. Let your guests compose their own plate or bowl, then sit down and enjoy the meal together. Tip a glass to my aunt Pah Pui while you're at it. Cheers!

Your Rice Cooking Options

Rice is the staff of life for most people on earth. Thai cooks have many ways to prepare the grain, and there are many varieties to choose from.

What kind of rice to cook? Growers in Thailand cultivate countless types of rice, including heirloom varieties and fanciful ones with cute names like "Forget Your Husband," which promises a flavor so enticing that you might abandon a marriage in search of the rice. Keep your eyes open during your travels and shopping adventures because there's a wide range of aromas, textures, colors, and flavors. Below is just a small sampling of Thai rice.

- **Jasmine rice** is what's commonly enjoyed with most Thai meals because it absorbs flavors well. Fragrant white jasmine rice is more popular than **brown jasmine rice**. A basic recipe for cooking white jasmine rice is on page 256.
- **Young "green" jasmine rice** is harder to source but worth the effort to find. The pale-green tinge on the unhusked grains reflects their youth. It is more tender than brown jasmine rice. I source young jasmine rice from Bangkok vendors. At Nahm, we cook it in jasmine flower-scented water for a very special treat.
- **Red Cargo rice**, a whole-grain rice, is not a type of jasmine rice. It requires more time and water than white jasmine and cooks up with a nutty flavor.
- **White sticky rice** is enjoyed with many Isaan dishes, such as laab and grilled gai yang chicken (pages 106 and 208). The rice is typically soaked for hours before steaming, but for the small amount needed for recipes in this book, use the quick microwave sticky rice recipe on page 257.
- **Thai black sticky rice** is a handsome whole-grain rice. It requires special handling and is only for certain dishes.

See page 27 for more tips on sourcing jasmine and sticky rice.

Rice Noodles 101

Here are some shopping and prep tips for the rice noodles called for in this chapter's recipes.

Flat rice noodles for stir-fries and noodle soups are sold at Asian and some international markets. When they are dried, the noodles are labeled "rice sticks" in English and "bánh phở" in Vietnamese.

- For the drunken noodles on page 260, check Chinese and Vietnamese markets for fresh rice noodles, known as chow fun, in or near the refrigerated noodle case. Or boil pappardelle-size wide dried flat rice noodles that are about ½ inch (1.25cm) wide; they're sometimes labeled "XL."
- To prepare crab sen chan (page 263), shop for fresh "pad Thai" noodles at Chinese and Southeast Asian markets or dried sen yai—medium-size flat rice noodles (think fettuccine size)—which are easier to find. Dried noodle packages labeled "pad Thai," "Chantaboon," or "Jantaboon" are suitable for stir-frying. Of note, Chantaboon is the historic name of the province of Chantaburi, where the style of chewy-tender noodle originated.
- When serving duck noodle soup (page 273) with rice noodles, any size of rice noodles works, though many people serve sen lek, narrow flat rice noodles (think linguine size). They're often labeled "S" for small. If wider noodles are handier, use them!

Round rice noodles for the kanom jeen recipes on pages 265 and 269 are mostly available as dried noodles labeled as "vermicelli," "rice sticks," or "bún" (in Vietnamese). The noodles come in different thicknesses, but the capellini-size ones are most similar to Thai kanom jeen rice noodles. Suggested brands include Pagoda, Three Ladies, and Golden Star.

To coil kanom jeen into spirals for efficient serving, after draining the boiled noodles, let them sit in cold water to cool briefly, about 5 minutes. Pick up a skein of noodles, holding them loosely (see photo), then dunk the skein back into the water a few times, gently slapping it back and forth in the water to line up and straighten the noodles. Gently release and coil the skein onto your other hand into a flattish spiral. Usher the noodle spiral onto a plate, then repeat with the remaining noodles.

ข้าวสวย | Khao Suay

Basic Jasmine Rice

MAKES 6 CUPS (1.5L), TO SERVE 4 TO 6

How to cook a pot of white jasmine rice? There are numerous methods. For instance, some people steam it, while others boil rice like pasta, which rids the grains of too much of the sweet starches that define their cozy texture and lovely flavor. At home, I only cook plain rice in a Zojirushi rice cooker or a Japanese donabe ceramic pot. However, Andrea often prepares white jasmine rice in a heavy saucepan on the stove, and here is her method. It involves a gradual lowering of the heat to ensure even cooking. She recommends preparing your rice in the same pan on a regular basis, because with practice, you'll soon be eyeballing the water level instead of measuring it. The Notes offer tips for troubleshooting and more.

380g | 2 cups raw jasmine rice
600ml | 2½ cups water

Rinse the rice: Measure the rice into a medium saucepan. Add water to cover by about 1 inch (2.5cm), stir with your fingers to loosen excess starch, then pour off the water. Repeat two or three times, or until the water runs mostly clear, then dump into a fine-mesh strainer. Shake the strainer to remove excess water, then return the rice to the pan. Add the water and note the rice and water levels in your pot to eyeball future batches.

10-10-10 cook: Bring the pot to a boil over high heat, stirring often with a silicone spatula to prevent clumping. Lower the heat slightly to maintain a brisk simmer, stirring often to scrape the bottom and circulate the grains, until the grains expand and swim about in the starchy, thickish liquid, 1 to 3 minutes. It's normal for a few craters to form on top. Turn down the heat to low, cover, and cook for 10 minutes. Turn off the heat and let sit for 10 minutes to finish cooking. Fluff the rice, re-cover, and let rest again for 10 minutes. Keep covered and warm for up to 30 minutes. Re-fluff before serving.

NOTES

If the cooked rice is too firm and dryish, sprinkle with water, cover, and set over low heat for 10 minutes to hydrate; then fluff. If the rice is mushy, decrease the water by 1 Tbsp per 1 cup (190g) of rice when you make your next batch. Find the best rice-to-water ratio for your tastes and the rice itself (for example, new-crop jasmine rice requires slightly less water than usual).

When preparing rice specifically for fried rice, turn the cooked rice onto a sheet pan, spreading it out to allow the grains to dry quickly so they will fry up nicely. Let cool completely, uncovered, for 1 to 2 hours, before frying. Or, cover the baking sheet and refrigerate overnight.

Plain rice is cooked unsalted in Thailand because the rice is meant to accompany other dishes that are boldly flavored. To cook a half batch of rice, use a small saucepan and the same cook times.

ข้าวเหนียวนึ่ง | Khao Niew Neung

Microwave Sticky Rice

MAKES ABOUT 2 CUPS (480ML), TO SERVE 4 AS A SIDE

Before this book, I only reheated rice in the microwave. However, we needed small batches of sticky rice for enjoying with laab, green papaya salad, grilled chicken, and the like. The rice is typically soaked for hours, then steamed, but Andrea has a rogue microwave steaming method to deliver sticky rice to the table in about 30 minutes. Now you can make sticky rice on the fly! For minimal cleanup, simply soak, steam, and serve in the same vessel. Sticky—also called glutinous and sweet—rice is sold at Asian markets. You'll need an inexpensive microwave vented splatter cover (see Notes).

200g | 1 cup raw sticky rice
About 240ml | 1 cup water

Measure and soak: Weigh the rice in a microwave-safe medium bowl, glass storage container, or casserole dish (see Notes). Give the rice a quick rinse to remove excess starch then drain well. Set the bowl on the scale and set the scale to tare (zero). Return the rice to the bowl, and then slowly add the water until the total weight reaches 450g (1 lb); you may not use all the water. Let soak at room temperature to hydrate for 15 minutes.

3-4-5 cook: Slide the bowl into the microwave and cover with a vented splatter cover. Cook on medium-high power (I select setting 8 on a scale of 1 to 10, from low to high) for 3 minutes. Use a silicone spatula to swiftly stir and fold the rice, which currently resembles undercooked risotto with little liquid visible. As you stir, the rice absorbs the lingering water. Scrape the vessel walls clean if needed.

Re-cover the vessel and microwave on medium-high power for 4 minutes. Remove from the microwave. The grains should now be sticky and tender firm, with no hard, opaque grains. Gently fluff and fold the rice with the spatula. Tightly cover the rice (I favor a silicone lid) and let sit for 5 minutes to further soften the grains.

Check and correct: If there are still some unpleasant hardish grains, gently fold in 1 Tbsp water, re-cover, and microwave on medium-high power for 1 to 2 minutes. Remove from the microwave, cover tightly, and let rest for 3 to 5 minutes before rechecking softness. The amount of water needed depends on the sticky rice used and your microwaving equipment. Jot down what works for you.

Keep the rice covered until serving time. Leftover rice can be stored in an airtight container in the refrigerator for up to 3 days. To reheat refrigerated rice, sprinkle with a little water, cover with the splatter cover, and microwave on medium-high power until warm and softened, 1 to 2 minutes.

NOTES

Don't have a microwave vented splatter cover yet? Cover the bowl with a plate, ensuring a crack of space for ventilation.

A medium cooking vessel holds 3 to 4 cups (720ml to 1L). When scaling up, adjust the vessel size and add more water. For instance, use a 5- to 6-cup (1.25 to 1.5L) vessel to cook the following:

1½ batches: 300g | 1½ cups sticky rice plus water to total 675g (1½ lb)

2 batches: 400g | 2 cups sticky rice plus water to total 900g (2 lb)

Do the 3-minute microwave steaming twice, stirring in between. That ensures the grains have sufficiently hydrated before the final 4-minute zap and 5-minute rest.

ข้าวผัดน้ำพริกไข่เค็ม | Khao Pad Namprik Kai Kem

Salted Egg Yolk–Shrimp Fried Rice

SERVES 4

Cooked namprik relishes such as ones featuring salted egg yolk or prickly ash (pages 130 and 127) are great little Thai seasonings to keep on hand. They function like condiments to perk up foods but are also fabulous for a flavorful, fast fried rice like this one. Instead of shrimp, use another protein, like leftover pork or chicken. Season and add it to the wok as usual. If the protein is raw, stir-fry it for about 2 minutes, just until cooked, before adding the rice. The Variation spotlights using curry paste for fried rice too. Regardless, add crispy fried eggs to your rice plate for Thai-style eating.

225g | 8 oz peeled and deveined large shrimp

1 tsp plus 1 Tbsp fish sauce, divided

450g | 3 cups lightly packed cold cooked long-grain rice

2 Tbsp neutral oil, such as rice bran

60ml | ¼ cup Namprik Kai Kem (Salted Egg Yolk Relish, page 130)

50g | ½ small red or yellow onion, cut into thin half-moons

Thinly sliced green onions, for garnish (optional)

Cilantro sprigs, for garnish (optional)

Serving sauce made by mixing 1½ Tbsp lime juice, 1½ Tbsp fish sauce, 1 Tbsp chopped fresh Thai chilies, and 1 Tbsp thinly sliced shallots (optional)

Prep the shrimp and rice: Rub the shrimp with 1 tsp of the fish sauce. Break up the rice to separate the grains. Set near the stove with the oil, relish, red and green onions, and cilantro (if using). If desired, make the serving sauce and set at the table.

Fry the rice and serve: Set a large wok over medium-high heat on your biggest burner. When the pan is hot (to test, flick in a couple of drops of water; they should sizzle and evaporate within seconds), add the oil and swirl the pan to coat with the oil. Add the namprik kai kem and red onion and stir-fry until fragrant and the onion is just beginning to soften but is still firm, about 1 minute.

Add the shrimp and stir a few times, then dump in the rice and swiftly stir-fry, tossing the rice to coat all of the grains with the seasoning. Spread the rice out along the bottom and up the sides of the wok to fry and caramelize the grains a bit, about 45 seconds, then stir and fold. Repeat the spreading and caramelizing one or two more times until the shrimp are just cooked. Pour the remaining 1 Tbsp fish sauce around the perimeter of the wok to season the grains, then stir to incorporate.

Turn off the heat, and dish out onto a plate or into bowls. Garnish with the green onion and cilantro, if using. Enjoy with the serving sauce, if desired. Sprinkle the sauce onto the rice to brighten and add a bit of zing.

VARIATION

ข้าวผัดน้ำพริกเห็ด | Khao Pad Namprik Hed Northern Curry and Mushroom Fried Rice

Season 8 oz (225g) chopped or hand-torn mushrooms (any kind) with ¼ tsp fine sea salt. Follow the main recipe but swap the salted egg yolk relish for 2½ Tbsp Prik Gaeng Mueng (Northern Curry Paste, page 184). Season the rice with 1 Tbsp Thai thin soy sauce (instead of fish sauce) and big pinches of salt. For the optional serving sauce, mix together 1½ Tbsp lime juice, 1½ Tbsp Thai thin soy sauce, 1 Tbsp chopped fresh Thai chilies, and 1 Tbsp thinly sliced shallots.

ข้าวผัดน้ำพริกกะปิ | Khao Pad Namorik Gapi

Namprik Gapi Fried Rice

SERVES 2

When you have leftover namprik gapi (shrimp paste relish), use it for this quick and delicious khao pad (fried rice). Instead of boiled egg, take time to fry a Thai herb omelet (page 179; part of the sour curry recipe) before frying the rice. You'll have a heavenly rice plate.

If a green mango or tart apple is handy, finely julienne a cheek of it to mix into the rice as you eat for a fruity, tangy burst. Initially frying the moist relish dirties up a stove fast. Put newspaper down in front of the stove to minimize cleanup. Scaling this recipe up or down is easy. Just remember not to crowd the wok.

300g | 2 cups lightly packed cold cooked long-grain rice

2 Tbsp neutral oil, such as rice bran

3 Tbsp Nampik Gapi (Standard-but-Not-Ordinary Shrimp Paste Relish, page 119)

Thinly sliced green onions, for garnish (optional)

Cilantro sprigs, for garnish (optional)

1 or 2 hard-boiled eggs or salted duck eggs (optional)

1 or 2 lime wedges

Break up the rice to separate the grains. Set a large wok (or skillet) over medium-high heat on the biggest burner. When the pan is hot (to test, flick in a couple of drops of water; they should sizzle and evaporate within seconds), add the oil and swirl the pan to coat with the oil. Turn down the heat to medium-low, add the namprik gapi, and stir swiftly to slightly mellow the raw garlic, about 20 seconds. Stand back and be careful because the mixture will spit.

Dump the rice into the wok, increase the heat to medium-high, then stir and mix all of the ingredients to heat the rice and coat the grains with gapi funky goodness, about 2 minutes. Turn off the heat and dish out onto a plate or into bowls, then garnish with the green onion and cilantro, if using. Add the egg (cut it in half if you like), if using, and serve with the lime wedges to brighten the flavor.

NOTE

No leftover rice around? Do what recipe tester Peter Luong did and order take-out rice from a nearby Thai restaurant. At home, spread it out on a quarter sheet pan and freeze it, uncovered, for about 15 minutes to cool down and firm up the grains so they're ready for fried rice.

ผัดขี้เมา | Pad Kee Mao

Drunken Noodles (with Any Meat)

SERVES 4

Easy to make and versatile, these stir-fried noodles suggest inebriation to the extent that after a night of drinking, many people crave noodles like these—salty, garlicky, spicy, and herbaceous. In other words, pad kee mao is good-times food! Extra-large rice noodles are my first choice (noodle buying tips are on page 255), though I've also made this recipe with pastas like spaghetti and linguine. The Notes include tips for using dried noodles; the next page contains a tofu rendition.

- Seasoning sauce made by mixing 3 Tbsp fish sauce, 1½ Tbsp Thai oyster sauce, 2 tsp Thai black soy sauce, and 1½ Tbsp water
- 225g | 8 oz ground meat (any kind)
- ⅛ tsp baking soda
- 1 pinch of granulated sugar (optional)
- 20g | 3 Tbsp thinly sliced shallots
- 10 to 15g | 6 to 8 fresh Thai chilies, to taste
- 2g | 2 tsp coarsely chopped cilantro root (optional; see Notes)
- 40g | ¼ cup garlic cloves
- 450g | 1 lb fresh chow fun rice noodles (see Notes)
- 3 Tbsp neutral oil, such as rice bran
- 45g | ½ small yellow or red onion, cut into wedges ½ inch (1.25cm) thick
- 75g | 1 cup thickly sliced mini sweet peppers or other mild chilies
- 45g | 2 cups fresh holy or Thai basil leaves, plus tender tips for garnish
- Lime wedges, for serving (optional)

Prep the meat: Mix the seasoning sauce in a small measuring cup, then spoon 1½ tsp of it into a medium bowl. Add the ground meat, baking soda, and sugar (if you want a touch of sweetness) to the bowl, then mix and massage the seasonings evenly into the meat.

Ready the remaining ingredients: Using a mortar and pestle, pound together the shallots, Thai chilies, and cilantro root to a coarse, rough texture. Add the garlic and pound to flatten, then scrape into a small bowl. Separate and fluff the noodles, dropping them into a medium bowl. Set the noodles by the stovetop along with the pounded garlic mixture, oil, seasoned meat, reserved seasoning sauce, onion, sweet peppers, and basil.

Stir-fry and serve: Set a large wok or skillet over medium-low heat on the biggest burner. When the pan is hot (to test, flick in a couple of drops of water; they should sizzle and evaporate within seconds), add 1 Tbsp of the oil, swirl the pan to coat with the oil, and add the pounded garlic mixture. Let it gently sizzle, stirring continuously, to tease the garlic and mellow its harsh raw edge, 30 to 60 seconds. Take care to avoid burning. Return the garlic mixture to its bowl. Rinse and dry the wok.

Return the wok to high heat. When the pan is hot, add the remaining 2 Tbsp oil and swirl the pan to coat with the oil. Add the seasoned meat, spreading it out into a layer, and cook until browned, 30 to 45 seconds, then break up the meat into small pieces.

Add the onion and stir for about 15 seconds to mix well. Dump in the noodles and garlic mixture, drizzle half of the remaining seasoning sauce around the perimeter of the pan, and then stir-fry to combine, 30 to 45 seconds.

Add the sweet peppers, pour in the remaining seasoning sauce, and stir and fold for 45 seconds just to soften the peppers. Add the basil and incorporate quickly to wilt, about 20 seconds.

Turn off the heat, transfer to a platter, garnish with the basil tips, and enjoy with squeezes of lime for bright tang, if desired.

NOTES

If you don't have cilantro root, just skip it; no need to bother with subbing cilantro stems.

Instead of fresh rice noodles, boil 7 oz (200g) wide dried flat rice sticks (see Rice Noodles 101 on page 255 for sourcing tips). Rinse and drain well, then transfer to a sheet pan or plate, and season with ¼ tsp fine sea salt and 2 tsp neutral oil, such as rice bran. Use right away, or refrigerate in an airtight container for up to 2 days, then return to room temperature before stir-frying.

VARIATION

ผัดขี้เมาเจ | Pad Kee Mao Jae
Drunken Noodles with Tofu

Instead of ground meat, use 8 oz (225g) super-firm tofu, crumbling it into pieces no bigger than ½ inch (1.25cm). For the Seasoning Sauce, mix: 3 Tbsp Fast Fake Fish Sauce (page 23), 1½ Tbsp vegetarian oyster sauce, 2 tsp Thai black soy, and 1½ Tbsp water. Season the tofu crumbles with 1 Tbsp of the seasoning sauce, the sugar, and for an umami boost, add 1 tsp of Saam Kleur (page 57); omit the baking soda.

Gently cook the garlic mixture as directed in the main recipe. Reheat the wok over high heat, swirl in 3 Tbsp oil, coating all over. Add the tofu, spreading it out as a layer to sear and brown here and there, about 1 minute. Flip and repeat to sear the tofu more. Continue as usual to phase in other ingredients and finish the stir-fry.

เส้นจันท์ผัดปู | Sen Chan Pad Pu

Crab Sen Chan Noodles

SERVES 4

There are great pad Thai recipes out there, so what you really need to add to your repertoire is crab sen chan. Originating in the eastern town of Chantaburi, where seafood is abundant, the popular stir-fry is that area's equivalent of pad Thai. The two noodle dishes share similar flavors, but crab sen chan celebrates the purity of crab without muddling it with peanuts or dried shrimp.

I love to prepare this recipe during Dungeness crab season so I can cook and pick the crab myself. That way, the meat is at its sweetest and there's tomalley (the flavorful soft, yellowish curds in the shell) for the sauce; see the Note for a tomalley substitute. Buy lump crabmeat when fresh crab is unavailable. Either way, use the maximum amount of cooked crab for a deluxe experience. At the table, season sen chan with lime to brighten its signature sweet spiciness.

---

200 to 225g | 7 to 8 oz dried pad Thai or Chantaboon rice sticks, or 300 to 340g | 10 to 12 oz fresh pad Thai noodles (see page 255)

60ml | ¼ cup Nam Makam (Tamarind Liquid, page 52)

3 Tbsp fish sauce

60g | 3 Tbsp firmly packed Thai palm sugar

3 Tbsp neutral oil, such as rice bran

40g | 1 medium-large shallot, thinly sliced

8g | 2 garlic cloves, chopped

2.5g | 1 tsp sweet paprika or coarse gochugaru (to boost color)

100g | ⅓ cup crab tomalley (see Note)

80ml | ⅓ cup water, plus more if needed

180 to 225g | 6 to 8 oz cooked crabmeat

180g | 6 oz mung bean sprouts

120ml | ½ cup cut fresh garlic chives, or 180ml | ¾ cup cut slender green onions, in 2-inch (5cm) lengths

Prik Pon (Toasted Chili Flakes, page 46), for finishing

Lime wedges, for serving

Prep the noodles and sauce: If using dried noodles, soak them in hot water until pliable and opaque, about 20 minutes, then drain well. If using fresh noodles, separate and fluff them, dropping them into a medium bowl. Meanwhile, mix together the tamarind, fish sauce, and sugar in a microwave-safe measuring cup. Microwave on high power for about 1 minute to melt the sugar. (Or combine in a butter warmer and heat on the stove.) Line up the noodles, sauce, and all of the remaining ingredients by the stovetop.

Stir-fry the noodles and serve: Set a large wok over medium-high heat on the biggest burner. When the pan is hot (to test, flick in a couple of drops of water; they should sizzle and evaporate within seconds), add the oil and swirl the pan to coat with the oil. Add the shallot and swiftly stir-fry until just softened, about 30 seconds. Lower the heat to medium, add the garlic and paprika, and stir for a few seconds to release aroma and color. Then add the crab tomalley and stir-fry until all the ingredients coalesce, 45 to 60 seconds.

Add the noodles and stir to combine. Add the sauce and stir and toss to coat the noodle strands evenly. Add the water, cover, and cook for 1 to 2 minutes. The noodles should be chewy-tender. If they are not, add 1 Tbsp water, re-cover, and cook briefly. Add the crab, gently folding in about half of it and leaving the remainder in nicely sized lumps. Add the bean sprouts and garlic chives and use tongs and a spatula to mix evenly. Transfer to a platter, sprinkle with some prik pon, and serve with lime wedges.

NOTE

If crab tomalley is unavailable, substitute a mixture of 1 large egg, 1 large egg yolk, 2½ Tbsp water, 1½ tsp fish sauce, and ½ tsp freshly ground black pepper.

ขนมจีนน้ำยา | Kanom Jeen Nam Ya

Fish Curry "Velouté" with Rice Noodles and Vegetables

SERVES 4 TO 6

My aunt Patum Snitwongse kept meticulous kitchen notes. Inside her recipe notebooks were neatly written gems such as this Central Thai noodle classic that features tender kanom jeen rice noodles, a mildly spicy fish nam ya curry sauce, and assorted vegetable mix-ins for diners to customize their noodle experience.

The origin of kanom jeen nam ya is attributed to Chao Chom Waen, a princess from Vientiane (modern-day Laos) who became a consort to King Rama I, who reigned from 1782 to 1809. Today, there are many renditions prepared in Thailand and Laos, but I'm partial to Pah Tum's extra-rich version, which involves the old-school method of simmering dried chilies and aromatics directly in the coconut milk instead of making a paste and blooming it like for other curry sauces. Because grachai (fingerroot; page 28) defines the nam ya's aroma and flavor, wait until you can find the fresh or frozen rhizome to make nam ya properly. Pounding the fish aerates and creates a fluffy, fine mixture, which when added to curry, yields a sumptuous, creamy velouté-like sauce.

One 400ml | 13.5-oz can coconut milk, unshaken

240ml | 1 cup coconut water or regular water

60g | 2 oz grachai (fingerroot), coarsely chopped

60g | 2 oz shallots, peeled but kept whole

30g | 1 oz garlic cloves, peeled but kept whole

18g | 3 Tbsp coarsely chopped lemongrass (from 1 medium stalk)

16g | 0.6 oz seeded dried prik chee fa or puya chilies

7g | 2 tsp thinly sliced, peeled galangal

5g | rind from 1 large makrut or Persian lime

50g | ¼ cup salted mackerel flesh (optional; see Notes)

225 to 300g | 8 to 10 oz sole, cod, rockfish, or other white fish fillet, using the maximum if omitting mackerel

120ml | ½ cup water

2 to 3 Tbsp fish sauce

Fine sea salt

Simmer the curry broth: Collect ½ cup (120ml) thick coconut milk from the top of the can and set aside in a small bowl. Pour the remaining coconut milk into a medium pot and add the coconut water, grachai, shallots, garlic, lemongrass, dried chilies, galangal, and lime rind. Bring to a boil over high heat, then adjust the heat so the liquid softly bubbles to release essences. Let cook until the liquid is reduced by roughly 20 percent, 30 minutes or so. The coconut milk will turn pale orange.

Poach and pound the fish: Add the salted mackerel (if using) and fish fillet to the curry broth and cook until just done, 3 to 5 minutes. To test for doneness, use a slotted spoon to scoop up a piece and check to see if it easily flakes when pulled on. Turn off the heat. Transfer all the fish to a plate and let cool until it can be handled, about 10 minutes.

Using a mortar and pestle, and working in batches, pound the fish, removing any errant bones. Aim for a coarse paste-like mixture that pulls and sort of suctions up against the pestle. Or flake the fish with your fingers or two forks, discarding any errant bones.

Finish the curry sauce: Using a blender, whirl the curry liquid and solids into a silky orange sauce (expect tiny flecks of chili). Return the sauce to the pot. Add the water to the blender and whirl to collect any remaining traces of the curry sauce, then add the extra liquid to the pot.

Add the pounded fish and reserved thick coconut milk to the curry sauce, stir to mix well, then season with up to 3 Tbsp fish sauce for a strong savory note. Beyond that, add big pinches of salt to avoid a sauce that tastes too strongly of fish sauce. The sauce texture will resemble a creamy French velouté or American chowder. The flavor and aroma of grachai should be present, followed by a bit of chili heat.

CONTINUED

FOR SERVING

340g | 12 oz small dried round rice noodles (see page 255)

180g | 1 small Chinese bitter melon (optional; see Notes)

Fine sea salt

One 225 to 300g | 8- to 10-oz package pickled mustard greens (see page 267)

225g | 8 oz mung bean sprouts

120g | 4 oz green or long beans, trimmed and thinly sliced on the diagonal

8 to 10 lemon or Thai basil sprigs

Ready the accompaniments for serving: Bring a medium-large pot of unsalted water to a boil, add the noodles, and boil until tender firm; the timing depends on the brand. Drain the noodles in a fine-mesh strainer, then submerge in a bowl of cold water until cool enough to handle, about 5 minutes. Pick up the noodles as small skeins, then coil them into 15 to 20 spirals (see page 255 for tips), arranging them on a large platter. Cover to prevent drying.

If using the bitter melon, halve it lengthwise, then cut each half crosswise to yield 4 pieces from each half. Use a spoon to scrape out and discard the spongy flesh and seeds from the center of each piece, add the pieces to a medium bowl, and then gently massage ½ tsp salt into the pieces. Add water to cover, swish a few times to remove some bitterness (the water may cloud up), then drain and rinse. Bring a medium saucepan of salted water to a boil over high heat. Ready an ice bath in a medium bowl and set near the stovetop. Add the bitter melon pieces to the boiling water (set the skimmer on top to keep the pieces submerged) and boil until jade green and slightly soft but still crisp, about 2 minutes. Drain and submerge in the ice bath to halt the cooking and set the color. Pat dry with paper towels, then thinly slice crosswise. Put the slices on a large platter.

Rinse the pickled mustard greens with cold running water and squeeze gently to expel excess liquid. Trim the core, then very thinly slice crosswise, including the leafy green parts if you like their chew. Add to the bitter melon platter along with the bean sprouts, green beans, and basil.

Reheat and serve: Bring the nam ya curry sauce to a boil over medium-low heat, stirring often to prevent scorching. Retaste to verify saltiness, then add pinches of salt if needed.

Kanom jeen noodles are traditionally served at room temperature, but if you like, warm the noodles in the microwave on high power for 1 to 2 minutes. Ladle the curry into a communal bowl and serve with the noodles and vegetables. Invite diners to put a few noodle spirals and a generous amount of curry on their plate, then mix in bean sprouts and green beans for crunch, pickled mustard greens for salty tang, and bitter melon to cool and curb the bit of chili heat that will sneak up on you.

NOTES

Keep the shallots and garlic cloves whole when cooking the sauce because they are aromatics that are pureed in the blender later.

Salted mackerel (pla kem) imported from Thailand is often sold in vacuum-sealed packages at Chinese and Southeast Asian markets, typically in the refrigerated case near dried shrimp and dumpling skins. Aside from this sauce, the preserved fish is used in certain Teochew-Thai fried rice and stir-fried dishes.

For a shortcut, substitute a good ½ cup (140g) Prik Gaeng Ped (Red Curry Paste, page 144) for the shallots, garlic, dried chili, lemongrass, galangal, and lime rind. Add to the coconut milk with the grachai.

If you dislike bitter melon or cannot fined any, swap in 2 cups (480ml) sliced radicchio or spicy radishes cut into matchsticks.

Get ahead. Cook the curry sauce up to 2 days in advance, or cook it and freeze it for up to 1 month (thaw in the refrigerator before reheating). The noodles and raw vegetables can be prepped a day ahead.

PICKLED MUSTARD GREENS 101

A tangy source of umami, pickled mustard greens in chartreuse-colored brine are sold in shelf-stable clear plastic packages. Shop for them at Chinese or Southeast Asian markets in the produce section or dried mushroom aisle. Choose a package with a lot of pale, thick stems, which have plenty of crunch. If you can, source one without food coloring.

ขนมจีนน้ำพริก | Kanom Jeen Nam Prik

Rice Noodles with Shrimp-Coconut Sauce

SERVES 4 TO 6

My indulgent childhood Sunday lunch was this over-the-top rendition of kanom jeen nam prik, with its rice noodles (kanom jeen), a sweet, salty, umami-rich shrimp coconut sauce (nam prik), crispy batter-fried leaves and shrimp, and sautéed and raw vegetables. Mixed together on a plate and enjoyed Thai-style with spoon and fork, this dish covers all the textures, flavors, and food groups. You don't need a bunch of unusual ingredients, but you do need time. (See the Notes for timing tips and more.) This is an impressive one-dish meal for family and Thai-food friends.

We serve this kanom jeen nam prik at Nahm in Bangkok, much to the delight of diners who rarely get to experience the heritage favorite. One Sunday, I brought my rendition home to my mother, who has dementia. She tasted it and memories from decades ago flooded back to her palate. Unaware that I was the chef, she said, "This tastes just like Khun Yai's recipe. We should order it from that restaurant again."

GENTLE CHILI OIL

- 120ml | ½ cup neutral oil, such as rice bran
- 1½ tsp mildly spicy Prik Pon (Toasted Chili Flakes, page 46)
- ½ tsp sweet paprika or coarse gochugaru (optional; for color)

Make the chili oil: In a small saucepan, combine the oil, prik pon, and paprika. Set over medium-low heat and heat until the oil turns orange-red and begins sizzling with tiny bubbles, then remove from the heat. Let cool briefly, then strain through a fine-mesh strainer to yield about ½ cup (120ml).

SHRIMP-COCONUT SAUCE

- 50g | ¼ cup dried split (hulled) mung beans (see Notes)
- 20g | 0.7 oz unsweetened dried coconut flakes (about ⅓ cup)
- 90g | 2 large shallots, unpeeled
- 25g | 5 large garlic cloves, sliced
- 25g | 2½ Tbsp finely chopped, peeled galangal
- ¼ tsp fine sea salt
- 900g | 2 lb very large head-on shrimp (see Notes)
- 500ml | brimming 2 cups coconut milk
- 120ml | ½ cup water
- 1½ Tbsp virgin coconut oil
- 2 large makrut limes, halved and seeds removed (optional)
- 5 to 10 lime leaves (use maximum if makrut limes are unavailable)
- 80g | ¼ cup firmly packed Thai palm sugar, plus more to taste
- 3 Tbsp fish sauce, plus more to taste
- 20g | 2 Tbsp Nam Makam (Tamarind Liquid, page 52)
- 1 Tbsp makrut or Persian lime juice (see Notes)

Prep the beans and coconut: Rinse the saucepan and the strainer you just used. Put the mung beans into the pan, add water to cover generously, swish the beans around in the water, and then drain in the strainer and return them to the pan. Add water to cover by 1 inch (2.5cm), bring to a boil over high heat, lower the heat to maintain a gentle simmer, and cook, uncovered, until the beans still hold their shape but can be easily smooshed, 22 to 30 minutes. To test the doneness, use the back of a spoon to press some beans against the wall of the pan. Drain the beans in the strainer, let cool, and then dump the very soft beans into a small bowl (it's OK if they look nearly pureed).

Meanwhile, in a medium pot over medium-low heat, toast the coconut, stirring occasionally, until golden brown, 3 to 5 minutes. Remove from the heat, let cool, and then add to the bowl with the mung beans.

Make the shrimp-coconut sauce: Over a high flame on a gas stovetop, char the shallots one at a time, turning often, until the skin blackens in many areas, 3 to 5 minutes. (Alternatively, use a perforated skillet or vegetable grill pan over the gas flame, place under the broiler close to the

CONTINUED

heat source for 5 to 8 minutes, or use a ripping-hot cast-iron pan on the stovetop.) Let cool briefly, then peel and trim, scraping off all the blackened areas. Finely chop the slightly smoky, still partially raw shallots. You should have about 2.5 oz (75g). Transfer to a mortar, add the garlic, galangal, and salt, and pound to an aromatic paste (a food chopper or processor cannot do this job as well).

Choose 8 handsome shrimp to fry. Twist off their heads and peel off their shells, leaving the tail shell segments intact for easy frying. Transfer their heads and shells to a medium pot. Completely peel the remaining shrimp, dropping their heads and shells into the same pot.

Devein all of the shrimp, setting the frying ones aside. Cut the others into ¾-inch (2cm) chunks. For intriguing texture, I favor triangular pieces. Cover and refrigerate all of the shrimp.

Set the pot of shrimp heads and shells over medium-high heat. When the shells and heads are hot, use a potato masher to vigorously press and stir them. You want to toast the solids and release their pink-orange juices, which will take about 3 minutes. Stir in the coconut milk and bring the cantaloupe-colored liquid to a boil, then turn off the heat.

Strain the liquid through a coarse-mesh strainer set over a large measuring cup. Smoosh the solids with the potato masher to extract as much liquid as possible. Return the solids to the pot, stir in the water, and then repeat the straining. You should have about 1¾ cups (420ml). Discard the solids.

Rinse the pot and reheat over medium heat. Add the coconut oil, and when it has melted, add the pounded paste of shallots and other aromatics. Cook, stirring often, until fragrant, 2 to 3 minutes. Add the shrimp-coconut broth plus the cooked mung beans and toasted coconut. Add the makrut limes and the leaves, crumpling the leaves as you drop them into the pot. Bring to a simmer and cook gently, stirring occasionally, until slightly thickened, about 5 minutes.

Add the sugar, fish sauce, and tamarind and return to a brisk simmer, then stir in the cut-up shrimp. Turn off the heat, wait for a few minutes for the shrimp to cook, and then taste the sauce. It should be slightly sweet with a salty finish. If needed, work in fish sauce and sugar by the 1 tsp. Stir in the lime juice to brighten it a bit, then cover the pot with the lid ajar while you prep the other components.

FOR SERVING

2 or 3 large eggs (optional)

340g | 12 oz small dried round rice noodles (see page 255)

180g | 6 red radishes, unpeeled, or 3 peeled watermelon radishes

180g | 6 oz green or long beans (see Notes)

Neutral oil, such as rice bran, for stir-frying and deep-frying

Fine sea salt

24 tender leaves and flowers (such as spinach, arugula, shiso, and nasturtium), spun dry

100g | ¾ cup tempura batter mix, such as Gogi brand

Ice water, for making the tempura batter

2 Tbsp cornstarch, for dusting shrimp

2 dried prik jinda or árbol chilies, for garnish (optional)

1 handful morning glory (ong choy) stems, cut into 5-inch (12.5cm) lengths, quickly blanched, and then sliced lengthwise into thin strips (optional)

60ml | ¼ cup fried shallots, for garnish (optional)

Boil the eggs and noodles for serving: If including the eggs, bring a large pot of water to a boil, add the eggs, and boil to the doneness of your choice, then transfer to an ice bath to cool. Once they are cool, peel and set aside until serving.

Return the pot of water to a boil, add the noodles, and cook until tender firm; the timing depends on the brand. Drain the noodles in a fine-mesh strainer, then submerge in a bowl of cold water until cool enough to handle, about 5 minutes. Pick up the noodles as small skeins, then coil them into 15 to 20 spirals (see page 255 for tips), arranging them on a large platter. Cover to prevent drying.

Ready the vegetables: Using a knife or mandoline, very thinly slice the radishes, submerge them in an ice bath, let soak briefly to crisp, then drain and pat dry. Trim the green beans, then slice very thinly on the diagonal into small ovals.

Heat a large wok over medium-high heat. When the pan is hot, add 1 tsp oil and swirl the pan to coat with the oil. Add the beans, a pinch of salt, and a tiny splash (1½ tsp) of water and stir-fry until bright green, 1 to 2 minutes. Transfer to a small plate. Rinse and dry the wok.

Fry time: Pour oil to a depth of a generous 1 inch (2.5cm) into the wok and heat over medium-high heat to 350°F (175°C). Line a sheet pan with paper towels and set near the stovetop.

While the oil heats, using paper towels, pat any excess moisture from the tender leaves and flowers and the whole shrimp. In a medium bowl, using chopsticks, mix the tempura mix with enough ice water to create a runny batter. If using Gogi brand, you will need about ¾ cup (180ml) water. Put the cornstarch into a small bowl. Arrange all of the leaves and flowers and the shrimp, tempura batter, and cornstarch near the stovetop.

When the oil is ready, fry the leaves and flowers in batches of 3 or 4. Dip each leaf or flower into the batter, coating lightly and letting the excess drip off (or drag on the bowl rim) before adding to the hot oil. Fry, turning once, until crisp and golden, about 1 minute. As each batch is ready, transfer it to the towel-lined sheet pan to drain, then let the oil return to temperature before adding the next batch.

Now fry the shrimp in two batches. Lightly dust each shrimp with the cornstarch, then dip in the batter, coating lightly and letting the excess drip off, and then add to the oil. Fry, turning occasionally, until crisp and golden, 2 minutes tops. As each batch is ready, transfer it to the towel-lined sheet pan with the leaves and flowers, then let the oil return to temperature before adding the next batch. If using the chilies for garnish, briefly fry them in the oil and add to the pile of shrimp.

Assemble and serve: Arrange the fried goodies on a serving platter. Warm the shrimp-coconut sauce and taste to verify the flavor, adding a touch more lime juice to brighten if needed. Ladle into a serving bowl. Include the cut limes and a few of the lime leaves if you like, though they aren't edible. Spoon on the chili oil to film the top (yes, that's Thai-style), then crown with the fried chilies (if using).

Kanom jeen noodles are traditionally served at room temperature, but if you like, warm them in the microwave on high power for 1 to 2 minutes. Serve the sauce with the noodles, tempura leaves and flowers, shrimp, beans, radishes, morning glory, and eggs (if using, cut the eggs in half). Invite diners to put a few noodle spirals on their plate, ladle a generous amount of sauce over the noodles, and enjoy with the fried, stir-fried, boiled, and raw accompaniments for textural and flavor contrast.

NOTES

Head-on shrimp impart the best flavor and color to the curry sauce. If you must, use headless shrimp, but you'll be missing some of the magic.

Split (hulled) mung beans are yellow, whereas the unhulled whole bean is green. At Indian markets, it is called moong dal. Try to purchase mung beans devoid of food coloring.

For the makrut lime juice, it's fine to squeeze it from the fruits before adding the fruits to the sauce.

Vegetable swaps: To substitute winged beans for the green beans, cut them crosswise into thin pieces, then stir-fry as directed. Instead of radishes, offer thinly sliced green mango, or cut the cream-colored tender inner petals of banana blossom into bite-size pieces and soak in salted water to prevent discoloration until ready to serve.

Get ahead. Make the chili oil up to 1 week ahead and cook the sauce a day in advance. The noodles and raw vegetables can be prepped a day ahead too. Wokking and tempura frying go fast, so have a buddy help you.

VARIATION

ก๋วยเตี๋ยวแห้ง | Kuey Tiew Hang
"Dry" Duck Noodle Soup

To serve "dry" duck noodle soup, assemble the bowl as usual, adding pounded roasted peanuts for textural richness. Serve the broth on the side.

ก๋วยเตี๋ยวเป็ดตุ๋นนครชัยศรี | Kuey Tiew Ped Nakhon Chaisri

Nakhon Chaisri Duck Noodle Soup

SERVES 10

Aside from symbolizing long life, noodles are a fun, celebratory food, so how about hosting family and friends for Thai-style duck noodle soup? To put together this special noodle dish without getting cranky, cook the broth and duck days ahead so you can relax as you welcome guests. (Assign them to bring snacks and dessert.) Set up a mini noodle soup shop by lining up all the ingredients for assembling kuey tiew ped, and then show guests how to make their own bowls. Everyone will sit down to a noodle-filled feast like you would in Nakhon Chaisri, a town west of Bangkok where this noodle soup originated.

The spicing for this rich, aromatic noodle soup has a myriad of healing, healthful properties. Dried longans and goji berries also add fruity sweetness (if unavailable, season the broth with extra sugar). Thai touches such as galangal and pandan tame the strong flavor and aroma of duck, while fresh and toasted chilies add heat at the table. This duck noodle soup works well with Chinese egg noodles too. For easy prep and consistent flavors, weigh most of the ingredients.

SPICE BAG

15g | 3 large cinnamon sticks

7g | 6 to 8 whole star anise

5g | 4 tsp Sichuan peppercorns, or 5 tsp makwaen (mắc khén)

8g | scant 1 Tbsp black peppercorns

30g | large 1-inch (2.5cm) chunk galangal (skin on or off), sliced

50g | ⅓ cup garlic cloves

10g | 1½ Tbsp cilantro root, or 3 Tbsp chopped cilantro stems

4g | 1½ tsp dried sand ginger slices (optional)

25g | ¼ cup dried longans (optional)

5g | 2 tsp goji berries (optional)

Prep the spice bag: Using a mortar and pestle, gently crush the cinnamon sticks. Transfer to a spice bag (or a piece of muslin). Repeat with the star anise and Sichuan and black peppercorns, gently pounding them together, then add to the bag. Repeat with the galangal and garlic to activate and release their magic, then scrape into the bag. Add the cilantro root, sand ginger, longans, and goji berries, if using, and cinch up the bag (or tie up the muslin with kitchen twine).

DUCK SOUP

One 2.5kg | 5½-lb whole duck

120g | generous ⅓ cup firmly packed Thai palm sugar

30g | 1 oz pandan leaves, tied into two or three big knots

55g | ¼ cup Shaoxing rice wine

50g | 2½ Tbsp Thai oyster sauce

30g | 2 Tbsp Golden Mountain Seasoning Sauce

40g | 2 Tbsp fish sauce, plus more to taste

20g | 1 Tbsp Thai black soy sauce

20g | 4 tsp fine sea salt, plus more to taste

Ready the duck: If the duck came with its neck, head, and feet attached, use a meat cleaver to detach them (or ask the butcher to do that for you). Save the parts.

Caramelize the sugar and make the broth: Select a big pot wide enough to accommodate the duck, such as a 12-qt (12L) stockpot or 8-qt (8L) oval Dutch oven. Chop or break up the sugar into small pieces, then add them to the pot. Add 2 Tbsp of water, and then heat over medium-low heat, stirring frequently, until the sugar has melted and is fully dissolved. Then allow the sugar to bubble and caramelize to a mahogany brown, 6 to 8 minutes after melting. Lower the heat if needed to prevent burning.

Add 1½ cups (360ml) water to the pot and stir to loosen and dissolve the now-hardened caramel. (If this seems daunting, use a small saucepan to caramelize the sugar, add the water, and then pour into the big pot.)

Add the duck, breast-side down, plus any reserved parts. Drop in the bag of spices and pandan and pour in 4 qt (4L) water. Add the wine, then add the oyster, Golden Mountain, fish, and soy sauces and the salt and stir a bit to distribute evenly. Keep the duck submerged in the liquid by weighting it down (I use the Chef's Press described on page 34). Bring to a boil over high heat, then lower the heat to simmer, partially covered, for 1½ hours. At the 1-hour mark, use tongs to turn the duck over.

Check the doneness of the duck by wiggling a leg. Does it move easily with only little resistance? If not, continue simmering, checking every 10 to 15 minutes (total simmering time shouldn't exceed 2 hours). When the duck is ready,

CONTINUED

use tongs to transfer it to a sheet pan (it's OK if it falls apart). Partially re-cover the broth and keep it gently simmering.

Let the duck cool, uncovered, for 15 to 30 minutes, then take the meat off the bones and tear it into large bite-size pieces about as thick as your index finger. No need to separate the skin, unless you don't want it. Leave the legs intact for some lucky diners. Put the legs and meat into a medium bowl, cover, and refrigerate.

Break apart the carcass and return it to the broth pot, along with any unwanted skin (it's full of great collagen, so don't waste it). Add 2 cups (480ml) water, bring to a boil over medium-high heat, lower the heat to a simmer, cover partially, and simmer until you have a flavorful, rich broth, 1½ to 2 hours.

Turn off the heat. Harvest most of the fat from the surface of the broth, transferring it to a glass measuring cup, and let it settle. Pour the broth through a fine-mesh strainer set over a large pot. You should have about 4 qt (4L). If there is too much, boil it down. If there's not enough, add water. (If not serving soon, refrigerate the duck, the broth, and the fat separately for up to 3 days.)

FOR SERVING

50g | ⅓ cup chopped garlic

900g | 2 lb fresh flat rice noodles, or 675g | 1½ pounds dried flat rice noodles (any width; see page 255)

340g | 12 oz mung bean sprouts

120g | 4 oz chrysanthemum greens, tender tops only (optional)

240ml | 1 cup thinly sliced green onions

240ml | 1 cup coarsely chopped cilantro sprigs

240ml | 1 cup coarsely chopped fresh sawtooth herb (optional)

Prik Pon (Toasted Chili Flakes, page 46)

Nam Som Prik Tum (Chili Garlic Vinegar, page 54)

Fish sauce

Fry the garlic for serving: Pour ½ cup (120ml) of the duck fat into a small saucepan and add the chopped garlic. Set over medium-low heat, bring to a gentle sizzle, and fry, frequently swirling the pan, until the garlic is buoyant, crispy, and light blond, 5 to 7 minutes. Near the end, pick up the pan to slow the cooking and avoid burning. Remove from the heat, let the garlic finish frying in the pan, and then, using a slotted spoon, transfer to a bowl to finish crisping and darken further (or pour into a fine-mesh strainer set over a small heatproof bowl). Save the fat for stir-frying or other dishes.

Set up a noodle soup station: If using dried rice noodles, soak them in warm water until opaque and pliable, 10 to 30 minutes; the timing depends on the size. Drain the noodles (dried noodles can be soaked hours in advance). Fresh noodles do not need to be soaked. Set the noodles near the stovetop.

Bring a medium-large pot of water to a boil and reheat the broth. Place the following nearby: cooked duck, fried garlic, bean sprouts, chrysanthemum greens (if using), green onions, cilantro, and sawtooth herb (if using). At the table, set out the prik pon, chili garlic vinegar, and fish sauce.

Assemble and serve: For each portion, use a vertical noodle or pasta strainer to blanch a handful of bean sprouts in the boiling water until just softened, then deposit the bean sprouts into an individual serving bowl. Repeat with the noodles to blanch them until tender firm, then dump into the bowl, spreading them out flat. Top with some duck and garnish with some chrysanthemum greens (if using), green onion, cilantro, and sawtooth herb (offer extras at the table). Ladle about 1½ cups (360ml) of hot broth into the bowl. Add about 1 tsp fried garlic and serve. Invite diners to season their bowls with chili flakes for heat, vinegar to cut the richness, and fish sauce for extra savoriness. Remind them to add any extra vegetable garnishes for refreshing notes too.

NOTES

Shop for sand ginger, dried longans, and goji berries at a Chinese market or herb shop, which will fill your apothecary chicken soup prescription (page 202) too.

If you like, swap another type of Asian noodle for the rice noodles. Short on duck? Add a halved hard-boiled egg to each bowl. Freeze leftover broth to seed future batches with extra flavor.

ข้าวซอยไก่ | Khao Soi Gai

Khao Soi with Chicken

SERVES 6

Around the turn of the twentieth century, my paternal grandfather migrated to Thailand from Swatow, on the southern coast of China. A goldsmith by trade, he followed a relative to the opulent northern provinces, an area rich in teak, rice, and gold. There he met a Thai woman from a Chiang Mai merchant family who would become my grandmother. In those days, Chinese immigrants customarily married within the diaspora community, so their story was quite an epic romance. This is why I always say that my love of Northern Thai food is encoded in my genetics.

Warmly perfumed with spices in a creamy, coconutty broth, this Chiang Mai–style khao soi recipe is dedicated to my khun ya (paternal grandmother). The bowls are traditionally served with an aromatic chili oil and other garnishes to allow diners to stoke the chili flames and add piquancy. Khao soi shops in Thailand may feature the dish with various stew-worthy meats, such as duck legs or beef short rib, shank, or oxtail. Chicken khao soi, however, is always a winner.

At my restaurants, we prepare a special curry paste for khao soi. This simpler but no-less-tasty version is what I make at home. Put your larder ingredients, prik pon and prik laab, to great use for this recipe. You'll also need curry paste and a masala, so make them in advance to easily bring things together.

SOUP

1 to 1.2L | 4 to 5 cups coconut milk, plus more to taste

100g | mounded ⅓ cup Prik Gaeng Ped (Red Curry Paste, page 144)

1 Tbsp Hunglay Masala (page 181) or Madras curry powder

1.5g | 1 small Chinese black cardamom, cracked open (see pages 32 and 33)

20g | 1-inch (2.5cm) chunk peeled ginger, bruised

60ml | ¼ cup fish sauce, plus more to taste

1 tsp firmly packed Thai palm sugar, plus more to taste

1L | 4 cups water

1.4kg | six 8-oz (225g) chicken leg quarters

Simmer the soup: Spoon ½ cup (120ml) of the coconut milk into a large Dutch oven or similar size pot. Set over medium heat and heat, stirring now and then. When the coconut milk bubbles, breaks, and begins releasing oil, after 1 to 2 minutes, add the curry paste and stir actively until aromatic, 1 to 2 minutes. Stir in the masala, fry briefly to bloom its fragrance, and then add 3½ cups (840ml) of the coconut milk along with the cardamom, ginger, fish sauce, and sugar.

Pour in the water and add the chicken. Increase the heat to high and bring to a boil, then lower the heat to a gentle simmer, cover partially, and simmer until the chicken is cooked through, 30 to 45 minutes (cook for a shorter time for chewy-tender flesh and a longer time if you prefer falling-off-the-bone flesh).

If you prefer to serve the chicken off the bone, use tongs to transfer the pieces to a plate, let cool briefly, and then cut (or tear) the meat, discard the bones, and return the meat to the pot.

Taste the soup. If needed, add about 1 cup (240ml) coconut milk to soften the chili heat. Return the soup to a boil and recheck the flavor. It should have an edge of fire, a mild, pleasant saltiness, and fragrant spice notes. If needed, add fish sauce or palm sugar by the 1 tsp. (If making the soup in advance, keep the meat and broth separate and refrigerate for up to 3 days or freeze for up to 3 months. Bring the broth to a simmer, then add the chicken to heat through.)

CONTINUED

FOR SERVING

2 Tbsp Prik Pon (Toasted Chili Flakes, page 46)

1 Tbsp Prik Laab (Northern Thai Chili-Spice Blend, page 49)

60ml | ¼ cup neutral oil, such as rice bran, plus more for deep-frying

450 to 675g | 1 to 1½ lb fresh flat wonton egg noodles (linguine width)

6 dried prik chee fa or puya chilies (optional)

One 225 to 300g | 8- to 10-oz package pickled mustard greens (see page 267)

2 limes, cut into wedges

240ml | 1 cup very thinly sliced shallots

240ml | 1 cup fried shallots

240ml | 1 cup coarsely chopped fresh cilantro

Fish sauce, for serving

Make the chili oil for serving: While the soup cooks, combine the prik pon and prik laab in a small heatproof bowl. Heat the ¼ cup (60ml) oil in a small saucepan over medium-high heat until smoking. Carefully pour the oil over the chili blend, pausing to stir halfway before adding the remaining oil. Let cool completely, uncovered, to develop flavor. (The oil can be made in advance and stored in a tightly capped glass jar in a cool place for up to 3 months.)

Fry the noodles and chilies: Rinse the saucepan and return it to the stovetop. Pour in oil to a depth of 1¼ inches (3cm) and heat over medium-high heat to 350°F (175°C). Line a medium plate with paper towels and set it near the stovetop. Measure 2 oz (60g) noodles and use your fingers to loosen and untangle them. Working in three or four batches, pick up the noodles with your fingers and drop them into the hot oil. Fry, turning once or twice, until crispy and golden, about 30 seconds. As each batch is ready, transfer it to the towel-lined plate to drain and return the oil to temperature before adding the next batch.

When all of the noodles are fried, turn off the heat and, if using, add the chilies and fry gently until puffed and crisp, 20 to 30 seconds. Transfer to the plate with the fried noodles. (The noodles and chilies can be fried up to 2 days in advance. Store them in separate airtight containers at room temperature.)

Boil the noodles: Bring a large pot of water to a boil over high heat. Add the remaining noodles and boil until chewy-tender. Eat a noodle to test because package cooking times are seldom correct. Drain the noodles, rinse with cool running water, and set aside.

Prep the garnishes: Rinse the pickled mustard greens with water, then squeeze gently to release excess moisture. Trim off the core and then very thinly slice crosswise; include the leafy green parts if you like their chew. Put the mustard greens on a medium plate with the lime wedges and place on the table along with the chili oil. Set the raw and fried shallots and cilantro near the stove.

Assemble and serve: Bring the soup to a swift simmer over medium-high heat. While the soup is heating, divide the boiled noodles evenly among six individual serving bowls. Then divide the chicken and soup among the bowls, avoiding the ginger and cardamom. Crown each bowl with some raw and fried shallots and cilantro (serve the extras at the table). Add a tangle of fried noodles and a fried chili (if using) to each bowl.

Serve with the pickled mustard greens, chili oil, lime wedges, and fish sauce. Encourage guests to break up the fried noodles and freely add the greens for tangy funk, squirts of lime for uplifting notes, and chili oil for aromatic heat. Extra raw and fried shallots and cilantro are often welcome too! If you've included fried chilies, crumble then into the soup for extra excitement. Slurp away.

NOTES

If you have other kinds of noodles in your pantry, feel free to use them. Rice noodles would work for gluten-free diners, for instance.

Any extra broth can be frozen for up to 6 months to quickly whip up a small batch of khao soi.

10 ของหวาน

Desserts

80
Kg

Sweet Adaptations and Innovations

Now that we are almost at the end of *Cooking Thai*, I can confess to you that I don't really know how to make Thai desserts. It's not that I don't like to eat them. I LOVE them. It's just that knowing how to make Thai desserts entails knowing how to make them properly—with the right flavors, the perfect balance, the correct texture. All of that is an enterprise of its own, mostly often left to Thai dessert experts.

It probably doesn't help that, unlike Western desserts with their precise measurements and prescribed techniques, most Thai desserts depend on ingredients that don't lend themselves to precise measurements. For example, palm sugar ranges in viscosity, and freshly milled rice flour differs from its commercially bagged kin. Everything, almost even more so than in the savory kitchen, depends on the feel in the hand and the texture and viscosity that are difficult to describe to someone who has never tasted the dish or cooked with the ingredient before. Many of my favorite desserts also rely on the freshness of coconut milk. So unless you can find coconuts of a certain (that is to say, correct) age and you're willing to crack them open, grate the flesh, and squeeze it fresh, it's a no-go.

What, then, do I do when I miss the sweet taste of home? I focus on straight-up simple classics that can be done with ingredients available outside of Thailand. Refreshing som chun (page 283), a gingery granita served with zippy fresh ginger, seasonal fruits, and a wee bit of fried shallots, is a royal Thai treat easily crafted with the aid of modern refrigeration, a blender, and canned tropical fruit. Seemingly daunting sankaya faktong (page 286), a custard steamed inside a small pumpkin, and bua loy (page 284), multicolored boba-like mochi balls in salty-sweet coconut milk, may look difficult to achieve, but they just take patience and a sense of adventure.

In addition, in this chapter I bring Thai flavors into desserts I adore, infusing verdant pandan into madeleines (page 290) and coconut mochi cake (page 289), or flavoring Basque-style cheesecake with Thai tea. I also incorporate some of the interesting pantry ingredients we make in this book, like prik laab (page 49), the Northern Thai chili-spice blend, to craft rich, addictive chocolate cookies.

We are living, cooking, and eating in an era when ideas and ingredients fluidly move across borders. You've fed your culinary curiosity by coming this far in the book, so I encourage you to try your hand at making these desserts. While you're at it, whip up a batch of my Thai iced tea (page 295) so you'll have extra fuel for your journey. All of the recipes are well worth the effort.

ส้มฉุน | Som Chun

Ginger Granita with Fruit and Fried Shallots

SERVES 6

The ginger syrup in this recipe forms the base for many iced desserts in Thai cuisine. My aunt Pah Tas, who taught me this recipe, is the mistress of Thai chilled treats. Her specialty, graton loy gaew—santol (cotton fruit, *Sandoricum koetjape*) carved into delicate flowers and served floating in iced sweet-salty gingery syrup—was my childhood favorite. For an easy-to-achieve modern take, I turn my aunt's ginger syrup into a granita-like concoction and serve it with lychees and a variety of citrus fruits (no fruit-carving skills required). Other fruits would work too. For instance, instead of lychees, use rambutans or longans plus one or two other fruits so you can mix sweet and tart. And don't skip the shallots. They add a savory edge that makes this dessert special.

GINGER SYRUP

35g | chubby 2-inch (5cm) section ginger, peeled, thickly sliced, and smashed

130g | ⅔ cup granulated sugar

¼ tsp fine sea salt

160ml | ⅔ cup water

Simmer the gingery syrup: In a small pot, combine the ginger, sugar, salt, and water and bring to a simmer over medium heat, stirring to dissolve the sugar. Lower the heat to a gentle bubble and continue to cook for about 5 minutes to develop the flavor. Remove from the heat, cover, and steep until pleasantly gingery, about 30 minutes (there's raw ginger later, so no worries now about not having enough of a gingery bite).

Strain the syrup through a fine-mesh strainer set over a measuring cup, pressing firmly on the solids, then discard the solids. Let cool, uncovered, to room temperature, then cover and chill until very cold, at least 3 hours or up to 1 week.

300g | 2⅓ cups ice (15 standard cubes)

25g | 1½-inch (3.75cm) section peeled ginger, cut into fine matchsticks

One 565g | 20-oz can lychees in heavy syrup

2 or 3 clementines, mandarins, tangerines, or small blood oranges

1 grapefruit (such as red, pink, or Oroblanco; optional)

2 tsp fried shallots

Make the granita: Using the "ice crushing" setting or pulse function on a blender, whirl together the ice cubes and syrup until an opaque crystally mixture forms, pausing to stir and scrape as needed, about 45 seconds total. It's OK if it's a little liquidy. Transfer to an airtight container and freeze until firm, 1 to 2 hours. Use a fork to scrape, stir, and mix the granita to even out the texture, then refreeze for at least 1 hour before serving. The finished granita keeps well in the freezer for up to 1 month for som chun on demand.

Assemble and serve: Let the granita sit at room temperature for 10 minutes to soften slightly. Meanwhile, put the ginger matchsticks into a small bowl, add enough syrup from the canned lychees to cover, and leave to soak.

Peel the small citrus fruits, then cut crosswise into circles about ⅓ inch (8mm) thick, removing seeds as needed. Place in a medium bowl. Cut a slice off the top and bottom of the grapefruit, if using, and stand the fruit upright. Following the contour of the fruit, slice downward to remove the peel and pith in wide strips, rotating the fruit as you work. Then cut along each side of the membrane between the sections, letting each freed section (supreme) drop into the bowl holding the citrus slices. Remove seeds as needed.

Build the som chun: Divide the granita among six dessert bowls. Arrange the lychees, citrus slices, and grapefruit supremes around the granita. Add some of the soaked ginger matchsticks, drizzle on some of the now-gingery lychee syrup, and then finish with a pinch of fried shallots. Eat up pronto!

บัวลอย | Bua Loy

Rainbow Mochi "Boba" in Coconut Milk

SERVES 6

Many people adore boba, and this traditional Thai dessert has all the joys of bubble tea. My version of bua loy is prepared by poaching pillowy balls of glutinous rice flour tinted with purple and orange sweet potato and then briefly soaking the balls in a sweet-salty coconut milk. Shaping the boba-like balls takes a while, but it is a fun group project for cooks of all ages.

- 120g | about ½ small unpeeled orange sweet potato, halved lengthwise
- 120g | about ½ small unpeeled purple sweet potato, halved lengthwise
- 200g | 1½ cups Thai glutinous rice flour, divided
- 500ml | brimming 2 cups coconut milk
- 360ml | 1½ cups coconut water (pinkish water yields blushing color)
- 40g | 2 Tbsp firmly packed Thai palm sugar
- 60g | 5 Tbsp granulated sugar
- ¾ tsp fine sea salt
- 2 pandan leaves, snipped into 3-inch (7.5cm) lengths (optional)

Make the two doughs: To cook the sweet potatoes, set up a large Chinese steamer, a tall pot with a collapsible steamer insert, or a pasta pot and strainer insert. Add water to a depth of about 1½ inches (3.75cm) to the pot and bring to a boil. Place the sweet potatoes skin-side down on the rack, cover, and steam until tender and you can easily pierce them with a fork, about 20 minutes. Meanwhile, divide the rice flour evenly between two medium bowls, one for each color of balls.

Let the potatoes cool for a few minutes, then remove and discard the peel. Press the warm orange sweet potato through a coarse-mesh strainer set over a small bowl, pressing firmly and mashing with a wooden spoon or silicone spatula. Stop when you have 2 oz (60g) mashed potato, then snack on the leftovers. Add the mashed orange sweet potato to one of the bowls holding rice flour. Repeat with the purple sweet potato, adding it to the other bowl of rice flour.

Bring a small saucepan of water (about 1 cup | 240ml) just to a boil over high heat, then turn off the heat. Scoop out ¼ cup (60ml) of the very hot water, add to the bowl of mashed orange sweet potato, and stir vigorously. When a dough starts forming, after about 1 minute, switch to using your hand to knead aggressively until a dough much like a Play-Doh forms. It should crack a little when squeezed. Transfer to a work surface and knead into a smooth peach-colored dough. Moisten your hand with water and continue kneading to work in extra moisture if needed. Cover the dough to prevent drying out.

Repeat to make the purple sweet potato dough. You'll need closer to 5 Tbsp (75ml) of very hot water to form the dough because the purple potato is drier than its orange kin. It will still crack a bit, so remember to knead hard. (The dough can be shaped into balls immediately. But if you have time, wrap each batch of dough separately in plastic wrap and refrigerate for 8 hours or up to 5 days. Resting the dough helps further hydrate it, making it easier to shape.)

Shape the balls: Working with one dough at a time, pinch off a ½-inch (1.25cm) nub, smoosh it between your fingers, and then roll between your palms into a ball the size of a small to medium blueberry. As you work, set the finished balls on a plate or small sheet pan. Once shaped, the balls can be cooked right away, or they can be refrigerated for up to 3 days or frozen. (To freeze the uncooked balls for up to 3 months, arrange in a single layer on a sheet pan and slip the pan into the freezer. When the balls are frozen, transfer them to a ziplock bag and return to the freezer. No need to thaw them before poaching.)

Make the coconut milk: In a medium pot, combine the coconut milk, coconut water, palm and granulated sugars, and salt. Add the pandan (if using). Bring to a simmer over medium heat, stirring to melt the sugars. When the sugars are fully melted, pull off the heat and cover to keep warm. As needed, remove the pandan from the coconut milk, pressing it well to extract as much flavor as possible. (The coconut milk can be cooled, transferred to an airtight container, and refrigerated for up to 5 days. Reheat over medium-low heat before using.)

Poach the balls: Fill another medium pot half full with water and bring to a boil over high heat. Ready an ice bath in a medium bowl and set it near the stovetop. Working in two or three batches, add the balls, stir once or twice to separate, and then lower the heat to medium to steady the cooking. When the pot returns to a boil and the balls float, let them cook until they've brightened in color and expanded by about 50 percent, 1 to 2 minutes. Using a fine-mesh skimmer, transfer the balls to the ice bath to halt the cooking and slightly firm up the texture. Let sit for 3 to 5 minutes. Repeat until all the balls are cooked.

Assemble and serve: Transfer the cooked balls to the warm coconut soup. Let sit for a few minutes, then ladle into shallow bowls and dive in with spoons. Bua loy is best enjoyed warm or slightly above room temperature.

สังขยาฟักทอง | Sankaya Faktong

Pumpkin Coconut Custard

SERVES 8

Five ingredients are all it takes for this classic Thai sweet, which tastes like a silky coconutty flan with a slightly sweet vegetal contrast from the tender pumpkin. You'll need a petite kabocha squash for this recipe; I also sometimes use tiny kuri squash. Finding the right size can be hard, and farmers' markets are my favorite source, as are small Asian grocers. See the Notes for a workaround if your squash is bigger. Gentle steaming is key to this favorite, so don't rush it.

---

500 to 900g | 1 small kabocha squash (no wider than 5 inches | 12.5cm)

100g | ⅓ cup firmly packed Thai palm sugar

1 Tbsp water

120ml | ½ cup thick coconut milk (see Notes)

¼ tsp fine sea salt

4 large eggs

Hollow the squash: If the squash does not sit flat and steady, trim off a paper-thin slice from the bottom. Using a sturdy, sharp paring knife, carefully cut a 2-inch (5cm) square from the top of the kabocha. Pop out the "lid" and set aside. Using a pointy teaspoon, scrape and scoop out all the stringy bits and seeds from the middle of the squash (it's like carving a mini Halloween pumpkin). Set the hollowed-out squash on a shallow heatproof dish for steaming; place the "lid" on the side.

To cook the squash, set up a large Chinese steamer, a tall pot with a collapsible steamer insert, or a pasta pot and strainer insert. Whichever setup you use, make sure the dish sits well in the pot with the lid on and the squash does not touch the lid. Add water to a depth of about 1½ inches (3.75cm) to the pot; ideally, the water does not touch the dish the squash sits in.

Make the custard: Chop up the sugar and put into a microwave-safe bowl, sprinkle with the 1 Tbsp water, and microwave on high power for 20 to 40 seconds to soften, stirring once at the midpoint. (If a microwave is unavailable, finely chop the sugar.)

In a blender, combine the coconut milk, salt, and eggs and process until well mixed. Add the sugar and blend until smooth. If the custard is very frothy, pour it through a fine-mesh strainer set over a large measuring cup to eliminate most of the bubbles. Pour the custard into the hollowed-out squash, filling it to just below the bottom of the opening you carved. If you have leftover custard, pour it into a ramekin to steam separately.

Steam and serve: Put the squash into the steamer, cover the steamer, and turn on the heat to medium-high. Once the pot is vigorously steaming, lower the heat to medium to maintain a steady, visible flow of steam to cook the custard without bursting the squash.

Steam until the custard puffs to form a slight dome, 30 to 60 minutes, depending on the size of the squash. (As needed, every 20 minutes or so, replenish the pot with very hot water.) To check for doneness, press on the custard with a fingertip or back of a spoon. It should feel springy and bounce back. Or insert a metal cake tester into the center, which should come out clean.

Turn off the heat, remove the steamer cover, and let the squash rest until cool enough to handle, 15 to 20 minutes. Remove the dish and squash from the pot and don't forget the "lid" too. Let rest to enjoy slightly warm or at room temperature. Expect the custard to shrink as it cools. It may detach from the squash walls, but once you cut the wedges and reposition the custard, it will fall into the squash walls, so no one will know—the flavor will be just as good!

Cut into wedges and serve with spoons to scoop up and enjoy the squash flesh and custard, leaving the skin behind. Cover and refrigerate any leftovers for up to 2 days.

NOTES

For the thick coconut milk, collect it from the top of an unshaken can of coconut milk.

If you cannot find a petite kabocha, use 2-inch (5cm) chunks of peeled kabocha or kuri squash. Arrange them in a layer in the bottom of a soufflé dish or heatproof bowl that measures 6 inches (15cm) wide and at least 3 inches (7.5cm) deep. Pour the custard on top, then steam as directed in the recipe.

เค้กบ้าบิ่นใบเตย | Babin Bai Toey

Coconut Pandan Mochi Cake

SERVES 12 TO 16

Everyone needs an impressive dump-and-stir cake in their back pocket, and this one is mine. Flavored by verdant pandan and rich coconut, it has a gently crisp top and chewy interior, thanks to rice flour and toasted coconut flakes. I serve this striking green cake at home as well as at Nari.

You can easily buy frozen pandan leaves and sweet rice flour at Asian markets. Used only in this recipe, mochiko sweet rice flour is ground from dry grains of short-grain glutinous rice, so it is slightly coarser than the water-milled Thai glutinous rice flour; Blue Star brand by Koda Farms works great. Use the extra pandan leaves for madeleines or duck noodle soup (pages 290 and 273).

225g | 1½ cups mochiko sweet rice flour, preferably Koda Farms

280g | scant 1½ cups granulated sugar

1 tsp fine sea salt

½ tsp baking powder

240ml | 1 cup coconut milk

120ml | ½ cup whole milk

50g | 1.7 oz pandan leaves, snipped into 1-inch (2.5cm) pieces

2 large eggs

1 large egg white

60g | 4 Tbsp butter, preferably salted, melted

75g | 1¼ cups unsweetened dried coconut flakes, toasted (see page 56)

Prep the pan and dry ingredients: Position a rack in the middle of the oven and preheat the oven to 350°F (180°C). To make unmolding the finished cake a cinch, line the bottom and sides of an 8-inch (20cm) square baking pan with parchment paper, letting it hang over two sides (like a sling). In a medium bowl, whisk together the rice flour, sugar, salt, and baking powder.

Make the pandan milk: In a blender, combine the coconut milk, whole milk, and pandan and process until a smooth jade-green liquid forms.

Mix the batter: In a large bowl, whisk together the whole eggs and egg white. Position a fine-mesh strainer over the bowl and pour in the pandan milk, scraping all the bits into the strainer. Stir and press firmly with a silicone spatula to force out as much liquid as possible. Rinse the spatula and then scrape the back side of the strainer to get all the goodies off and into the bowl. Go in with your hand to push and squeeze on the solids until nothing else comes out of your fistful of green fuzz. If needed, repeat scraping the back side of the strainer.

Add the butter and whisk until well mixed. Then add the flour mixture in three portions, whisking vigorously after each addition until no traces of white remain.

Set aside a big handful of toasted coconut, then stir the remaining coconut into the batter. Scrape the batter into the prepared pan. Shimmy the pan to level the batter. Sprinkle the reserved coconut flakes on top, then gently press them into the surface.

Bake, let cool, and serve: Bake until golden and done to the touch, 40 to 45 minutes. To test for doneness, touch the dry top. It should be set but still have a slight wobble in the center. A metal cake tester inserted into the center should come out clean. Let cool in the pan on a wire cooling rack for 30 minutes. As needed, run a dinner knife around the edge of the pan to loosen the cake sides from the pan. Lift the parchment with the cake from the pan. Enjoy warm or at room temperature, cut into 2- or 3-inch (5 to 7.5cm) squares. Store leftover cake tightly covered at room temperature for up to 2 days, or refrigerate for up to 1 week.

ขนมไข่ใบเตย | Kanom Kai Bai Toey

Pandan Madeleines

MAKES ABOUT 24 MADELEINES

The Portuguese introduced many European baked goods to Thailand, including petite madeleine-like cakes called kanom kai, which are traditionally cooked on a special griddle with shell-, star-, or flower-shaped molds. Like Proust, I have long adored madeleines, but I prefer mine accented with bai toey, the aromatic leaves also known as pandan (see page 28 for sourcing tips) that taste of coconut and vanilla. They flavor a wealth of South and Southeast Asian dishes. When the leaves are used to make pandan butter for the madeleines, the results are superb; you can use pandan extract (see Notes), but the cakes will not be as good. Included in the photo on page 288, the madeleines bake up best in a standard-size madeleine pan that contains a dozen 3-inch-long (7.5cm) molds. I have included a mini-muffin pan tip in the Notes in case you don't have the pan. Weigh the ingredients (even the milk) for easy prep and consistent results. The batter needs a long chill, so make it hours (or up to 2 days) ahead of baking.

PANDAN BUTTER

225g | 1 cup salted butter, cubed (see Notes)

50g | 1.7 oz pandan leaves, snipped into 1-inch (2.5cm) pieces

Make the butter: In a small saucepan, combine the butter and pandan. Set the pan over low heat to melt the butter slowly. After about 20 minutes, just when the fragrant butter begins to boil, remove from the heat. Set aside to infuse for 1 hour.

Transfer the infused butter to a blender and process until the pandan is pulverized and a jade-green liquid has formed. Pour through a fine-mesh strainer set over a small bowl, scraping out all the bits from the blender jar. Using a silicone spatula, stir and press firmly to extract as much butter as possible. Set the butter aside.

FOR THE MADELEINES

200g | scant 1½ cups all-purpose flour or pastry flour

2 tsp baking powder

4 large eggs, at room temperature

120g | scant ⅔ cup granulated sugar

80g | ¼ cup honey

50g | ¼ cup whole milk

3 Tbsp salted or unsalted butter, at room temperature, for greasing the molds

Prepare the batter: In a medium bowl, sift together the flour and baking powder. Set the dry ingredients aside.

In a stand mixer fitted with a balloon whisk, or in a large bowl with a handheld mixer, beat together the eggs and sugar, starting on medium and gradually increasing the speed to high, until lusciously thick and pale and the whisk leaves tracks in the mixture as it turns, 5 to 8 minutes. Pause the mixer, add the honey, and then beat on low speed until incorporated.

If using a stand mixer, remove the bowl from the stand. Using a silicone spatula, transfer a good one-fourth of the batter to the bowl of dry ingredients, stir vigorously until no clumps remain and the mixture is homogenous, and then pour into the whisked batter remaining in the mixer bowl. Gently fold the flour-batter mixture into the whisked batter by sweeping the spatula down the side of the bowl and along the bottom and then bringing it up and folding the batter over on itself. Rotate the bowl a quarter turn clockwise and repeat the sweeping and folding motion. Continue rotating the bowl and sweeping and folding the batter until all the ingredients are well mixed. Next, gently fold in all the pandan butter. Last, fold in the milk. Stop when you have a beautifully smooth, shiny batter.

Scrape down the sides of the bowl, smooth the batter surface, and then press a piece of plastic wrap directly on top of the batter to cover. Cover the bowl tightly with a second piece of plastic wrap and refrigerate for at least 3 hours or up to 2 days.

Bake the madeleines: Position a rack in the middle of the oven and preheat the oven to 400°F (200°C). Butter a standard-size madeleine pan, making sure to coat the molds evenly and thoroughly, then flour the molds, tapping out the excess flour. (I prefer metal madeleine pans over the silicone ones. And I always butter and flour my mold even when using nonstick pans.)

To fill the molds, use a 2-Tbsp cookie scoop or employ 1 or 2 soupspoons. Fill each mold with a scant 2 Tbsp of the batter, placing it slightly more toward the wider end. You'll form a 1½- to 2-inch (3.75 to 5cm) oval of batter. When not filling a pan, keep the batter chilled to ensure madeleines with handsome bumps.

Place the pan in the oven and bake until the edges of the cakes turn a bit darker than golden brown, 10 to 12 minutes. Remove from the oven and immediately unmold by tapping the pan on the countertop to loosen the madeleines. Slide each cake out of the pan and place on a plate to serve. Rinse the pan with cold water to rid it of baked-on bits and to cool it down, then dry it well, butter and flour it, and bake the remaining batter.

For the best flavor, serve the madeleines warm out of the oven. If you must, let them cool completely before storing in an airtight container at room temperature for up to 2 days.

NOTES

If you don't have pandan leaves, you can melt 14 Tbsp of butter and cautiously add pandan extract ¼ tsp at a time until you achieve good flavor without a Day-Glo color. The madeleines will not be as elegant as when made with the actual leaves.

If you have only unsalted butter on hand, add ½ teaspoon of fine sea salt to the pandan butter.

Resting the batter at least overnight ensures the beautiful characteristic madeleine bump.

Without madeleine pans, bake in mini muffin pans, filling each well about two-thirds full. Test bake two madeleines to determine the bake time.

Rinse and trim any brown ends from the pandan leaves before using. Unused leaves are great for the mochi butter cake on page 289.

If your honey has crystallized, microwave it on high power for 10 to 20 seconds to warm and melt. Briefly cool before using.

sfwater.org

คุ้กกี้ช็อคโกแลตพริกลาบ | Cookie Prik Laab

Lanna Spicy Chocolate Cookies

MAKES 36 COOKIES

Looking to put a Thai imprint on a Western classic, I added Northern prik laab to a chocolate cookie to create this extra-fun treat. You have the chili-spice blend in your larder, yes? The delicious tartare on page 68 and artichoke laab on page 110 depend on it, and so does this delicate, chewy-crisp cookie. I created this fail-safe recipe as an homage to Lanna (Land of a Million Rice Fields), a wealthy self-ruling kingdom that once spanned all the area of present-day Northern Thailand and into parts of Myanmar and Laos. Lanna culture left its mark in and around Chiang Mai, as it does in this easy, sweet pleasure that you'll be making over and over.

250g | 1¾ cups unbleached all-purpose flour

50g | 1.7 oz unsweetened cocoa powder (any kind)

2 tsp Prik Laab (Northern Thai Chili-Spice Blend, page 49), divided

2 tsp cream of tartar

1 tsp baking soda

½ tsp fine sea salt

225g | 1 cup salted butter, at room temperature (see Note)

300g | 1½ cups granulated sugar

2 large eggs, at room temperature

50g | ¼ cup turbinado or other coarse sugar

Make the dough: In a medium bowl, whisk together the flour, cocoa, 1 tsp of the prik laab, the cream of tartar, baking soda, and salt.

In a stand mixer fitted with the paddle attachment, or in a large bowl with a handheld mixer, beat together the butter and sugar on medium speed until creamy, pale, and fluffy, 2 to 3 minutes. Pause to add the eggs, then continue beating on medium speed until smooth. If using a stand mixer, remove the bowl from the stand.

Using a silicone spatula, stir the flour mixture into the butter mixture until a dough forms with no visible dry patches. Divide the dough in half. Place half of the dough on a sheet of plastic wrap (or waxed or parchment paper) and shape into a log about 9½ inches (24cm) long and 1½ inches (3.75cm) in diameter. Roll up the log in the plastic wrap (or paper) and twist the ends to secure. Repeat with the second half of the dough, then refrigerate the logs for at least 6 hours or up to 3 days. (Or freeze them for up to 3 months, thawing them in the refrigerator before continuing.)

Slice and bake: Position racks in the upper third and lower third of the oven and preheat the oven to 350°F (175°C). Line the bottom of two large sheet pans with parchment paper (these cookies spread too much to bake them on silicone baking mats).

On a small plate, mix together the turbinado sugar and the remaining 1 tsp prik laab. Slice the firm, cold dough logs into pucks ½ inch (1.25cm) thick. If you like, neaten them into perfect rounds (I don't). Press one of the cut sides in the spiced sugar, then place, sugared-side up, on the prepared sheet pans, spacing them about 2 inches (5cm) apart. Sprinkle with any leftover spiced sugar.

Bake the cookies for 5 minutes, switch the pans between the racks, and then continue baking until the cookies are crisp at the edges and dry to the touch in the middle, about 5 minutes longer.

Let cool on the pans on wire cooling racks for 1 to 2 minutes, then transfer the cookies to the racks to cool completely. Eat promptly and then store the extras in an airtight container at room temperature.

NOTE

If you have only unsalted butter, increase the amount of fine sea salt to 1 tsp.

ชีสเค้กชาไทย | Cheesecake Cha Thai

Thai Tea Cheesecake

SERVES 8

Years ago, San Francisco food writer and restaurateur Patty Unterman of Hayes Street Grill gifted me a Basque cheesecake recipe obtained from a chef in Spain. I've since tinkered with it, adding Thai flair to make the recipe my own.

Two points to note: Rich Philly cream cheese works best, and the resulting cake is beautifully browned from high-heat baking, not from broiling. You cannot screw this recipe up, though do have the cream cheese and eggs at room temperature to facilitate blending. To serve this cheesecake for dinner, bake it in the morning or a day ahead. It needs time to rest so that the center can slightly set.

300ml | 1¼ cups heavy cream, plus more to taste

24g | ¼ cup ChaTraMue brand Thai tea mix (from 6 sachets)

Two 225g | 8-oz packages Philadelphia cream cheese, cubed and at room temperature

180g | scant 1 cup granulated sugar

3 large eggs, at room temperature

1 large egg white, at room temperature

18g | 2 Tbsp all-purpose flour (any kind, even a one-to-one gluten-free blend)

½ tsp fine sea salt

Infuse the cream: In a small saucepan, combine the cream and tea mix. Set over medium heat and warm, stirring continuously to release the tea flavor, color, and vanilla-like aroma. When tiny bubbles appear at the pan edge, turn off the heat and let sit, uncovered, until the cream is an intense rusty orange, about 5 minutes. Strain through a fine-mesh strainer set over a measuring cup, firmly pressing against the solids with the back of a spoon to extract as much flavor as possible (a little tea in the cream is forgivable). You need a generous 1 cup (250ml) total. If you're short, splash some cream into the strainer, stir, then press through. Let the cream cool, uncovered, until tepid.

Prep the oven and pan: Meanwhile, position a rack in the middle of the oven and preheat the oven to 450°F (230°C; no convection, please!). For a handsome cake, use a high-sided 8-inch (20cm) round pan with a removable bottom. (My pan is 3 inches | 7.5cm tall.) Line it with two 12 by 16-inch (20 by 40cm) pieces of parchment paper, crisscrossing them. Use your fingertips to press the paper firmly onto the bottom and up the sides to set the edges and minimize the space between the parchment pieces. When done, the parchment should extend about 2 inches (5cm) above the rim.

Make the batter: In a blender or food processor, combine the tepid cream, cream cheese, sugar, whole eggs, egg white, flour, and salt and process until smooth. Pour the batter into the prepared pan. It should fill a good 1½ inches (3.75cm) below the rim to allow space for the cheesecake to rise. Tap the pan on your counter to remove any air bubbles, then place it on a sheet pan.

Bake, chill, and serve: Slide the sheet pan into the oven and bake the cake until dark brown, cracked at the perimeter, and wobbly in the center but dry to the touch on top, 35 to 45 minutes. Transfer the round pan to a wire cooling rack and let cool for about 1 hour, then unmold and leave to cool completely before serving. If not serving the cake the same day, cover and refrigerate and return to room temperature to serve.

ชาเย็น | Cha Yen

Thai Iced Tea

SERVES 4

Recipes don't get easier than this one. Make your tea and then add some sweetened condensed milk diluted with whole milk. Most renditions use either evaporated milk or non-dairy creamer, but to be honest, they taste awful. At Kin Khao, we make "Thai cream"—a one-to-one blend of sweetened condensed milk and regular milk and add that to our brewed tea. (For a vegan option, use a coconut condensed milk and a plant-based milk.)

But whatever you choose for your Thai cream, use what I and many Thais choose for the tea: ChaTraMue brand Thai tea mix. Practically a household name, it's been around since 1945 and is what we prefer at my restaurants. According to the label, the mix contains mostly Assam red tea plus a smidgen of sugar, vanilla flavoring, and food coloring. The food coloring helps create Thai tea's signature reddish-brown color, and commercial Thai tea formulas include coloring in their signature blends. Premeasured sachets are useful because you don't have to fuss whatsoever to craft perfect glasses of Thai iced tea, which can be sweet enough to be dessert but for a nice pairing, enjoy it with Lanna spicy chocolate cookies, as photographed on page 292.

24g | ¼ cup ChaTraMue brand Thai tea mix, or 6 sachets

720ml | 3 cups just-boiled water

120ml | ½ cup sweetened condensed milk

120ml | ½ cup milk (any kind)

Ice cubes, for serving

Steep the tea: Put the tea (or sachets) into a large heatproof measuring cup. Add the hot water and steep, uncovered, for 4 to 5 minutes. Strain and discard the spent tea leaves (or discard the sachets). Let the brewed tea cool to room temperature before using, or cover and chill for up to several days (it's just tea!).

Make Thai cream: In a measuring cup, stir together the condensed milk and milk.

Assemble and slurp: For each drink, fill a tall glass with 5 or 6 ice cubes. Add about ⅔ cup (160ml) tea and ¼ cup (60ml) Thai cream (or as much as you like!). Stir the ombré tea and drink up!

Acknowledgments

Life is like a tennis game; when you play with someone who's better than you are, your game is elevated to match. I am so grateful to this team of ace players who helped me put together this book you are reading. I am every so proud of the work we produced together.

The biggest thanks, of course, goes to Andrea, my old friend, co-writer, editor, cheerleader, therapist, and occasional school mistress. It's been quite a thrilling and eventful journey for us these last few years. This book would never be this good without your hand in it.

Kudos, also, to the whole house at Ten Speed Press, from publisher Aaron Wehner, who has been a fierce supporter of *Cooking Thai* since he heard the pitch, or maybe even before, to our editor Molly Birnbaum, whose guidance helped us shape this book, to our copy editor Sharon Silva, production editor Serena Wang, editorial assistant Laine Whittier, production manager Phil Leung, managing editor Kristin Sargianis, production designer Mari Gill, publicist Kristin Casemore, and marketer Emily Hotaling.

A special appreciation must go to our photographer Ed Anderson, food stylist Alison Attenborough, and MVP art director and designer Betsy Stromberg, who all brought so much talent to the table, yet never let it get in the way of listening to my ideas and vision. Alison, Betsy, Ed, this work is our true collaboration. I cannot forget our prop stylist, Glenn Jenkins, who curated a beautiful collection of items for the images in this book. I am also grateful to all our assistants, especially Chantael Takeuchi, who helped to make our photoshoot go smoothly. I am so happy to have you all on my team.

To our cadre of intrepid recipe testers, new friends and old from across the world (even including our photographer Ed and designer Betsy) who peeled and pounded your way diligently through every single recipe in this book, your insightful notes, sharp suggestions, and delightful compliments meant everything to Andrea and me. You have our eternal gratitude, and when our readers try the recipes in this book, you'll have theirs too.

Ed Anderson
Alex Ciepley
Todd Claybaugh and Betsy Stromberg
Gudrun Enger
Diane Estes
Alyce Gershenson
Doug and Candace Grover
Paulina Haduong and Colin Hart
Megan Hoang
John Lau
Peter Luong
Laura McCarthy
Nancie McDermott
Hugh McElroy
Cate McGuire
Emily Nevitt
Josie Nevitt
Namthip Paine
Robyn Pearson
Lisa Rossi
Nathan and Kate Schmidt
Allison Solomon
Heidi Swanson
Cathy Thome
Supawat Thongthip
Sean Timberlake
Maki Tsuzuki
Tina Ujlaki
Jennifer Yee Collinson

I want to recognize my past and present kitchen teams at Kin Khao, Nari, and Nahm. Your contributions, your ideas, and your palates have helped shape the flavors and development of my food. Thank you Meghan, Mike, Narciso, Adam, Cecile, Nikko, Intu, Nik, Matt, Jakob, Kevin, Kevin, Sean, Joh, Peace, Pop, Jan, Pat, and all who've worked over fire with me through the years. This book is yours too. I'm also grateful to my front of house teams; you kept our guests happy and fed so I could focus my energy on this book. Sam, Jackson, Alyx, Katie, Brian, Aaron, Mary, Will, and the rest of the team, I owe you a drink, or a few!

I wouldn't be this person I am without the love and support of my family and friends who have cultivated and contributed to my culinary being. Some of those people are still here with me while others have passed on to the next life. I am so grateful to have had this opportunity to learn so much about my heritage, our cuisine and be able to pass along that knowledge in this printed form. I am a proud link in this delicious chain. พลับขอกราบขอบคุณป๋า แม่ คุณตา น้าดี ที่เลี้ยงลูกดูหลานมาจนเป็นตัวเองนี้ ขอบพระคุณคุณยาย ป้าปุ้ย ป้าทัศน์ คุณป้าทุม คุณป้าใหญ่ พี่ปลา พุด พี่กุ้ง แม่ครัวทั้งน้านวยและป้าเบียบ ที่ทำอาหารให้กิน ส่งของมาให้ลอง สั่งสอนสืบความรู้ครัวไทยให้มาตั้งแต่เป็นพื้นฐาน ขอบคุณส้ม หนึ่ง น้าเจี๊ยบ ที่เชื่อมือกันมาตั้งแต่เริ่มต้นที่กินข้าว ขอบพระคุณอาจารย์ท่านผู้เขียนตำราอาหารทั้งเก่าทั้งใหม่ ทั้งเพื่อนเชฟหลายคน ที่แบ่งสอนความรู้ทั้งทางตรง ทางครูพักลักจำ จะไม่ลืมคุณของทุกท่านค่ะ

I've been so lucky to have such strong support from so many friends, and the two I'm most indebted to for this project are David and Allison Solomon, who let us take over their kitchen for two whole weeks to produce the gorgeous hero shots of all the recipes in this book. Dave and Allie, you are both mad and I love you for it.

My heart is so full of love and gratitude for my adoring husband, Mark, who, a decade ago, promised to hold my hand through dreams and nightmares. My hand is in yours, forever and always.

Index

D

E

F

G

H

N

O

P

Q

R

S

T

V

W

Y

Ten Speed Press

An imprint of the Crown Publishing Group
A division of Penguin Random House LLC
1745 Broadway
New York, NY 10019
tenspeed.com
penguinrandomhouse.com

Typefaces: Cadson Demak's Anugrom, Narrow Type's Girona, and Monotype's Neue Plak

Library of Congress Cataloging-in-Publication Data

Names: Techamuanvivit, Pim author | Nguyen, Andrea Quynhgiao author
Title: Cooking Thai : heritage and modern recipes from my kitchen notebooks / Pim Techamuanvivit with Andrea Nguyen.
Identifiers: LCCN 2025044453 (print) | LCCN 2025044454 (ebook) | ISBN 9780593836583 hardcover | ISBN 9780593836590 ebook
Subjects: LCSH: Cooking, Thai | LCGFT: Cookbooks
Classification: LCC TX724.5.T5 T375 2026 (print) | LCC TX724.5.T5 (ebook) | DDC 641.59593—dc23/eng/20260114
LC record available at https://lccn.loc.gov/2025044453
LC ebook record available at https://lccn.loc.gov/2025044454

Hardcover ISBN 978-0-593-83658-3
Ebook ISBN 978-0-593-83659-0

Acquiring editor: Molly Birnbaum
Production editor: Serena Wang
Editorial assistant: Gabby Urena Matos and Laine Whittier
Art director and designer: Betsy Stromberg
Production manager: Philip Leung
Production designer: Mari Gill
Food stylist and on set prop stylist: Alison Attenborough
Food stylist assistant: Chantael Takeuchi
Prop stylist: Glenn Jenkins
Copy editor: Sharon Silva
Compositor: Nick Patton
Proofreaders: Heather Rodino, Erica Rose, Katy Miller, Tess Rossi, and Navorn Johnson
Indexer: Stephen Callahan
Publicist: Kristin Casemore
Marketer: Emily Hotaling

Thai talisman graphic © Wasarat - stock.adobe.com

Manufactured in China

10 9 8 7 6 5 4 3 2 1

First Edition

The authorized representative in the EU for product safety and compliance is Penguin Random House Ireland, Morrison Chambers, 32 Nassau Street, Dublin D02 YH68, Ireland, https://eu-contact.penguin.ie.